Tom Stoppard and the Craft of Comedy

Theater: Text/Theory/Performance

Enoch Brater, Series Editor
University of Michigan

Editorial Board

This series focuses on playwrights and other theater practitioners who have made their impact on the twentieth-century stage. Books in the series emphasize the work of a single author, a group of playwrights, or a movement that places dramatists in new aesthetic or historical contexts.

Around the Absurd: Essays on Modern and Postmodern Drama
edited by Enoch Brater and Ruby Cohn

Tom Stoppard and the Craft of Comedy: Medium and Genre at Play
by Katherine E. Kelly

Tom Stoppard and the Craft of Comedy

Medium and Genre at Play

Katherine E. Kelly

Ann Arbor

THE UNIVERSITY OF MICHIGAN PRESS

1994   1993   1992   1991   4   3   2   1

Library of Congress Cataloging-in-Publication Data

Kelly, Katherine E., 1947–
    Tom Stoppard and the craft of comedy : medium and genre at play /
    Katherine E. Kelly.
        p.   cm.   —   (Theater—theory/text/performance)
    Includes bibliographical references and index.
    ISBN 0–472–10188–9 (cloth : alk. paper)
    1. Stoppard, Tom—Criticism and interpretation.   2. Comedy.
I. Title.   II. Series.
PR6069.T6Z73 1991
822′.914—dc20   90–24217
                                                            CIP

Acknowledgments

I wish to express my appreciation to the following for their invaluable assistance: Richard Corballis for his generous and intelligent criticism of this book; Jeffrey Cox for his incisive response to parts of the manuscript; the College of Liberal Arts and the Department of English at Texas A&M University for travel and other support that enabled me to visit archives in London; the staffs of the British Newspaper Library and the National Sound Archive (London); Deborah Archer and Michelle White for their help in compiling a bibliography of primary and secondary works; LeAnn Fields of the University of Michigan Press for her encouragement and support; and the editors of *Modern Drama* for permission to reprint parts of chapters 1 and 2.

To Michael, Megan, and Patrick with gratitude

Contents

Introduction

In their meticulous and painstaking revision of comic subgenres, Tom Stoppard's plays have helped to define a post-Beckett era on the contemporary British stage. Two of the most significant pressures shaping that era, from the late 1950s to the present, have been Beckett's experiments in formal minimalism and Brecht's epic theory as applied by political playwrights using the theater to generate social change. Over a decade ago, the late Kenneth Tynan astutely placed Stoppard's work in relation to these two pressures. In extending his description of the cultural energies infusing these plays, this book hopes to contribute to the growing scholarship on Stoppard's comedy by presenting its valorizing of craftsmanship as an authentic response to the London stage as he found it in the mid-1960s and as he has helped to shape it in the 1970s and 1980s. My interest in understanding Stoppard's sense of craft as the representation of artistic skill, signaled most pointedly by the self-announcing procedure of parody, has grown not simply from my admiration for these plays but more centrally from the failure of both strictly "formalist" and political readings of them to account for the tensions they signify.

Catherine Itzin's 1980 description of Stoppard's plays exemplifies the British radical left's dismissal of his work: "Stoppard opted for 'human solidarity' rather than 'class solidarity,' " and was concerned with "freedom and freedom of speech from a liberal or right-of-centre perspective" (185–86). It is quite true that, when Stoppard first began writing in the 1960s, he defended his work against the call for "committed art" by staking his position as what his detractors would call a "liberal humanist." But as I hope to demonstrate, his involvement with and concern for the artist's social responsibility has been rigorous and unfailing, although his sense of that responsibility diverges widely from those of radicals at either end of the political spectrum. Political dismissals of Stoppard's work leave a significant part of its energies unaccounted for, not only its acute attention to literary and cultural history through the operations of parody but also its critique of its own ideology of individualism expressed through the comic undercutting of the Stoppardian eccentric, as well as its resistance to monolithic stagings of "truth" and "meaning" through the conventions of satire and parody.

One of the more self-consciously "formalist" readings of Stoppard, Neil Sammels's 1988 study, argues that, at his best, Stoppard duplicates the defamiliarizing strategies of the Russian Formalists by deforming and thus critiquing the materials of his plays. My own reading of Stoppard is also indebted to Russian Formalism, specifically to the Formalists' theories of parody described by Victor Erlich and Peter Steiner, as a device for re-presenting literary history by rejuvenating our responses to the canon. But while I share Sammels's interest in the formalist vocabulary for describing parody as an intentional misreading of literary precursors, I am less confident than he that Formalism provides a ready-made discourse for reading Stoppard's plays. The fundamental formalist assumptions — first, that literary study can and should emulate the methods of science, and second, that the ultimate value of parody lies in the improving of literature by renewing exhausted forms (Steiner 1984, 27, 61) — arose from an intellectual climate peculiar to the Russia of the early decades of the twentieth century, a climate markedly distinct from our own post-technological age. While Stoppard's parodies always engage the literary and theatrical past, they do not always do so to the end of improving upon it. *Artist Descending a Staircase,* to take one example, does not provide a better alternative to Duchamp's *Nude Descending a Staircase* but questions its avant-garde assumptions about the making and the value of art. Further, it makes fun of the implied playwright's alternative to those assumptions as backward turning and retrograde. The historical and narrative lines coincide in their circularity.

In attempting to avoid rigidly political and formalist readings of Stoppard's work, I may well be courting another kind of danger in the form of a heavy reliance upon what the playwright has said about himself and his plays in interviews and written essays. While Stoppard has occasionally seemed to contradict himself when describing his work, sometimes referring to it (and all art) as profoundly moral and other times as lacking in conviction (for which read, resisting declamation), he has tended on the whole toward consistency; indeed, many of his interviews appear to be duplicates of one another. While I rely heavily on such interviews with the author, I attempt to read them skeptically where there is cause to do so. For his own part, Stoppard himself has acknowledged the hazards of giving "statements of truth" about himself and his play writing during interviews (Interview with David Gollob and David Roper 1981, 13).

Again taking the cue from Tynan and from the playwright himself, we learn that young Stoppard, determined to make the leap from journalism to fiction and play writing, read the London art scene in political terms: "I used to feel out on a limb, because when I started to write you were a shit if you weren't writing about Vietnam or housing" (quoted in Tynan 1980, 47). In choosing not to write plays about poverty, race relations, or class conflict, but instead to write an imitation of Beckett ("my first play . . . called *The Gamblers* . . . was really *Waiting for Godot in the Condemned Cell*" [Interview with Editors of *Theatre Quarterly* 1974, 4]), Stoppard was doing two things: recognizing the nature of his talent and ability, and actively and deliberately resisting a political imperative that required a display of social conscience. This resistance did not spring from a naive rejection of the artist's social responsibility but from a refusal to endorse a single form of acceptable political engagement. From his earliest stage and radio plays, what I shall, with a small *f,* call Stoppard's formalism, was in part a defense against political programs that would limit artists' and spectators' stagings of experience. The hero of early Stoppard is less the smug aristocrat Lord Malquist than the individualist anarchist Mr. Moon whose solution to the faceless inhumanity of the modern world is to set off a bogus bomb. The "hero" is the dialogue between the two choices of withdrawal or impassioned participation. In focusing upon Stoppard's formalist preoccupation with genre and medium, with the "how" of artistic production, I do not share Terry Eagleton's assumption that any formalism presupposes a neglect or superceding of the content of literary works—"content is merely a function of form" (1976, 23). Rather, I read Stoppard's formalism as the product of his concern with the integrity of the artistic process, including its reception by an audience. In Stoppard's terms, art should demonstrate the conditions of its making by displaying the skill with which it was made and the conventions that helped to make it. "Form," in the Stoppardian sense, is the hypothesis of art's fictional coherence that marks it off from the extra-artistic world. The permeability of the division between art and life is itself brought under question in his more recent plays, particularly *The Real Thing*.

Stoppard has consistently written plays from the vantage of consciously resisting an ideological position that would dictate the artist's choice of medium or matter, or that would restrict the space of the imagination by defining the kinds of operations literature should be allowed to perform. Stoppard's formalism is thus the product of an authentic engagement with his own past as a Czech emigré, with his experience as a journalist, and with his view of himself as a divided observer. For the other side of his political conservatism is expressed as a nagging—even obsessive—doubt concerning the right of the artist to exist both inside and outside society at once; to be both an active concerned citizen of his world and a detached observer of it; to create elegant dramatic structures of no immediate use to those contemplating them. One of the goals of this book is to document that doubt as it is expressed by Stoppard's virtuoso display of comic tropes, especially the trope of parody.

If we accept Tynan's reading of the profound influence Stoppard's early flights from totalitarianism must have had in shaping his political values, then we can reasonably ask what effect his early childhood migrations have had on his artistic methods. One less obvious expression of Stoppard's hostility toward totalitarianism lies in his dislike of the declamatory in others' work and, by extension, his dread of the overly explicit in his own work. This dread has contributed, in the case of *Hapgood*, to the near failure of the play before audiences bewildered by a plot too convoluted and implicit to permit their ready comprehension. Another expression of his resistance to didacticism lies in Stoppard's insistent use of the open-ended debate structure in several of his major plays, even when, as in *Travesties*, the implied playwright's position on the question under debate emerges in spite of a conceptual "tie." The obligation of artists to imagine a worldview hostile to their own is taken most seriously by this playwright, even when treated in a comic spirit.

Parody, another of Stoppard's formal expressions of aversion to the declamatory, gives him the means to engage the literary past in a particularly controlled way while avoiding didactic and explicit statements of his opinion of that past. In his plays up to and including *Travesties*, Stoppard solved his relation to dramatic and theatrical precursors in part by demonstrating that he could duplicate consciously their achievements. However, he also knew that virtuosity alone did not an artist make—that the ability to imitate what others before him had done forged a link between his own work and the cultural legacy, even in cases where his imitation mocked its model.

The second and more elusive attribute of the artist—talent—has always been for Stoppard a mysterious and forbidden subject of inquiry. As he told a New York audience in 1988, "Work informed by the subconscious is the most successful. . . . What you're working on can lose its force if you become too aware of your editorial stance . . . " (quoted in Interview with Leslie Bennetts 1988). He developed his writing skill gradually while working as a journalist and play reviewer for Bristol newspapers. As a drama and film critic, he began to learn the rules by which comedy works and became intrigued with the actor's mysterious and powerful art of presenting a role. From his earliest days as a playgoer, the theater presented him with both the formal challenge of deciphering the rules motivating comic art and the intriguing mystery by which that art can suggest both the real and the unreal, the expected event and the surprise event, the familiar text suddenly made strange.

Aside from a brief but suggestive comment by Joan Dean, who attributed Stoppard's "inclination towards parody" (1981, 6) to his profession of journalism, full-length studies of Stoppard's art have, until recently, excluded an extended discussion of both his generic renovations and of his earliest journalistic writing. Neil Sammells's recent book lucidly describes some of the early journalism and its possible influence on later plays. But as Sammells characterizes Stoppard's overall achievement in terms of the principles of Russian Formalism, he largely neglects the implications of medium or of specific comic conventions on particular plays.

In this study, I hope to throw a backlight on Stoppard's work to date by shifting the emphasis of the predominantly thematic studies of his work. Starting in chapter 1 with his signed theater and film reviews, I locate thematic and formal preoccupations that turn up later in obvious places like the spoof on drama reviewers, *Real Inspector Hound,* and in less obvious places, such as the more naturalistic *Night and Day.* Stoppard's stories form the link between the journalist and the artist, drawing in several specific ways upon his experiences with Bristol newspapers, while his novel features a note-taking auto-interviewer mimicking the narrator of Joyce's *Ulysses.* Chapter 2 looks at Stoppard's work for what he considered to be secondary media—radio and television—where he began his training as a stage writer. The limits of the radio and television media drove him toward experimenting both with voice and rhythm and with visual and aural suggestiveness in ways that enriched his powers as a writer for the stage.

In his earliest stage works, described in chapter 3, Stoppard begins his customary borrowing from precursor texts. Ironically reworking the soap opera conventions of domestic melodrama, *Enter a Free Man* rewrites *Look Back in Anger* by placing greater emphasis on the unsinkable quality of the British character. *Rosencrantz and Guildenstern Are Dead* resists both *Hamlet* and *Waiting for Godot* by repeating its lines and gestures with difference. *The Real Inspector Hound* mocks the entire genre of whodunits, first flaunting and then circling back to reinforce its central clichés, while *After Magritte* mimics the verbal-visual play in the Belgian's *This Is Not a Pipe* by accompanying a bizarre visual tableau with banal domestic dialogue. The result is not Magrittean menace but a comic wink at the painter's evocative mysteries. *Jumpers* shows

Stoppard reaching for a new comic synthesis by submitting the characters and situation of manners comedy to the extreme distortions of farce. As Stoppard's first example of an extended mock-philosophical argument, *Jumpers* is important not for what it says about God or Bertrand Russell but for its interlacing of contrasts, situations, and character types that conditions our reception of the argument. *Travesties* is the fullest, most uninhibited example to date of Stoppard's play with specific texts. Hitching *Travesties* to *The Importance of Being Earnest* for practical and theoretical reasons, Stoppard both signals his affinity with and subverts Wilde's art-for-art's-sake ideology by insistently questioning the artist's role in politics. *Travesties* marked a watershed in Stoppard's play writing, after which he began to explore the conventions of psychological realism and nonverbal expression as a critique of his earlier practice.

Chapter 4 considers the three plays Stoppard wrote for and about Eastern European dissenters under the genre designation satire. As always, these are neither pure nor simple examples of a genre, but critical adaptations using standard genre markers. The essential feature of these satires is their clear definition of a target for ridicule: officials of totalitarian governments. But the moral norm essential to satire is implied, rather than militantly announced in these plays, by the heroes' resistance to official conformity. Stoppard's experiment with the "militant irony" of satire drove him toward nonverbal modes of expression in an effort to implicate his spectators in resisting monolithic texts and interpretations. Consequently, the eastern comedies make new use of gesture, music, and mime to signify artists' determination to express their reading of the world, especially when that reading conflicts with officially sanctioned versions of the real or the true.

In titling chapter 5 "Postmodern Polyphony," I am referring to the most recent examples of Stoppard's tendency, shared by many contemporary artists, to multiply the textual voices participating in and simultaneously commenting upon the dramatic event. In spite of their shift toward greater verisimilitude, both *Night and Day* and *The Real Thing* extend the use of parody as a method for evoking and remaking prior texts and their conventions. Further, they both expose the procedures by which art and life intersect and mimic one another. Parodic echoing in *Night and Day* serves to create the illusion of a relatively direct relation between events and newswriting, while parody in *The Real Thing* supports an indirect and metaphorical expression of the relation between art and life. *Hapgood* takes metaphor as its subject and method, foregrounding the "as if" make-believe of theater in an extended and rich comparison between particle-wave physics, the operations of double, triple, or even quadruple secret agents, and the interpretive efforts of spectators.

In omitting from this study Stoppard's adaptations of works by Federico Garcia Lorca, Graham Greene, Vladimir Nabokov, and others, I am implicitly treating them as minor examples of Stoppard's comic craft. As adaptations, they expose how Stoppard handles received texts, but they do not tell us as much about his recycling as do his major parodies that have fully engaged him in a critical review of the British tradition he has received and is helping to transform. On other counts, too—Stoppard's figuring of women, his use of language as performance, his preoccupation with children, and so on—I am largely silent in this book. But as Stoppard continues to write, so we can continue to reflect on his work as the comedy of our interpretive play.

Chapter 1

The Playwright Prepares:
Journalism and Fiction

The Early Journalism: Inside and Outside Society

At the age of seventeen, Tom Stoppard left school to join the *Western Daily Press* (*WDP*) as a reporter, feature writer, humorous columnist, and reviewer of plays and films. The move was to be decisive for his future as a playwright. Not only would his apprenticeship encourage young Stoppard to develop and cultivate a prose style but it would introduce him to actors at the Bristol Old Vic and lesser provincial theaters where he would gradually learn the practical business of stagecraft by observing a multitude of plays succeed and fail before live audiences. He entered the news profession hoping eventually to lead a danger-filled life as a foreign correspondent, a grand dream[1] at which he later poked fun: "I wanted to be Noel Barber on the *Daily Mail* or Sefton Delmer on the *Daily Express* — that kind of big name, roving reporter. Noel Barber actually got shot in the head in Budapest, which put him slightly ahead of Delmer as far as I was concerned" (Interview with Editors of *Theatre Quarterly* 1974, 4). While he does not mention Ernest Hemingway, one of his earliest literary heroes, Stoppard may also have had in mind Hemingway's successful career as a reporter, Paris correspondent, and, later on, roving free-lance feature writer covering wars in Europe and China. Stoppard never became famous as a reporter, but he managed to pay his bills while finding the time to write fiction and plays. He also developed the reviewer's habit of becoming immersed in the works of a single writer, a habit that may have triggered his deforming repetitions of others' texts. As he explained to Ronald Hayman in 1974, reading gave him something to write about. As a journalist, one "read[s] the works of Norman Mailer in fourteen days in order to write an article of 1200 words" (Hayman 1979, 1). With some important exceptions, Stoppard still finds his material for plays as he would for reviews, largely outside of his personal life and frequently in the works of other writers.

In his four years with the *Western Daily Press*, 1954–57, Stoppard wrote without a byline, but probably began to use the initials "D. D. F." shortly before resigning, which, in his second job with the *Bristol Evening World* (*BEW*) became the full-blown pseudonym, "David Foot."[2] He also occasionally reviewed plays as what I would assume to be a third-string reviewer (the prototype for Puckeridge of *The Real Inspector Hound?*) as two other regularly featured drama reviewers wrote under a byline at this time, and a third (Stoppard?) wrote without one.

During this period, he made friends at the Bristol Old Vic and discovered the work of Peter O'Toole, which began his serious interest in observing and writing for the theater. Several years later, in 1962, Stoppard would make O'Toole the subject of a long and admiring interview in which the actor described his commitment to serious contemporary theater by announcing his post–*Lawrence of Arabia* plans to produce works by Brecht, Beckett, and Anouilh, with little or no pay. This O'Toole, free-spirited champion of radical but still literary theater and performer of rare intensity was, to take Kenneth Tynan at his word, single-handedly responsible for turning Stoppard toward writing plays (1980, 59).

Like his fictional reviewer Moon from *Real Inspector Hound*, young reporter Stoppard hoped to work his way up the journalistic ladder. Junior reporters could do this by establishing a specialty, getting a byline, and building a reputation for a particular kind of reporting. Unfortunately, neither drama reviewing nor soccer reporting were likely to make his fame in the newspaper business, where city or political reporting were considered the pathways to eventual editorship of a paper. It seems unlikely that young Stoppard would have aspired to editorship of a provincial paper, so his upward path lay in establishing himself as an extraordinary writer. For that, he eventually would have to go to London. Early in 1958, after four years with the *Western Daily Press,* he accepted an offer from the rival *Bristol Evening World* to write a soccer column, features, and film reviews. This represented a step up (and a raise in salary), as he was now writing front-page general news as well as continuing regularly to write soccer news and theater and film reviews. During January and February of 1958, the byline "David Foot" appeared on front-page stories and on the soccer column.[3] Sometime during 1959 or early 1960, Stoppard's own name began to appear as a byline under some theater reviews; other reviews, as well as many soccer columns, were signed "David Foot."

Stoppard's *BEW* drama reviews show that he was initially attracted to the theater by observing the actor's art; his comments on acting tended to be especially acute. Describing an appearance by Noël Coward in Graham Greene's film, *Our Man in Havana,* young Stoppard praised Coward's self-conscious portrayal of the gentleman: "There is a gem of a performance by Coward, an immaculate well-bred vision of correctness that is not quite parody. This is how others see us, and this, Coward suggests skillfully, is how some of us really are" ("Guinness Seems," 1960). Both qualities of the Coward performance — its elegant polish as well as its presentational surface ("this is how some of us really are") — would eventually become features of his own articulate heroes and heroines, aware of themselves as actors presenting themselves to spectators. In the same review, Stoppard laments Alec Guinness's underplaying of his role, suggesting that comic material cannot bear too much subtlety. Guinness's performance, he writes, "is meticulously thought out, but so subtlely projected, so soft-pedalled that the comedy . . . is at times refined out of existence." In attempting to sort out the successful comic performance from the near miss, the critic is training the playwright: to get a laugh, a performance must be sufficiently but not excessively broad; urbane but accessible; artificial but authentic. We can even find in these reviews clues to later Stoppard characters such as Rupert Purvis, the quietly desperate double agent in the radio play, *The Dog It Was That Died* (1983), who, like the type of inspector Stoppard claims to prefer, runs toward "clean-collar decency" and an "unostentatious yet efficient air that makes the more familiar tough-talking . . . American-influenced wonder boys look the cardboard cut-outs they are" ("It's a Joy," 1960). (The American wonder boy would later appear as Waites, the black intelligence agent in *Hapgood.*)

Even in these early journalism years, Stoppard had a keen nose for detecting the bogus in art. An early story on a self-proclaimed group of Bristol "beat" writers who had abandoned society in disgust drew the reporter's comment, "There is something stagey about a roomful of people all acting as if they are alone" ("Tom Stoppard Treads," 1960). In addition to exposing the pseudo-artistic enemies of society, critic Stoppard suspected the motives of a commercial film about teenage sexual abuse that appeared to claim credit for fighting social evils: "It is all too easy for a film to lay claim to a penetrating inquiry into a social problem, when all it's doing is making hay with a nasty — but commercially alluring — subject" ("Teenage Problem," 1960). These two reviews touch on a question that will continue to haunt Stoppard: are artists responsible for commenting directly upon the social world within which they write, or may they choose to behave as if their art were self-contained and distinct from that world? The Bristol beats are inauthentic because they have answered the question too simply: withdrawal from the world is sanctioned by their dismissal of nonartists as an inferior tribe. On the other hand, some artists pretend to be socially responsible by virtue of choosing to write about particular topics—housing, sexual abuse, unemployment. The real test of responsibility, Stoppard implies, is not the issue written about but the vantage from which it is viewed. Stoppard's plays have posed the question of the artist's responsibility from various angles, but no single angle can provide an answer. The journalist and the artist must keep one foot in fantasy, the other in reality; they both stand "inside and outside society," granted this privilege by virtue of talent—and luck.

Besides admiring the art of the actor, Stoppard's *BEW* theater and film reviews mockingly praised the deft use of comic plots and characters. When describing a classic tearjerker film in 1960, reviewer Stoppard wrote: "I . . . admire the genius of a scriptwriter who, without strain or artifice, . . . brought so many stock ingredients out of cold storage and packaged them up into a whole that bears the stamp of sincerity" ("Tear-jerker," 1960). In hindsight, his contempt for the automatic assembling of stock devices predicted his own determination to use them in thoroughly original ways.

What would become thematic preoccupations in his creative work also began to surface during his days with the *Bristol Evening World*. Stoppard complimented an early Richard Attenborough film, *The Angry Silence*, with a nearly literal prefiguring of his own comic hybrid. The film blended "entertainment and education as completely as a row of chorus girls explaining Einstein's theory of light" ("As a Shout," 1960). (*Travesties* would later feature a beautiful Wildean heroine explaining Lenin's theory of value.) But the reviewer's stronger attraction to the film lay in its central subject: a machinist who refuses to join a strike because he objects to the organizers' methods. After veiled threats, the worker initially gives in to the strikers, but when he is warned not to step out of line in the future, he rebels and returns to work alone. Eventually murdered by union thugs, he could be the prototype for independent reporter Jacob Milne of Stoppard's *Night and Day* who refuses to join the National Union of Journalists' strike against a Grimsby newspaper and is eventually killed by gunfire while covering a story about a civil war. The basic opposition between the lone outsider and the group in power prefigures many of Stoppard's plays beginning with *Enter a Free Man,* where unemployed inventor George Riley refuses to compromise his independence by accepting a government handout. (Riley's heroism is finally equivocal, as his independence is purchased at the cost of his daughter's and wife's enslavement to dreary jobs.) In the 1983 radio play, *The Dog It Was That Died,* double agent Purvis rejects both England and Russia in favor of standing on independent, and therefore uncertain, ground. Double agents, artists, and journalists, living "both inside and outside" of society, emerge as the type of the Stoppardian hero.

While this 1960 review of Attenborough's film hints at Stoppard's libertarianism, others, written in the same year and later, reveal his staunch support of minor or marginal figures in British theater and film. Speaking in defense of the British actress ("I know where to choose my friends," he quips), reporter Stoppard asks why her French and Italian counterparts must be imported to lend continental sheen to a British comedy like "Inn for Trouble." Why must the maid in *Upstairs and Downstairs* be French? "Was it really essential for Pier Angeli to play Richard Attenborough's wife in 'The Angry Silence?' " ("Was Their Journey?" 1960).

In a similarly slanted *BEW* film review, he touted a number of small, new British film companies begun by artists such as actor Richard Attenborough and director Joseph Losey, determined to produce quality films outside the commercial establishments of Hollywood and Pinewood: "Bryanston, Beaver, Allied, Cambria—all new names, names that you possibly have never heard of. . . . But you *have* heard of their products. And you are going to hear a great deal more." Stoppard takes sides with these small companies who represent the power of the actor triumphing over the power of moronic "front office" "big boys." "There is an important point in their make-up. In nearly every case the company has been started by actors" ("Look Out for," 1960). Thus, contrary to the opinions of his detractors eager to ally him with unthinking conservatism (Roberts 1978, 85), Stoppard's taste and sympathies have always been with independent and adventurous artists—both in England and abroad.

By March of 1960, when Stoppard's name had begun appearing regularly under film and theater reviews, he had been writing fiction and drama on his own. He had come to a parting of the roads and decided, in July of 1960, to attempt to make his living as a writer rather than a journalist. It was a difficult decision for several reasons, but primarily because it would remove him even further from the center of the traditional working world than had the profession of journalism. Eight years later in a *Sunday Times* interview, he explained his hesitation in this way: "I feel some guilt about being a writer. Probably all artists feel guilty. . . . Artists are made to feel decorators, embroiderers, who . . . don't in fact contribute in a way that one can contribute a bicycle or a pound of butter, who somehow are in a business that can barely justify itself until we have enough butter and all that butter stands for" ("Something to Declare," 1968). Not until *Travesties,* his ambivalent assertion of the artist's freedom from social and political claims, would Stoppard partially exorcise this guilt.

Stoppard has candidly admitted to the journalist Jon Bradshaw that he was never good at journalism: "I wasn't much use as a reporter. I felt I didn't have the right to ask people questions. . . . For me, it was like knocking at the door, wearing your reporter's peaked cap, and saying: 'Hello, I'm from journalism. I've come to inspect you. Take off your clothes and lie down' " (Bradshaw 1977, 47–48). (Is it merely coincidental that Ruth Carson does just this—twice—with reporter Wagner?) The ethical problem involved in exposing people's private lives in the public press did trouble Stoppard deeply enough to inform one of his short stories (called "The Story") in which a child abuser commits suicide after being written up in a newspaper. But he was also disappointed with what passed as journalism. The beginnings of his disillusionment with actual newswriting can be traced to his move from provincial Bristol to London. Expecting Fleet Street to be filled with brilliant writers, Stoppard discovered instead that most reporters wrote badly and, worse, they didn't much care: "I misunderstood the nature of Fleet Street. It wasn't until I had been there and looked about that I realized that people weren't actually that good; most of them were terrible, and would have been well down the batting order in Bristol" (Interview with Mark Amory 1974, 68). In spite of his disappointment with Fleet Street, Stoppard has remained a devoted fan of journalism—even a self-styled "groupie"—on the one hand dazzled by the glamor of roving correspondents and on the other ideologically committed to the principle of press freedom as the primary guarantor of human rights.

After quitting the *Bristol Evening World,* Stoppard free-lanced for various papers between July of 1960 and August of 1962, among them the *Western Daily Press* (again!) where he wrote drama reviews under the editorship of A. C. H. Smith, who told Amory that he had found them "marvellous, extraordinary" (Interview with Amory 1974, 66). Stoppard himself dismissed this period of his review writing as embarrassingly egotistical: "There is a sort of second-rate journalism that presents the journalist more than the subject. I did that" (Interview with Amory, 66). He accepted a final reviewing position with *Scene,* an upscale arts magazine for which he wrote numerous essays and essay-interviews during its short life, from September of 1962 to April of 1963. During the *Scene* period, Stoppard continued to support noncommercial theater, singling out the Bristol Old Vic, the New Arts, Joan Littlewood's Theatre Workshop, and the Royal Court as worthy of a greater share of resources and recognition than they had been receiving. In a long *Scene* piece, Stoppard laments the lack of support, governmental and private, for fringe theaters whose enviable New York off-Broadway counterparts were offering plays by "Brecht, Genet, Ionesco, Williams, Beckett, Albee, two or three unknowns and a selection of satirical revues . . . " ("Off the Shaftesbury Fringe," 1962). He also began to assert his judgments of artistic quality more forcefully, distinguishing between authentic and falsely imposed directorial concepts and ranking plays as major, minor, or "in between" works of theater. He rarely praised a poorly crafted play, the exception being novelist Edna O'Brien's first stage attempt, *A Cheap Bunch of Nice Flowers.* The O'Brien piece, like its predecessor at the New Arts, Muriel Spark's *Doctors of Philosophy,* violated Stoppard's ground rules for stagecraft but still won points for literate writing and sound characterization ("Fine Hand at Work," 1962). Implicit in this review is Stoppard's belief that the playwright should master the conventions of traditional stagecraft—writing for a stable set, creating consistent characters, and driving the plot toward a plausible conclusion—before undertaking experiments in moving walls and disappearing characters.

> Miss Spark's assault [on the technical canons of stagecraft] was grandiose, involving mobile walls, characters stepping in and out of the play, and so on. The trouble was that all this did not grow out of the play but was imposed upon it, and it is significant that after the first night these tricks were done away with and the play worked better as a straightforward and literate comedy. (19)

Good playwrights avoid retreating into the safety of formulaic writing while at the same time displaying a mastery of formulae adequate to set off their improvements upon them.

The growing seriousness and intensity of Stoppard's reviews reflect a major change taking place in his role as a writer. Having become a fellow playwright as well as judge, he commented more freely and passionately upon the London theater in which he had a stake. By the end of 1960, his first play, *A Walk on the Water,* later revised as *Enter a Free Man,* had been optioned by H. M. Tenant. And while it would take three years to secure a production, and then on television rather than the stage, Stoppard's first play nevertheless transformed him from reviewer-as-critic to reviewer-as-playwright. Consequently, the tone of his reviews sharpened, reflecting his impatience with that segment of the contemporary British theater that refused to take seriously the craft of writing and staging plays.

Typical of this impatience are the *Scene* reviews dismissing "formulaic" writing. His concern was not that play-writing formulae should be avoided altogether, but that they should be avoided as a means of simplifying the writing or viewing of plays. Contempt for "canned" writing runs consistently throughout the *Scene* reviews: "*Big Fish Little Fish* . . . lays itself open to the suspicion of having been assembled from a tried-and-tested theatrical cookbook . . . " ("Big Fish Little Fish," 1962). When reviewing a comedy starring Sir Laurence Olivier, Stoppard is more explicit: "Described as 'a satirical comedy,' [this] play . . . bestride[s] the gap between the smart ridicule of the Fringe fringe and the conventional plot-riddled uproar of domestic crisis. (There is something about the current writing scene which encourages this sort of analysis, suggesting a given number of dramatic idioms to be used in any combination, like a Readymix . . .)" ("New Wave Olivier," 1962). He reserves a special contempt for what he calls "in-between" plays, those not good enough to occupy a commercial theater for profit but "too good" for radio or television: "I think of these plays as being not so much written as typed." He associates their mediocrity with a complacent efficiency, describing the "machined expertness" with which they "present a single situation-idea, turn it around, get a few laughs out of it and ring down the curtain on it." The edge of Stoppard's criticism in this review seems to follow from his belief that these are not honest, all-out efforts at good play writing but safe and sterile exercises in a proven technique ("A Case of Double Vision," 1963). He later faults an actor's performance in an adaptation of Gogol's *The Diary of a Madman* for having been pulled from "a bag of mechanical tricks" ("Tom Stoppard on the Strange Fact," 1963). It comes as no surprise that when this reviewer turned to writing plays, he aimed for comedy of the most self-conscious sort, subverting the expected use of a genre convention or a character type.

Not only canned writing but sloppy writing comes under attack. Even a largely favorable review faults the gratuitous gag. The "pointless jests" in James Saunders's script, *Next Time I'll Sing To You,*[4] prompted comparison with their Beckettian source: "In Beckett, everything counts, nothing is arbitrary" ("Tom Stoppard on a . . . New Writer," 1963). Tight construction and maximum density of language—two of mature Stoppard's criteria for well-crafted plays—were already conscious markers of quality. And the example of Beckett was foremost in Stoppard's mind when assessing the merits of contemporary plays, particularly those reflecting the Irishman's influence.

Perhaps most revealing of Stoppard's maturing sense of craft and of his seriousness as a judge and writer of plays are his reviews of playwrights he strongly admires: Brecht, Ibsen, Shakespeare, and Beckett. In these above all other *Scene* essays, the reviewer qualifies his admiration with a detailed accounting of where productions have failed to make the text visible in a new way. In each of these reviews, Stoppard isolates basic elements of play production—ideology, unity, action, technical realization—noting where they do and do not cohere to promote an authentically new reading of a script. Some of his commentary is overtly ideological. Marking the irony of Brecht's commercial success at the Royal Court, Stoppard praised his ability to "merge art and doctrine into a theater of genius" while arguing that Brecht's attempts to distance his audience (in this play, at least) were doomed to fail: "When he tried to dehumanize characters to caricature—'St. Joan of the Stockyards'—he failed as a playwright and his argument suffered in absurdity" ("Bits of Bert"). Ibsen's *Peer Gynt* is recklessly sprawling, wrote Stoppard of the Old Vic's 1962 revival starring Leo Kern, but the unity is provided by "the figure of Peer and his progress to his own epitaph: 'Life is a terrible price to pay for birth' " ("Peer's Progress," 1962).

In a tribute to Jack MacGowran's evening of Beckett excerpts at the New Arts, Stoppard revealed his admiration for the self-canceling effect of Beckett's serio-comedy, an effect that would inspire his own comedy of incertitude:

> At first there is something too arbitrary about assembling what is virtually a new bastard play by channeling speeches from eight sources into one character. But it works because Beckett's view of man's estate is consistent in all of them, a look of pity and ironic amusement. . . . caught between memory and desire. Everything is cancelled out ("Crying Till You Laugh," 1962).

But a later viewing of Beckett's *Happy Days* left critic Stoppard dissatisfied with Beckett's nearly complete eclipsing of dramatic action: "The statement has left the theater behind. . . . and dramatically it is not enough" ("Waiting for Scofield," 1962). Again, the critic's objection anticipates the playwright's practice. For Stoppard, *theater* means action, vivid dialogue, and spectacle, including song and dance.

While his admiration for Beckett has never truly flagged, Stoppard here signaled its limits. After all, his own preference and practice has been the antithesis of minimalism. Stoppard recognized early on that although Beckett's *Godot* had "redefined the minima of theatrical validity" (Hayman 1979, 6), his own talent, as well as the future of the theater he hoped to work in, lay in the surprise exploitation of the full range of effects available to the playwright. This is not to deny the anxious influence of Beckett on, especially, the young playwright Stoppard, whose first unpublished play, *The Gamblers,* he later described as pseudo-Beckett, and whose *Rosencrantz and Guildenstern Are Dead* parodies *Godot* in an attempt both to acknowledge and to resist its authority. This early critique of Beckett's tendency to "leave the theatre behind" would eventually support Stoppard's own efforts to leave Beckett behind.

Stoppard's *Scene* reviews of major Shakespearean productions are especially acute in judging where a director's concept proceeds from the play's language and where it adheres thinly to a few gags or tricks designed to dress up rather than rethink the play. Thus, Peter Brook's idiosyncratic *King Lear*, played by Paul Scofield as a "slightly dotty and ill-behaved old extrovert with a latent persecution complex," scores points in spite of excising lines and running for two hours without break to the end of the third act. The changes are justified, Stoppard argues, as they capitalize upon Lear's lopsided domination of the play. But the Royal Shakespeare Company's versions of *The Tempest* and *Julius Caesar* do not fare well, as their directorial concepts are imposed from without rather than developed from within the text. "In *The Tempest* the accent is on gags," writes Stoppard, citing "a white rat passing across the stage on a conveyor belt," "a stool rising out of the floor in time to meet Prospero's bottom," and "trapdoors all over the place" as just a few examples. Caliban, twice described in the text as fish-like, is gratuitously portrayed as a naked Negro ("Tom Stoppard on Why Directors," 1963).

Julius Caesar misses the mark by failing to use set, costume, and character effectively. What should be moving instead seems merely contrived: "John Blatchley has Cinna's murderers chuckling moronically, which is effective, and the killing ends with a rag dummy being hurled out of view, which is not." When Mark Antony enters in Roman running gear, he "looks as if he had to get out of his bath to answer the telephone, clutching a scrap of towel round him." The text alludes to Cassius as a man who "reads much" and "thinks too much," but this production cast Cyril Cusack in the role "who by his hands-on-hip stance and bullet-headedness" fails to suggest a lean and hungry intellectual. But "the abiding and fatal omission is any sense of place." Not only are the crowd scenes "pathetic" but Caesar's triumphant procession is "ludicrous." Miscast, poorly designed, and transparently gimmicky, the production found little favor with reviewer Stoppard ("Tom Stoppard on Why Directors").

When fully engaged by a work he respects, Stoppard's critical sense points to what would become his play-writing practice. In addition to his appreciation of wit, Stoppard clearly preferred plays dense with literary allusion and orchestrated with an ear to rhythmic variation. The Shakespeare reviews show him awed by the text even when critical of a particular director's production concept. It is no accident that *Rosencrantz and Guildenstern Are Dead*, its earliest version written two years after these reviews, transports blocks of Shakespeare's lines untouched into the context of *Godot*. *Hamlet*'s structure can be violated, but not its language.

As Joan Dean was the first to suggest, Stoppard's long apprenticeship as a theater critic may account for his attraction to parody as comic method and compositional technique (1981, 6). In recycling prior texts, parody establishes the ground of tradition against which Stoppard's surprise deviations become both visible and valuable. The merely mechanical tricks dismissed by critic Stoppard as well as the unthinking reliance on literary habit and stage convention can be opposed by the defamiliarizing effect of parodic recycling. Best of all, in openly declaring its literary debts, parody invites the spectator to observe familiar texts operating in a new frame.

Since *Scene*'s demise in 1963, Stoppard has continued to write journalistic essays, reviews, and letters,[5] many of them directing Westerners' attention to the plight of (pre-perestroika) Czechoslovakian and Eastern bloc so-called dissidents, for whom publicity in the West has sometimes made the difference between imprisonment and relative freedom. As a mature artist, he has come to view journalism as uniquely suited to accomplishing just this kind of short-range goal for social change (Interview with Editors of *Theatre Quarterly*, 14). But for the young Stoppard in Bristol, journalism was a back-door to the stage.

Fiction: The Road Not Taken

Two of the three stories Stoppard published in 1964 rely directly and in terms at least partly autobiographical on his experiences as a journalist. "Life, Times: Fragments" tells the story of a writer of fiction who subs for a daily newspaper while waiting to become famous. Some of the narrative details come directly, with minor changes, from Stoppard's own life – the decision to resign his journalism position at the end of a summer vacation; the move from the provinces to London; a disastrous interview with a newspaper editor;[6] and the ambition to write an audacious novel that would break with the old models. But the details are embedded in a frame loosely modeled on Beckett's *Krapp's Last Tape,* beginning with the writer's first days as a journalist, then skipping ahead to "the thirty-fourth year of his obscurity," and finally to his fiftieth year, when, still unknown, he has become the oldest sub in London. The whimsically un-Beckettian conclusion describes the writer's suicide after hearing an angel recite a rejection slip from God. His body is subsequently discovered and his corpus enshrined by the most famous critic in the land.

Stoppard's decision to narrate this story by alternating first and third person may have been inspired by Beckett's play, in which the voice of Krapp as narrator/commentator in the here and now alternates with the several taped voices of Krapp at younger ages. One senses in "Life, Times" the near identity of the two narrative voices; thus, the effect of switching between first and third person is that of the storyteller revising himself—a technique that will reappear in *Lord Malquist and Mr Moon*. The third person narrator takes an ironical view of the first person narrator, "Shouting into the teeth of the thirty-fourth year of his obscurity, he patrolled the battleground of fallen heroes . . . " (127) much as Krapp ridicules his younger self: "Just been listening to that stupid bastard I took myself for thirty years ago . . . " (Beckett, 24). Some of the comments made by the author/narrator/character are mischievously self-referential. At age fifty and still unknown, the first person narrator assures us that he puts on a brave face for the world in spite of his desperation: "You should see me, I am drowning with the panache of someone walking on the water. That's not bad. I could slip it in somewhere" (129). *A Walk on the Water*, Stoppard's first stage play written in the second half of 1960, had been adapted for television and broadcast one year earlier. In shaping his own version of the trendy fiction about fiction writing, Stoppard hit on his characteristic blend of farcical exaggeration and dry wit, mocking his own plans to write a radically new novel (commissioned one year earlier) that would make him famous:

> "Listen," he said, "the models are not good any more, we've had all that, we're on our own now," and bending into her profile . . . he said, "I will do it, yes, that much I know, I will do it and it will be for you," . . . *"I am—I feel—seminal!"* and she, getting up, faceless for the dark, said, "No, do you mind if we don't tonight. I've run out of the stuff." (128)

While cutting his ties with journalism to devote himself full-time to fiction and drama, Stoppard wrote a story about a sub journalist trying and failing to become a recognized author. But in spite of its comically forlorn hero, the story's effect is that of a happy, even exuberant testimonial celebrating the young author's membership in the down-at-heel tribe of writers.

"The Story," on the other hand, narrated by a journalist, painfully recalls a news story that resulted in a schoolmaster's suicide after his exposure as a child molester. In this story about a journalistic story, the narrator uses the tone and slang of the newsroom to reproduce for the reader the world in which the event occurred. He even includes in the second paragraph an explanation of how the Press Service and International-Express paid journalists for stories, a detail needed at the story's close. But for the most part, Stoppard takes care that the world and its rules emerge through the details of the story without calling particular attention to themselves.

Once the narrator begins to dramatize the events of the story haunting him, his characters'—both journalists— professional disregard for the story's subject becomes blatantly obvious:

> "Much about?"
> "No, even sin seems to be on the way out."
> I said, "I had a teacher on an indecency."
> Diver stopped slapping (the paper). It was just like that.
> "Did he go down?"
> "No, twenty-five quid."
> "Oh well, I don't know. What school?"
> So I told him that.
> Diver said, "Christ, that's worth a line. What was it all about?" (133)

The narrator's strict adherence to the story's details, his refusal to comment on the fact that its publication in most of the August 9th papers preceded by one week the schoolmaster's suicide, is masterfully ironical in the style of Hemingway, one of Stoppard's heroes at this point in his life. But more significantly, the narrator's drive to tell the story in the first place, his need to confess his complicity in a man's death, shows Stoppard to have been as preoccupied with the moral consequences of writing in his work of the 1960s as he has been in the 1970s and 1980s. The narrator's concluding tally of his earnings from the story, listed in pounds, shillings, and quid, draws the reader into his guilt as we register his failure to state the implied moral:

> About a month after that I got a check for a guinea from the Broking daily. Inter-Ex paid out 18s. for the paragraph and there was 23s. 6d. from P.S. That made £3 2s. 6d. I don't know what I spent it on. It got mixed up with my other money and at the end of the month I was broke as usual. (136)

Stoppard's ability as a "straight" storyteller was considerable, but storytelling was not suited to his gifts as a writer. He clearly views these stories as failures, having described them to Mel Gussow in 1984 as "bad Hemingway stories." "I was passionate about Hemingway when I started writing. . . . I think he's still my favorite American writer" (Gussow 1984, 28). The missing ingredient in "The Story" is the sense of play and distance typical of most of Stoppard's works. "The Story" is not a parody of Hemingway—the reader is not invited to recognize in it a Hemingway model being resisted or distorted in some way — it is just an attempt to "sound like" him. As Stoppard told Gussow, "The more you like another writer the more you shy away from using him as a model — because it's a fatal attraction" (28). Stoppard's ability to write lean, understated dialogue would surface later with greater playfulness in his work for television and in his stage plays about Eastern European dissidents.

The third story to appear in the "Stories by New Writers" collection, called "Reunion," is the first and only serious treatment of romantic love he published before returning to it in 1982 with his stage success, *The Real Thing*. The narrator and central character are again nearly identical, with the narrator describing how the protagonist thinks and feels during his brief and painful reunion with a former lover. The fear of breaking apart, of being overcome by chaos and loneliness, play off in the protagonist's mind against the hope that he can locate a particular word which, "if shouted at the right pitch . . . would nudge the universe into gear" (123). He explains this compressed description of the Joycean "epiphany" to his remote lady friend using details that will surface again in *Lord Malquist and Mr Moon*, very likely being written during this same period. This special word, he tells her,

> would have to be shouted in some public place dedicated to silence . . . a monstrous, unspeakable intrusion after which nothing can be the same for the man who does it. . . . It must be stumbled upon, loudly and spontaneously, in exactly the right circumstances. It will probably turn out to be an obscenity. (123)

Stephen Hero, the probable model for this particular Moon obsession, searched among Dubliners' vulgarities for just the phrase or few sentences that would perfectly capture an emotion or thought (Joyce 1963, 211). But Stoppard's Moon does not share Stephen Hero's faith in language to capture and, in capturing, to elevate reality. (Moon's word does turn out to be an obscenity printed across a huge balloon inflated in the middle of Trafalgar Square during a public funeral.)

The story's dialogue consists of the protagonist's desperately witty attempts to win back his love and her nearly monosyllabic resistance to renewing the relationship. In an appeal that Stoppard will use later in *The Real Thing*, the protagonist woos her with words, putting before her small tributes of eloquence, bouquets of wit, as if to suggest that for him, love flows through language and language through love. But he fails to engage her in the invention game, and she finally turns him away with a blunt, "Shut up!" In closing off dialogue, she closes off love.

Although the weakest of the three stories, "Reunion" is of interest as a small-scale study of the novel's obsessions and as an example of Stoppard's difficulty with writing emotions, a weakness he defended during his 1971 interview with Kenneth Tynan: "I don't see any special virtue in making my private emotions the quarry for the statue I'm carving. I can do that kind of writing, but it tends to go off, like fruit" (64). When Stoppard wrote his novel, he avoided the emotional realism of "Reunion," preferring to stylize his characters in the direction of manners comedy and to equip them with concerns extending beyond their immediate emotional fortunes. The result is a compelling, if not entirely successful, mock epic that sums up Stoppard's early obsessions with the frightening gigantism of modern living, with the death of the individual, and with the expressive possibilities of art.

Lord Malquist and Mr Moon: A London Odyssey

"I used to interview the upholstery," Stoppard told Kenneth Tynan when describing his ambition as a young journalist hoping to make it to Fleet Street (1980, 58). In his first and only novel, *Lord Malquist and Mr Moon*, the auto-interview becomes one of Moon's anodynes along with his Uncle Jackson's bomb, which Moon will set off when he can no longer tolerate the accelerating expansion of modern life. The overwhelming complexity of the world is made particularly painful by his marriage to a beautiful cousin with no interest in sex (a prototype of Penelope/Dotty Moore). Stoppard had high hopes for his novel, commissioned in 1963 by Anthony Blond: "I liked it enormously when I wrote it—" he told the *New Yorker* in 1968, "I worked on it for months, all day and half the night . . . " (41). Published in the same week in August 1966 that *Rosencrantz and Guildenstern Are Dead* opened at the Edinburgh Festival, Stoppard firmly believed " . . . that the novel would make my reputation, and the play would be of little consequence either way" (Interview with Janet Watts 1973, 12). History has proven it otherwise. While the play made Stoppard's reputation as a dramatist, *Moon* had sold 481 copies as of April 1967 (Interview with Keith Harper 1967, 7). In writing *Moon*, Stoppard believed he was creating his masterwork, a diminutive, parodic *Ulysses*, cataloguing and juxtaposing with great energy and innovation his formal and thematic experiments of the early 1960s with images of the state of the British nation after Churchill's death. And while the novel has yet to capture a vast reading public, it has come due for its share of renewed critical attention as the prose precursor of the stage anthology, *Travesties*. As Ronald Hayman has commented on the novel, "style is one of [its] main subjects, and amusing reverberations are set up between the style of the narrative, the life-style of the characters and their prose-style, both in conversation and in what they write" (1979, 48).

Stoppard identifies his novel with Joyce's Dublin Odyssey, adapting some of the characters and narrative strategies of *Ulysses*, but forging his own postmodern epic on the smithy of literary parody. Largely confined to the twenty-four-hour period between 29 and 30 January 1965, *Moon* traces the hero's wanderings about London on the eve and day of an unnamed statesman's (Sir Winston Churchill's) funeral. Structured episodically, *Moon* does not so much tell a story as present a series of loosely connected events in the lives of London eccentrics which together signify something of the bizarre chaos of the modern world after the death of its heroes.

While the narrative avoids a strict chronology, occasionally doubling back on itself to present the same event from another character's point of view, a summary of the titles and key incidents in each chapter clarifies the novel's spatial pattern which, in turn, points to its overall significance. Chapter 1, "Dramatis Personae and Other Coincidences," introduces us to the characters' idioms and their obsessions. In the course of chapter 2, "A Couple of Deaths and Exits," located entirely within Moon's residence, two people are killed, Moon's wife and new client exit together with apparently amorous intentions, Moon sets off the twelve-hour fuse on his bomb, and accidentally incinerates the notebook in which he is recording (Boswell-like) the bon mots of his new client (and his wife's new admirer), Lord Malquist. The third and briefest of all chapters, "Chronicler of the Time," presents directly Moon's reconstruction of the destroyed Malquist journal—a narrative within the narrative—written in Moon's stiff, prissy prose and conspicuous in its failure to record even a single of Malquist's epigrams. Chapter 4, "Spectator as Hero," is relatively action-packed. Moon places the two corpses now wrapped in his living room rug on the back of the donkey provided by a wandering American who calls himself the "Risen Christ," and sends him out into the city; he departs for Malquist's residence where the earl's wife invites him to bed; he leaves to find her stray shoe in Green Park; and eventually he meets up with the other characters and most of London in Trafalgar Square where Churchill's state funeral is under way. We are close to the novel's catastrophic climax, when, in chapter 5, Lord Malquist and Jane approach Trafalgar Square in his coach and pair, with Malquist enumerating the public monuments they encounter in the manner of Leopold Bloom, "Mayor of Dublin" in the Circe episode of *Ulysses*. All are now proceeding toward the Square—the Risen Christ on his donkey, the two cowboys competing for Jane's affections, and Moon with his bomb. Nearly simultaneously, the bomb goes off, inflating a giant balloon inscribed with a two-word obscenity, the cowboys shoot one another to death, the Risen Christ's donkey is accidentally hit by a stray bullet, the carriage rocks into the square, and the funeral procession reaches its full ceremonial splendor and solemnity. In the sixth and final chapter, "An Honorable Death," all of the characters return to Malquist's house, each nursing his or her own obsession. While Lord Malquist and Jane retire to his bedroom, Moon borrows Malquist's hat, cape, and carriage and, mistaken for Malquist himself, is blown up by a real bomb thrown by the husband of a working-class woman run down by Malquist's coach in the opening chapter.

In organizing the novel spatially about the residences of Moon and Malquist, Stoppard established its dialectic to be a series of contrasts between the ninth earl and his would-be chronicler. Idealist Moon and aristocrat Malquist are attracted and repelled as are Bloom and Stephen Dedalus. Both Malquist and Bloom are the "last of a line," without living heirs or the promise of heirs. Stephen and Moon offer Bloom and Malquist a kind of immortality, Stephen by functioning as an adopted son, Moon by acting as Malquist's Boswell. But Moon's journal fails dismally to preserve Malquist's witticisms and Moon, the "son," has taken Malquist's place in his wife's bed just as Malquist is to take Moon's. Parallels to *Ulysses'* female characters are also conspicuously, if loosely, drawn. Laura Malquist, a charming alcoholic obsessed with her childlessness, has what appears to be countless lovers although perhaps not as many as the twenty-five listed by Bloom in the Ithaca episode of *Ulysses*. Moon's own wife, Jane, has been given Molly's theatricality, although Jane's sexual preferences are ambiguous. Either a voyeur or a nymphomaniac—the narrator leaves us guessing—Jane torments Moon with her suggestive posture whenever he encounters her with one of her suitors.

Stoppard's novel also contains several Joycean narrative features as well as a few of its own surprises. When introducing his cast of characters in chapter 1, "Dramatis Personae," Stoppard occasionally uses Flaubert's method, developed by Joyce in *Dubliners* (Lawrence 1981, 23), of presenting them in their own idiom complete with their limitations. The introduction of Jane Moon provides the best example:

Jane was sitting at her toilette, as she called it in the French manner, dreaming of might-have-beens. It was the height of the Season in London, and an onlooker might have been forgiven for wondering why it was that this mere slip of a girl with hair like spun gold, with exquisite features that proclaimed a noble breeding, should sit alone with sadness in her heart. (10)

The point of this technique is not to expose Jane as self-deluded nor to dismiss her as a ridiculous romantic but to let us in to her imaginary world where we see that, among other things, she plays at being a ridiculously romantic hero-ine. The world of *Moon* is one in which all characters deliberately and know-ingly wear masks and even drop or change masks from time to time as they see fit. Only Moon, or so he thinks, is authentic and reliable, although in this he underestimates and oversimplifies himself.

Each of the main characters is introduced mockingly in this chapter. The Risen Christ, leading his donkey to the city to preach The Word, is a mock simpleton:

> He hoped to find a fig-tree among the stunted hawthorns but there was food only for the donkey. He smiled gently at this reminder of the infinite workings that compensated all God's creatures for their limitations and checked them for their presumptions. He lay down on the grass and fell asleep. (9)

Laura Malquist, drunk and abandoned by her friends, wanders in an alcoholic daze over Green Park, "Her mouth and throat, her whole body, felt as if she had never had a drink in her life and all the dry years were compressed now into a terrible need" (8). Long John Slaughter and Jasper Jones, two bourgeois refugees from a pork 'n' beans commercial, ready to compete to the death for Jane Moon's love, square off for a near showdown. The narrator provides the telltale clichés, "Slaughter was a left-handed gun and he had the look of a man who had come a long way" (7). But when introducing us to Lord Malquist, the narrator uses direct discourse, quoting exactly the earl's epigrams and com-menting upon them parenthetically in a Nabokovian aside: " 'When the battle becomes a farce the only position of dignity is above it,' said the ninth earl (the battle raging farcically beneath him)" (3). The narrator pokes fun at Malquist's posing just as he does at his excessive care for style in dress and manners: "He took a grip (lilac-gloved) on the door-frame (rosewood, mother-of-pearl) as the pair of horses rocked the coach up Whitehall. . . ." (3). But the con-fidence of Malquist's epigrams, some of them direct quotes from Oscar Wilde, privileges his dialogue in the novel. Malquist speaks, as he dresses, with style, escaping the flattening treatment of most of the novel's characters.

Moon is presented to us in yet another way, through the narrator's description of his thought and action, suggesting a unique intimacy between Moon and the narrator: "Moon, snatching at the tail-ends of recollection, trust-ing the echo in his skull to reproduce a meaning that had not touched him, scribbled with a kindergarten fist against the sway . . . " (3). We come to know everything about Moon, but very little about the interior states of the other characters. Only Moon, and to a certain extent Malquist, appear to be self-dramatizing types whose antics amuse and move us. Like Malquist, Moon is given a high degree of self-awareness, if a low degree of linguistic confidence of the Malquist variety, as we learn from the narrator's report at the end of chapter 1: "He had tried to pin the image of an emotion against the wall but he did not have the words to transfix it. . . . he did not have the words to translate a certain fear about something as real as a coffee-pot . . . " (18). And in this echo of J. Alfred Prufrock imagining himself "formulated, sprawling on a pin" lies the crucial difference between Stoppard's and Joyce's epics.

Malquist's and Moon's divergent responses to the paralysis of Britain at the moment of Churchill's death correspond to those of the withdrawn aristocrat and the quasi-anarchist. The Wildean language of confidence spoken by Malquist is counterpointed by the tentative inarticulateness of Moon, who hopes to "solve the world," like the Joyce of *Stephen Hero*, through an epiphany triggered by a vulgarity. In a final parodic gesture, Moon's vulgarity blows up over Trafalgar Square.

Moon expresses his perpetual state of intellectual uncertainty through the auto-interview which gives him two voices (one of which frequently sounds like Malquist's), signifying his failure to know for certain what he thinks and why he thinks it:

> *So you carry this bomb about with you expressly for the purpose of throwing it at someone?*
> Well, yes. I suppose there's no getting away from that. . . . I mainly think of throwing it.
> *At whom?*
> I don't know. I've got a list.
> *Now why exactly—*
> I don't know exactly. . . .
>
> (12)

In this adaptation of Joyce's Ithaca catechism, the interrogating voice seems to be Malquist's, reinforcing the idea that the entire novel is based upon a dialogue between Malquist and Moon. But Moon also has a variety of narrative voices, all of them dramatizing himself at significant moments in the action. Preparing to bring Laura Malquist a forbidden bottle of whiskey, Moon narrates his moment of glory by comparing it to the performance of a trained dog:

And flashing the old retainer one of my sunnier smiles I legged it upstairs with the water of life clutched to my bosom, and grinning like a golden retriever coming back to base with the first pheasant of the season. (124)

Later, after lying with Laura Malquist, Moon announces the fact to himself in a variety of idioms, each corresponding to one of his imagined selves:

I've had it away, he thought, amazed. *I have lain with Lady Malquist (how poetical!). Tupped her* bragged Moon Jacobean, *been intimate with her* claimed Moon journalistic, *I've had sexual relations* thought Puritan Moon. (134–35)

He sees himself in a dramatic light, as do the other characters, although Moon complains to Malquist's coachman, a Black Irish Jew by the name of O'Hara, that none of *them* seem real:

"The thing about people is," said Moon, "that hardly anyone behaves naturally any more, they all behave the way they think they are supposed to be, as if they'd read about themselves or seen themselves at the pictures. The whole of life is like that now." (48–49)

This concern for authenticity may not be altogether authentic, as Moon's interior monologues suggest. But his description of natural and unnatural behavior perfectly fits Stoppard's characters drawn from the stockpile of comic types and aware of themselves as actors in a drama. One of the problems of which they are aware in his plays is the difficulty of being completely who they are, if they can discover who that is.

The novel finally parodies (in a mocking spirit) both the earl's confident epigram and Moon's vulgarity. In the place of Joyce's vast catalogue of idioms, rhetorical devices, and rhythmic variations Stoppard offers a choice between the hyper- and the sub-articulate, both eventually found unequal to the task of "solving the world." When Moon asks Malquist what he "stands for," the earl responds, "Style, dear boy . . . Style. There is nothing else." But Moon, refusing to let it rest, silently counters: "*There is everything else. Substance. I stand for substance.*" The narrator then steps in to amend Moon's response, revealing his sympathy with the novel's hero: "That wasn't true at all, he didn't even know what it meant. He stood for peace of mind. For tidiness. For control, direction, order; proportion, above all he stood for proportion . . . " (57–58). The narrator's need to find the words is much stronger even than character Moon's and constitutes his particular quirk or obsession. The narrator, like Moon, thinks that language can express some kind of truth.

Perhaps the shadow hero of the novel, as of the stories and earliest stage plays, is not James Joyce at all but Samuel Beckett, who freed himself from Joyce's linguistic virtuosity by embracing the minima of artistic ambition, preferring "the expression that there is nothing to express, nothing with which to express, nothing from which to express . . . together with the obligation to express" (Beckett 1965, 103). The link between Stoppard and Beckett is their mutual gravitation toward the incomplete, the unclear, the inexpressible in art. But Stoppard's response to the inexpressible is to stage a series of verbal displays or feints, cheerful but doomed attempts to capture and fix meaning. While the comic Stoppard would move very quickly away from Beckett's black humor, he would nevertheless continue to find heroic his characters' Beckettian willingness to admit that they cannot find the words to contain their chaos.

Chapter 2

The Plays for Radio and Television

Part I: Discovering the Media

The Fear of Falling: Early Radio Plays, 1964–72

Tom Stoppard typifies the postwar British dramatist in having written for the radio early in his career. The aural medium attracts the promising playwright for several reasons, not the least of which is the British Broadcasting Corporation's history of creating and promoting "serious" radio drama as a distinct genre (Drakakis 1981, 1–36). It has become commonplace to argue that virtually all important modern British playwrights started in radio, a medium more accessible than the stage or screen by virtue of the large numbers of plays it can accommodate, and one that promises the novice writer an audience that can number in the millions (Gielgud 1957, 30). The practical benefits of writing for radio are fairly obvious: it requires less time and money to produce for this medium than it does for the stage or screen, which in turn minimizes the risk of artistic failure. As a result, as many as six hundred new plays are produced annually by BBC radio alone (Drakakis, 219). But in addition to its accessibility, radio offers aspiring playwrights highly defined limits, both aesthetic and practical, within which to perfect their craft.

From 1964 to 1972, Stoppard wrote six radio plays, half of them for the BBC's "Third Programme," later called "Radio 3,"[1] through which he gradually developed his own rhetoric of radio drama as he discovered its suggestive possibilities. His first pair of plays, *The Dissolution of Dominic Boot* and *'M' is for Moon Among Other Things,* both fifteen-minute pieces written (unsolicited) in 1964 for the series "Just Before Midnight," showed sufficient promise to attract the attention of Richard Imison of the BBC, who commissioned further radio plays. *The Dissolution* has all of the hallmarks of early

Stoppardian dramaturgy: a self-effacing character trapped absurdly in a situation of his own devising and propelled logically, if ludicrously, toward complete dissolution. The continuous action consists entirely of Dominic, a young accountant, riding frantically about town in a taxi in an effort to pay off its running meter. Dominic loses the race, cut off from financial relief by his embarrassed efforts to conceal his poverty. While riding from bank to bank, stopping off to collect from indebted friends, to borrow (yet again) from his parents and even his fiancée, all to no avail, the meter continues to tick and eventually drives him to sell his clothes and furniture to the cab driver to settle his debt. He ends up unemployed, unengaged, and dressed in pajamas — clothing that seems to hold a special appeal for the playwright. The picaresque structure of the plot suits the spatial freedom of the medium while riveting our attention on the continuous passing of time as registered by the meter (inaudible in the broadcast I listened to) and Dominic's anxious counting of change. By the time his dissolution comes, it has the effect of a well-timed punch line. The meter joke, hardly the stuff of great drama, could not sustain a play much longer than this one, but, together with other time-marking techniques, it makes for an amusing fifteen minutes of sound play.

Broadcast approximately six weeks later, on 6 April 1964, the second in this set of plays is weaker in plot but stronger in characterization. *'M' Is for Moon Among Other Things* began, according to the author, as a short story and was later revised for the radio (Introduction to *Dog It Was*, 7). While Stoppard wrote *Dissolution* primarily as a one-character play, *'M'* requires two voices, Alfred and Constance, married, middle-aged, middle-class and childless. Stoppard gives each member of the couple a distinctive speech and preoccupation that manages to set the terms of their comic misunderstanding within the first few moments of air time. Constance, like Dominic, marks time by resorting to mechanical tasks. She has reached the letter 'M' in *The Universal Treasury of People, Places and Things* at the play's opening. She will turn exactly forty-two-and-a- half precisely at 10:30 P.M. that evening. "Forty-two-and-a-half, and all I've got is a headache." "Where's it all going?" (63), she wonders. While she ponders aging and the apparent pointlessness of her life, uncomprehending Alfred daydreams about owning luxury cars and rescuing young women in distress, particularly Marilyn Monroe, whose death by suicide is announced on the 10:05 P.M. news for 5 August 1962.

While Stoppard softens the comedy of this couple by developing the poignancy of their situation, he avoids sentimentality by undercutting their expressions of disappointment with comic non sequiturs. Each of them speaks in a public and a private voice. While their public dialogue is banal by even the most generous standards, their private utterances have the pathos and spice of grown-ups' childish fantasies. The humor comes from the crossing of private references. Constance mistakes Alfred's regret at the death of Marilyn Monroe as sympathy for her own malaise, and simple-minded Alfred mistakes Constance's habitual reading of *The Treasury* as a quest for knowledge. Typical of Stoppard as a non–illusionist playwright is the refusal to disguise the movement between inner and outer speech, suggesting instead their confusion for comic effect. The auditor's pleasure lies in listening to the characters mistake the one for the other.

If You're Glad I'll Be Frank, aired two years later in 1966, already shows a more ambitious and self-conscious use of the radio medium. The first scene opens with two voices: one of them a recording and the other, as it were, "live." Bus driver Frank calls TIM and recognizes the voice as that of his beloved wife Gladys, announcing the seconds, minutes, and hours. As Stoppard told the BBC's Peter Orr, this piece, like *The Dissolution,* which grew out of the running taxi meter gag, began with an "instant idea": revealing the person behind the apparently mechanical TIM voice. Frank's function in the plot will consist of his fruitless attempts to find and rescue Gladys inside the post office building where she has been literally entrapped as the "speaking clock." We have all heard such recordings on the telephone, but Gladys's announcement of the hours, minutes, and seconds encourages us to listen attentively to a voice we customarily accept as merely the audible extension of an inhuman mechanism. As we listen, we come to regard the play itself as a kind of timepiece. And no wonder, since the stage directions tell us that the actual time Gladys announces should be related to the number of minutes or seconds that have passed in the broadcast, thereby collapsing the distance between speaker and auditor.

In addition to its two major voices, the play assigns Gladys two voices as well. Against the background of her public voice announcing the "pips" and counting the seconds, Gladys speaks in what is now a fully developed private voice, meditating on the very activity of counting and marking time. The interior voice gives Gladys an instrument of lyric evocation tempered by an ironical sense of humor. Her private language, approaching the formality of poetry, expresses the pressure of her entrapment through a hypnotic utterance: "When you look down from / a great height / you become dizzy. Such / depth, such distance, / such disappearing tininess so / far away, / rushing away, / reducing the life-size to / nothing– / it upsets the scale you live by" (50). Stoppard suggests her isolation with a generalized spatial image of her distance from life. Discouraged from visualizing a specific object here, we instead supply from our memories, Gloucester-like, the recollection of looking down from great heights onto tiny objects below. Similarly, when Gladys describes what she hears on the other end as people call in for the time, "I can hear them breathe, / pause, listen" (61), we again supply echoes from our aural memories, sounds of breathing, pausing, even the weighted silence of listening, much like the auditor's own while attending to the play. Threatened with madness as she contemplates infinity, Gladys hopes husband Frank can bring her back down to earth, closer to the human scale. But Frank's bus schedule obligates him to catch up with the minutes and seconds just as literally as Gladys's position ties her to counting them. Thus, when Frank dominates a scene, the tempo is driven frenetically by the passing of clock time, whereas when Gladys's voice speaks, we hear her reflective meditation on eternity ironically foregrounded by her announcing of minutes and seconds. Time appears to speed up with Frank and to slow down with Gladys. This counterpoint controls the play's tempo as scenes alternate between the two voices. Finally, the madness of Lord Coot's Post Office, home of the speaking clock, prevails. Frank fails to rescue Gladys, who must resume counting for a world racing to beat the clock.

Stoppard's efforts to master the radio as a comic medium began with separating levels of speech and led to experimenting with recurring aural patterns as grounds on which to superimpose spatial images of perspective. The recurring pattern marks time and can be used to indicate changes in tempo, while the spatial images help construct the larger thematic interest of the play. In both *'M' is for Moon* and *If You're Glad,* the thematic center lies in the struggle between a desire for withdrawal in the form of fantasy, contemplation, or the complete immersion in mechanical tasks and the desire for involvement in the world outside the self. The award-winning *Albert's Bridge,* broadcast eighteen months later on the BBC's Third Programme, clarifies this conflict by combining spatial imagery and time marking in a more fully developed dramatic narrative. Gladys's view of herself as a remote consciousness looking down on humanity from a great height becomes the controlling image of this piece in which university drop-out Albert abandons philosophy for the more serene activity of painting—and repainting—the Clufton Bay Bridge. As in *If You're Glad,* Stoppard divides the scenes between Albert's private, lyrical monologues and the farcical dialogue of Clufton's officials who control the outcome of Albert's drama. The genesis of this piece probably lay in another "instant idea"—the notion of painting a bridge from one end to the other at which point its repainting must begin. The idea suggests both the comic futility of the painter's Sisyphean task and the continuous activity that will be used to mark time during the broadcast.

The play opens with an original and precise manipulation of auditory effect to suggest spatial arrangement. Four painters, arranged one above the other on a vertical member of the bridge, finish their day's painting and call to one another to begin their descent to the ground. Stoppard positions the microphone at Albert's level, the top, but the painter furthest from it, that is, closest to the ground, speaks first, calling to the man above him, who calls to the next higher, and so on. This creates the auditory effect of climbing the steel member, painter by painter, until reaching Albert, who fails to hear the others calling him. Happily self-absorbed, Albert croons fragments of moon lyrics, "How high the moon in June? / how blue the moon when it's high noon" (9).[2] As he approaches collapse, Albert becomes increasingly egocentric, losing all sense of his humanity in his desire to identify himself with the bridge: "Paint on my arm, / silver paint on my brown arm; / it could be part of the bridge" (27). His psychology and language are sharper and more developed than those of Stoppard's earlier radio voices. In a provocative sound painting of the chaotic city he has escaped, Albert describes the drowning of one sound by another:

> All conversation is hidden there,
> Among motors, coughing fits, applause,
> screams, laughter, feet on the stairs, [. . . .]
> Listen. The note of Clufton is B flat.
> The whole world could be the same.
> Look down. (27)

Like the first voice of Dylan Thomas's *Under Milk Wood,* Albert directs the imperatives "Listen" and "Look down" at the auditors, inviting us to "hear" the white noise in the air above Clufton and to "see" the purely imaginary dots of its landscape. His piling up of images conveys the impression of aural chaos without requiring that the listener hear each distinct sound. Albert seeks refuge in the aural monotony afforded by distance: "The whole world could be the same."

Fraser, a second voice in the play, acts as Albert's double. A would-be suicide when he first meets Albert on the bridge, his new vantage on life from afar restores his confidence. Once high above Clufton, Fraser finds "the idea of society just about tenable" (34). When Albert objects, "But it's my bridge —," Fraser responds, "You think only of yourself—you see yourself as the centre, whereas I know that I am not placed at all—" (39). Fraser has Gladys's vision of a world gone mad, and Stoppard wastes no time in proving him right.

The parallel plot in this play, hatched by City Engineer Fitch to maximize man power and paint, is about to dovetail with the Albert-Fraser story as 1799 painters march onto the bridge to complete the job of painting it in one day. Everyone's fears come true as the bridge wrenches and snaps under their weight, collapsing into the silence of the play's conclusion. Trapped in his fragmentary perspective, neither Albert nor Fraser sees his dilemma whole. The consequence of partial vision becomes audible with the collapse of the entire structure.

Nearly three years will pass before Stoppard again writes for radio. *Where Are They Now?*, produced in January of 1970, was specially commissioned for the BBC's Schools Radio, a series produced for school age people. Its audience in part determined its subject: an old boys' twenty-third annual reunion dinner for the graduates of Hove — an English preparatory school replete with public school traditions such as nicknames, school songs, war stories of youthful punishment, and a reverence for now dead pupils and masters. As usual, Stoppard crosses two plots for farcical effect. In the major plot, three of the Good Old Boys who had been the best of friends — each known by one of the Marx Brothers' names — recollect their school days together and reflect on their present fortunes over a salmon dinner. Scenes in the here and now alternate with flashbacks to a school dinner of twenty-four years earlier, marked by cruelties and humiliations that undercut the old boys' sentimental reveries. The minor plot concerns a Mr. Jenkins, retired graduate of Oakleigh House for the Sons of Merchant Seamen's Widows, who has mistaken Hove's banquet for Oakleigh's. The discovery of this mistake is the capstone to the play.

Stoppard's note to the printed edition explains his intention that the scenes should move between present and past "without using any of the familiar grammar of fading down and fading up; the action is continuous" (119). Alternating juvenile and adult voices signal time shifts suggested by fades in the traditional grammar of radio production. As in his stage plays, Stoppard will cut the unnecessary break in illusion if it can be accomplished by language or voice. Eliminating the conventional fade intensifies the action and creates an edge of surprise that Stoppard exploits in tandem with his theme of remembrance: Who are the Marx brothers and where are they now? In the first of the play's four flashbacks, the attentive listener will link the name Brindley to the school name "Chico." But the identity of the remaining two Marx Brothers remains ambiguous until the play's closing scenes. We will likely assume that Gale is Harpo — both are mute in the play's first scenes. It thus comes as a surprise to learn that the dejected youth Harpo has grown into the pompous ass

Marks, a "good old boy" who has denied his youthful misery so completely that he has sent his own son to suffer at Hove. We have been fooled into mistaking one old boy for another by the narrative's ambiguity as surely as Marks has been fooled by his selective memory. Stoppard will fool us again in similar fashion in *Artist Descending a Staircase,* where we will attempt to solve a perceptual mystery with an ambiguous set of clues.

As boys and as men, their temperaments fit their names: rebellious Groucho writes for newspapers; cheerful Chico serves the Church as a reverend; and silent Harpo, victim of former French master Jenkins's sadism, now complacently enjoys good silver and good wine. Each man's memories also define his character: in spite of remembering the cruelty of their French master, Brindley and Marks now excuse it as salutary. Only Gale refuses to sentimentalize the past.

This radio play is one of the earliest examples of Stoppard's interest in the mystery formula that will characterize his mature stage works. The major mystery in this piece has to do with the source of the flashbacks. The first of the four begins in the distant past and the remaining three move toward the present, becoming shorter as they grow nearer. But from whose point of view are they spoken? Since most of them contain incidents of cruelty or humiliation, Groucho (Gale), the most consciously resentful of the old boys, could be their author. But some of these scenes exclude Gale, and one of them, the scene in which Marks's son is being punished by young Crawford, could not have been witnessed by Gale. The flashbacks must then be the product of an implied author whose opinion of the school agrees closely with Gale's. The narrative line in this play is, with a few exceptions, controlled by Gale's recollection. But like most of Stoppard's narrators, Gale cannot fully be trusted. He has, for example, misremembered his days at Hove as uniformly unhappy, but the final scene containing the play's only cross-fade to the past is full of young Gale's shouts and laughter and the sounds of other boys calling for the ball—" 'Here, Gale! Gale, Gale!' " (139). The implied author even adds commentary for the reader's benefit: "It is a day he has forgotten, but clearly he was very happy" (139), suggesting that this point was not clear in performance.

In attempting to write for young voices, Stoppard—a one-time journalist for whom boarding school was a "negative" if not punishing experience— appears to have turned to his own childhood[3] and found, in the process of interrogating his memories, a ready subject and method for his play: the process by which one recollects and evaluates the past. Narrating from memory can be as unreliable as interpreting sound in this and the earlier radio plays. Neither Constance nor Alfred "hears" the real voice of the other; Albert hears one kind of sound while on the ground and another while in the air. Gladys's impersonal public voice counting the seconds conceals an anarchist's private voice that no longer believes in time as a measured flow. As Stoppard's first radio attempt to shuttle the action freely between present and past, *Where Are They Now?* prefigures the narrative structure of his next radio play, *Artist Descending a Staircase* (1972), as well as his 1974 stage success, *Travesties.*

Commissioned by the BBC as the first in an intended series of European radio plays celebrating Britain's entry into the European Economic Community (Brassell 1985, 163), *Artist Descending* appeared nine months after *Jumpers.* Aware that his radio plays *Albert's Bridge* and *If You're Glad I'll Be Frank* had been adapted for the stage at Edinburgh's 1969 Festival, Stoppard set out to write a "pure," unstageable radio play, which he has since himself adapted for a London stage debut in 1988. As he told the BBC's Richard Mayne, *Artist*'s genesis lay, accordingly, in a "tape gag." The play opens with a tape loop that has inadvertently recorded the fatal fall of aged artist Donner down his loft stairs. Roommates and fellow artists, Beauchamp and Martello, speak over the loop (and the corpse), accusing one another of having pushed Donner to his death. In search of a motive, they begin a retrogressive recollection of their lives and work, attempting to sort out quarrels, lovers and manifestoes in search of a clue. As in *The Dissolution,* the gag contains within it the structural and conceptual germ of the entire play, this time tuned exclusively for the ear.

As the artists perceive it, the Ur-loop's essential elements include the following, listed in Stoppard's stage directions:

> (a) Donner *dozing: an irregular droning noise* (b) *Careful footsteps approach.* . . . *A board creaks.* (c) *This wakes* Donner, *i.e. the droning stops* . . . (d) *The footsteps freeze.* (e) Donner's *voice, unalarmed: 'Ah! There you are* . . . ' (f) *Two more quick steps, and then Thump!* (g) Donner *cries out.* (h) *Wood cracks as he falls through a balustrade.* (i) *He falls heavily down the stairs, with a final sickening thump when he hits the bottom. Silence.* (75)

Beauchamp and Martello no sooner hear the loop and see Donner's corpse than they begin their "farce of accusation and counteraccusation" (77). Stoppard gives his tendency toward self-reference full play in this piece. The painters see themselves as dramatic characters performing in the public arena of the modern art world. They hear in their voices an habitual strain of modernist irony: "(God forgive my *brain*! —" complains Martello in an aside, "it is so attuned to the ironic tone it has become ironical in repose; I have to whip sincerity out of it as one whips responses from a mule!)" (77–78). And when Beauchamp accuses Martello of murder, he cannot resist judging the crime by theatrical standards: "(Y)ou ruined what would have been a strand in my masterwork of accumulated silence, and left in its place a melodramatic fragment whose point will not be lost on a jury" (78–79).

The exchange of insults gives way to a full-blown comedy of recollection, a sort of metatext containing the Ur-text. Stoppard constructs it with remarkable precision (as he describes in a note to the Grove Press edition): "The play is set temporally in six parts, in the sequence ABCDEFEDCBA A = here and now; B = a couple of hours ago; C = Last week; D = 1922; E = 1920; F = 1914" (73). As I have argued elsewhere (Kelly 1986), the temporal accordion structure, pivoting at Scene F, no doubt structurally echoes Marcel Duchamp's pictorial segmentation in "Nude Descending a Staircase," called by a hostile reviewer of the 1912 New York Armory Show, "an explosion in a shingle factory." But Stoppard himself had earlier experimented with fragmented recollection in *Where Are They Now?*, which he extends and shapes more purposefully in *Artist Descending.* In lieu of the adult-juvenile voice changes signaling temporal shifts in the earlier play, Stoppard has assigned a series of sonic signals to mark location and time, many of them signs that draw attention to their artificiality ("cliché Paris music," the clip-clop of horses' feet, the bouncing of Ping-Pong balls, etc.). The careful temporal design, achieved in part through these aural signs, eases the auditor through jumps in sequence.

The conceptual dead center of the metatext lies in the ill-fated love affair of blind traditionalist Sophie and relentlessly avant-garde Beauchamp. Like *Under Milk Wood*'s Captain Cat and *All That Fall*'s Dan Rooney, Sophie is a blind protagonist who "sees" with her mind's eye:

> I enjoy the view . . . as much as anyone who sits there with eyes closed in the sun; more, I think, because I can improve on reality, like a painter, but without fear of contradiction. (103)

When facing the Thames river, Sophie sees it as Turner painted it. Her lover Beauchamp, on the other hand, while professing to be an artist, hangs his reputation as an avant-gardist on eschewing the aesthetics of the eye: "I'm trying to liberate the visual *image* from the limitations of visual *art*" (98). Blind Sophie's idealism ill adapts her to the modern period, while Beauchamp thrives on the radical relativism of the avant-garde ethos: "Art consists of surprise."

All of the characters are trapped in a hermeneutic circle that Stoppard has signified in a variety of formal ways: by the temporal circularity of the narrative returning to the "here and now"; by Beauchamp's tape loop circling back on itself; by Martello's habitual use of the ironic tone; by Donner's fitful return to "traditional" art; and by Sophie's choice of a lover based upon her unreliable interpretation of a scene she saw dimly at the "Frontiers in Art" exhibit two years before falling to her death. Sophie's entrapment is the most poignant of them all as its consequences are the most serious and as she fails to acknowledge her role in constructing the trap she has sprung for herself. An excited spectator at the "Frontiers" show, she peered through thick glasses at the three artists and their pictures. As she later confides to Donner, she kept returning her gaze to one of them who became her secret love. Months later, after she has become completely blind, she visits the artists in their loft and attempts to identify which of them she had gazed upon, in spite of admitting to all three that she had been unable visually to distinguish them. The painters help her to reconstruct what she saw at the show:

> *Martello*: [. . .] [Y]ou want to know which of us was the one who posed against the painting you have described.
> *Sophie*: [. . .] It was a background of snow, I think.
> *Donner*: Yes, there was a snow scene. Only one.
> *Sophie*: A field of snow, occupying the whole canvas —
> *Martello*: Not the whole canvas —
> *Sophie*: No — there was a railing —
> *Beauchamp*: Yes, that's it — a border fence in the snow!
> *Sophie*: Yes! (*Pause.*) Well, which of you . . .?
> *Donner*: It was Beauchamp you had in mind.
>
> (102–3)

As Sophie saw it, the puzzle was solved. She had been looking at Beauchamp. But the auditor cannot be so confident. We learn in a later scene that Donner's painting of thick white fence posts with dark gaps between them also hung in the gallery. And Donner had earlier suggested to Sophie that the two of them had exchanged glances at the show. Donner could just as easily — more easily in fact — have been the figure Sophie had singled out. When Donner confesses his love to Sophie after Beauchamp has deserted her, she claims to be unable to return it — her capacity for love was used up entirely by Beauchamp. As the character most unable to negotiate change and ambiguity, Sophie is least likely to survive the modern period. Her past is what she believes it to have been, in spite of her awareness that she has, in part, authored it.

Stoppard's own implied view mediates between Sophie's traditionalism and the artists' avant-gardism. Sophie insists that the true painter must be different in kind from his or her non-painter fellows, while Beauchamp claims that "art should break its promises" and "is nothing to do with expertise." "Doing something well," he claims, "is no excuse for doing the expected" (104). Siding with Sophie on the question of artistic skill, implied playwright Stoppard nevertheless appears to share Beauchamp's love of surprise. In the play's closing scene, where we find Beauchamp and Martello once again attempting to put together the "facts" of Donner's death, a buzzing fly, heard earlier at several points in the action, interrupts their labors. While stalking it, Beauchamp unwittingly reproduces the sequence of sounds on the Ur-loop:

(a) Fly droning
(b) Careful footsteps approach. A board creaks.
(c) The fly settles.
(d) Beauchamp halts.
(e) Beauchamp: 'Ah! There you are.'
(f) Two more quick steps and then: Thump! (116)

Gleefully recollecting Gloucester's stoicism, Beauchamp quotes aloud, " 'As flies to wanton boys are we to the Gods: they kill us for their sport' " (116). We are once again returned to Gloucester's perspective: blinded, atop an imaginary cliff, listening to stories in the dark.

The fear of falling runs motif-like through nearly all of Stoppard's radio plays. Albert's precarious perch atop Clufton's bridge, Gladys's mental elevation above the flow of time, and Sophie and Donner's fatal falls, all signify the potentially destructive power of the human imagination in terms made especially vivid in the aural medium. Each of these victims has failed to balance his or her inner, imagined world against the chaos of the outer world. Each of them has embraced art (or its analogue) as a retreat from life rather than as a means to living at its border, "both inside and outside society." In falsely believing that art can protect them from the disorder and chaos of experience, they succumb to the different but equally powerful tyranny of their imaginations, which, in demanding absolute fidelity to the imaginary pursuit of beauty and order, eventually destroys them. In the claustrophobic and occasionally dark space of these radio plays, the auditors create a visual analogue to the sound score. We, too, see only with our mind's eye, guided by the playwright's suggestive use of sound. Our perspective, too, is flawed and necessarily partial, even if privileged relative to that of the characters.

Artist Descending a Staircase shows more clearly than any other single early piece for radio that Stoppard occasionally built complex large-scale stage plays directly upon a relatively simple foundation in another medium. In its precisely segmented narrative structure, its parodic repetition of source texts, and its critique of the avant-garde's dismissal of artistic material and skill, *Artist* directly anticipates the form and content of *Travesties*, which would appear two years later. *Travesties'* narrative regression, turnabout, and progressive return to the here and now prescribes an emphatic arc about the First War, the historical center of Henry Carr's narrative and the political-ethical watershed of the play's art-politics argument. In its multiple restarts, Henry Carr's recollection of Switzerland in wartime disrupts more radically the convention of linear continuity than does the narrative boomerang of *Artist*. But the inspiration for Carr's self-indulgent self-correction would seem to lie in the ironical retrospection of the aging avant-gardists of the radio play. "Really, Donner," complains Beauchamp, "your mind keeps wandering about in a senile chaos!" (83). The parodic impulse in *Artist* is realized through a series of major and more obscure avant-garde works—Duchamp's *Artist Descending a Staircase*, John Cage's tape loops as well as his celebration of silence, and pop sculpture of the 1960s.[4] The parody of *Travesties*, on the other hand, boldly deforms major literary and political works—*The Importance of Being Earnest*, *Ulysses*, Shakespeare's eighteenth sonnet, and Lenin's Collected Writings ([sic] does Stoppard here mean *Collected Works*?). The spokesman for the avant-garde in *Artist*—a pastiche of Marcel Duchamp and John Cage—gives way to the highly particularized (and therefore theatrically more powerful) figure of Tristan Tzara in *Travesties*, quoting from Tzara's works and displaying his reputed eccentricities. And finally, the debate between the avant-garde and the traditional ethos of art posed visually in *Artist* becomes a debate over the ideology of literary values in *Travesties*, widening and deepening Stoppard's early concern with the rights and responsibilities of the artist in western culture. Literary, political, and social history converge in the image of the artist protected from war by the orderly refuge of Switzerland, an image first suggested in *Artist* by the avant-gardists' bumbling vacation jaunt to the war frontier.

Before Stoppard would write a successful, full-length stage play, he would experiment in another "entry" medium. Like radio, television was relatively accessible to young writers, promising them instant audiences in the thousands and a greater number of opportunities to see work of short duration produced. As a visual medium, it encouraged Stoppard to develop a pictorial sense of humor, particularly at close ranges, and to submit his gift for literary eloquence to the decorum of the small screen where characters are expected to speak more or less like "real" (in other words, middle or working class) people and to become involved in "real life" intrigues involving sex, jealousy, and disappointment such as we might hear directly reported to us in daily life. How would this young playwright, for whom art represented a problematic withdrawal from "life," respond to the mimetic conventions of the small screen? Television did not encourage the best of Stoppard's early work, but it did reveal a somber underside of his high-spirited comedy. Stoppard never surrendered the seriousness that shows on the surface of some of his early television work, but he learned to manage it through the distancing effect of comic treatment.

Stoppard in Close Up: The Early Television Plays, 1965–67

A naturalist bias grew up with the TV play as it achieved status as a genre on British channels. By the mid-1950s, plays written exclusively for television had begun to gain popularity on the BBC channel, especially police and detective stories. By the mid-1960s, what became known as "kitchen sink" dramas — single plays and series depicting, often in minute and highly accurate detail, the daily struggles of the lower class (Self 1984, 9–10, 45) — had won critical praise and wide viewing interest. Naturalistic TV plays were promoted by the BBC's then head of drama, Sydney Newman, who favored "agitational contemporaneity," of which he considered John Osborne's *Look Back in Anger* to be an exemplary stage model (Self 1984, 45, 49). This milieu was not likely to call forth the best efforts of young Stoppard, wary of naturalism — "it leads you straight down to the dregs of bad theatre" (Tynan 1980, 64) — and suspicious of television's suitedness to serious art — "All my ideas [for ABC Television] . . . were 'too downbeat,' they said" (Interview with Editors of *Theatre Quarterly* 1974, 6). He was, therefore, likely to be particularly suspicious of television's tendency to create the illusion of unmediated reality (Brandt 1981, 23–28) prompted by the continuous flow of nonfictional material defining the majority of TV output. TV realism was and is at odds with the self-reflexivity of Stoppard's writing for all media.

Despite his inclinations, young Stoppard seized the opportunity to write television dramas, content to produce lesser pieces for radio and television while staking his reputation initially on his novel, *Lord Malquist and Mr Moon,* and later on his stage plays (Interview with Janet Watts 1973, 12). Most of his writing for television takes the form of the single play — the highest ranking genre in British television's hierarchy (Self 1984, 2) — which offered him relative freedom from the restrictions of subject and style imposed on authors writing the lesser ranked series and adaptations. As he began to learn the grammar of television writing, Stoppard adapted his comic characters and situations to the domestic themes and genres favored by television audiences: the soap opera, the spy thriller, and the "faction," a scripted play combining fiction and historical fact in a form distinct from the "drama-documentary," which concerns itself with issues of social inequity (Self, 17).

A Separate Peace, written in 1965, was the first of his television plays to be aired by BBC TV.[5] According to the author, it was the fictional half of an hour-long documentary on chess players co-written by Stoppard and Christopher Martin. As it turned out, the play dramatizes an attitude Stoppard considers to be the opposite of chess players' aggression: the desire for escape from the world into the ordered cloister of a hospital (Introduction to *Dog It Was,* 7). Beginning as an anatomy of chess players, it became an anatomy of the artist figure, here called by the pseudonym "John Brown," whose tentative relation to society comprises the subtext of much of Stoppard's early work for all media.

Stoppard showed himself a quick student of the medium by adapting the story of Brown's withdrawal to television's small screen preference for interior and close-up shots. As a low-budget studio product, his play had to make the most of severe limitations of setting and cast. The critical interest lies in how Stoppard negotiated these limits. Opening with Brown's arrival at the hospital and concluding with his departure, the play's nineteen scenes alternate between two sets: the Hospital Office and Brown's Ward. Brown's dilemma emerges as we view scenes in the Office where the staff are secretly attempting to locate his family followed by scenes in Brown's private ward where he is relishing his new found serenity. The dialogue consists primarily of duologues, usually intimate conversations suited to the close-up shot, between Brown and a staff member or between one staff member and another. The dual setting reinforces the central agon: the struggle between the artist who wishes to withdraw from society and the uncomprehending philistines who attempt to block his withdrawal. Brown's enemies in the Office eventually drive him out after contacting his family and announcing their imminent arrival. The doctor justifies his meddling with a parodic echo of E. M. Forster's *Howard's End:* "It's not enough, Mr. Brown. You've got to . . . *connect* . . . " (183).

Brown leaves behind a wall-sized pastoral mural, shown in several scenes as it is drawing closer to completion. Stoppard's use of the signifying power of a painting suggests that he had learned to exploit the economy of the visual image as he began to create in televisual terms. The mural's iconography, "competent but amateurish," is taken from pastoral — a simple scene of the

English countryside. And like that of other pastoral characters, Brown's withdrawal will be temporary, offering him a brief period of calm to reflect on the life of action. But in an ironical twist of the convention, Brown would prefer that it be permanent: "If I'd got four times as much money, I'd take four rooms and paint one for each season. But I've only got money for the summer" (178). In place of the woods, shepherds, and oaten flutes of the green world, Brown cherishes nurses, clean laundry and prompt meals. "Hospital routine in a pastoral setting," he muses to his friend, Nurse Maggie Coates. "That's kind of perfection, really" (180). Brown remembers his four years as a prisoner of war to have been equally happy: "It was like winning, being captured. . . . They gave us food, life was regulated, in a box of earth and wire and sky" (180–81). As Thomas Whitaker has suggested, *A Separate Peace* may reflect Stoppard's early infatuation with Hemingway and his ideal of the "clean, well-lighted place." But its inconclusive outcome implies not so much the moral superiority of the simple life as it does Brown's mistaken refusal to recognize that retreat must be a temporary step in learning to negotiate between the outer and the inner world.

For Ronald Hayman, Brown's dilemma faintly echoes that of any number of Beckett's static, indolent anti-heroes, most obviously Belacqua of *More Pricks than Kicks,* whose instinct was "to make himself captive" (quoted in Hayman 1979, 60). But where Beckett emphasizes the tragic, alien quality of his characters in exile, Stoppard's Brown turns whimsical in the face of absurdity. The last line of the play conveys this tone precisely. As Brown leaves the hospital, suitcase in hand, eager to dodge the reunification with his family prescribed not only by society's guardians but also by traditional comedy, he analyzes his dilemma with a droll sincerity: "Trouble is, I've always been so *well*. If I'd been *sick* I would have been all right" (183).

Brown's wish to drop out of the social world echoes that of all early Stoppard heroes as well as the young Stoppard himself, uneasy over his own definition of the artist as outsider. Brown knows his solution is wrong but he simply cannot find a better alternative. As he tells Nurse Coates:

Brown: A hospital is a very dependable place. . . . You need never know anything, it doesn't touch you.
Maggie: That's not true, Brownie.
Brown: I know it's not.
Maggie: Then you shouldn't try and make it true.
Brown: I know I shouldn't.

(179)

Like the bridge escapists in *Albert's Bridge,* Brown knows that seclusion from the madness of the world will not be tolerated, but he refuses to condemn it as wrong. As he sees it, "this is a private ward; I'm paying for it" (178). The reasoned tone of his rebellion lacks Albert's aggressive egotism and, ultimately, his conviction. Although his combination of common sense and radical conduct gives the play its humor, the character Brown finally fades out of the action, too gentlemanly to have made a deep impression. His subtlety may have reflected Stoppard's wish to avoid overdramatizing for the television medium.

Teeth, written for BBC 2's *Thirty Minute Theatre* in 1966 and broadcast in 1967, appeared at a turning point in Stoppard's career. Jim Hunter describes 1966 as "the year of Stoppard's arrival as a writer," and no wonder when one considers the amount and range of the year's creative activity: BBC Radio broadcast *If You're Glad I'll Be Frank* in February, the Royal Shakespeare Company performed Stoppard's adaptation of Slawomir Mrozek's *Tango* in May, and, within the space of days in August, BBC Television transmitted *A Separate Peace,* the Oxford Theatre Group performed *Rosencrantz and Guildenstern Are Dead* at the Edinburgh Festival Fringe, and Anthony Blond published Stoppard's novel, *Lord Malquist and Mr Moon* (Hunter 1982, 6–7).

Teeth shows evidence of the developing farceur in a plot that overlooks character development for the more ancient amusements of spouse-swapping and cuckoldry. Written under a thirty-minute time limit for a studio setting with minimal changes of place and heavy use of the close up, *Teeth* demonstrates Stoppard's ability to present the minima of farce in a televisually effective way. The play's central conceit lies in exploiting the power a dentist exercises over his helpless patient (who, in this case, happens to have been sleeping with the dentist's wife, mischievously named Prudence). Dentist Harry slowly tortures his rival, George (husband of Harry's dental assistant, Mary), with leading questions about the illicit affair. In response to these, George improvises with growing desperation a series of transparent and highly amusing lies. Mary enters to assist the dentist while chair-bound George helplessly watches a budding affair between his wife and the man repairing his teeth.

This highly condensed version of the marriage comedy, in which husbands and wives knowingly swap partners, has an elegant and leisurely counterpart in Noël Coward's comedy of manners, *Private Lives* (Ruskino 1986, 116). But Stoppard's approach belongs clearly to farce, specifically the farce of revenge, with its motive of cuckolding the cuckolder (Davis 1978, 43). Stoppard adapted this well-established stage genre to the small screen in several ingenious ways. The play opens with an establishing scene introducing us to the future victim, George Pollock, described in the dramatis personae as a "saloon-bar Lothario"—a braggart type Stoppard also used in *Enter a Free Man*. Pollock eavesdrops on two spinster patients while studying a bra and panty ad. The overheard dialogue between the two spinsters—a hybrid of clichés, soap opera confessions, and music hall cross talk—rapidly builds up comic momentum while establishing a link between teeth and the traditional farce signifiers, sex and violence.

> *Agnes*: I was brushing my teeth after dinner. It's only the two middle ones that come out—the rest's my own, what there is, but of course it's the *gap*, isn't it?
> *Flora*: Oh yes. It's the gap that'd give you away.
> *Agnes*: (*Recalling it with tragic clarity*) 'Agnes, . . . what have you done to your *teeth*?!' . . . It wasn't the same after that with Jack Stevens. A week later he'd got his third mate's papers and he was taken away, over the horizon, by a dirty black tramp—yeh Irene Castle from Cardiff, I still look out for her.
> *Flora*: Got all her own teeth, has she?
> *Agnes*: 'sa boat.
>
> (72)

In the last scene of the play, the waiting room, now containing two or three additional ancient and unattractive patients, is reintroduced to bring the play to conclusion. We are overhearing Flora describing an old lover she discarded after he'd lost his teeth when George reenters, smiling wanly, and we see a large gap where his middle tooth used to be. The patients all smile back in recognition, revealing identical gaps. George, formerly a ladies' man with a beautiful smile, has now joined the band of farce losers, the ugly, aged (and toothless) who go to bed lonely.

The suggestion of an endless series of repetitive actions, one of the conventions of farce absurdity, is repeated within the central drama as George submits unknowingly to Harry's vengeance. Prudence, it seems, or so Harry wishes George to believe, has had other lovers before George. Collins, a trainee from the dental hospital, had good teeth, Harry admits. But after he had exploited Prudence's youthful "innocence," the dentist took care of him in his own way: "Collins wouldn't be showing his face around the fair sex for quite a while to come . . . " (80). While stuffing George's mouth with instruments and probes, Harry reveals bit by bit his awareness of George's affair with his wife Prudence. Each of the revelations is accompanied by Harry's wielding of a malicious instrument, including, at one point, a mallet and chisel. In Stoppard's gentrified example of farce, literal beatings give way to the sublimated violence of the dentist's chair, the more amusing for its disguise as a form of medical treatment.

The comedy begins to spiral as Harry gradually reveals his knowledge of the affair and George lies to cover it up. At its most inventive, George's explanation of how Prudence came to be wearing a pair of Mary's shoes begins with his demonstrating a new line of life jackets at the Serpentine where he happens to see Prudence picking flowers for her flower-arranging class. They take a paddleboat ride during which her feet somehow land in the water after which George invites her, along with the three or four old people she was supposed to be visiting that afternoon, up to his flat for dry shoes and a spot of tea. As both Mary and Prudence wear the same size, the shoes somehow become switched. The capstone to the mounting humor and the symmetrical completing of the revenge farce occurs when the cuckold prepares to become the cuckolder, as Mary and Harry briefly disappear from the screen and return, in cheerful disarray, to finish their job on George.

Both the use of the close-up, focusing on George's eyes, frantically moving to left and right to see what Harry and Mary are up to, and the choice of teeth — a small and vulnerable part of the human anatomy associated with sexual attractiveness — show Stoppard adapting the revenge farce to television's fascination with the minute and mundane in human affairs as codified in the soap opera. He learned the soap formula first in the radio medium, having written four episodes in 1964 for the BBC Radio soap *The Dales*. The formula amounts to a series of unending, interweaving plots detailing domestic bliss and misery, usually conveyed through secrets, gossip, and confessions by conventional characters (Self 1984, 31–36).

Stoppard repeats the cuckold joke in his next 30-minute comedy broadcast on BBC-TV in June of 1967 under the title *Another Moon Called Earth.* Eventually to become the 1972 stage success, *Jumpers, Moon* provides the most direct evidence that Stoppard has built full-scale stage works from small-scale pieces in other media. Not only the characters but also the core of *Jumpers'* plot was modeled directly upon *Moon*. When *Moon*'s Penelope, the voluptuous and rich wife of historian Bone, no doubt linked by name to Molly Bloom's fictional precursor, suffers a breakdown following man's landing on the moon, she receives the daily visits of the dapper Dr. Albert Pearce, while the inattentive Bone attempts to move beyond the Etruscans in his penetrating history of the world. When Stoppard rewrote *Moon* five years later for the stage, he added elements of suspense and ambiguity associated with the detective thriller. *Jumpers'* Dotty is a prime suspect in the opening murder of Duncan McFee, but we never learn for certain who killed him. *Moon*'s Penelope, on the other hand, establishes early on that she pushed her nanny, Pinkerton, to her death from the window of their upper flat. *Moon*'s hall porter Crouch, the prototype for *Jumpers'* Inspector Bones, has no connection with the police and thus appears somewhat inexplicably at Bone's door to inquire about Pinkerton's body. *Jumpers'* Inspector Bones, on the other hand, has both a motive to call at the Moore's residence and a full-blown comic realization once he is on stage. As in *Jumpers, Moon*'s Albert functions as the third member of the triangle who covers up the Pinkerton murder to protect Penelope from the law.

The real mark of Stoppard's growth as a television dramatist lies in *Moon*'s witty use of the television as a central prop. This moves the play beyond the revenge farce formula of *Teeth* toward the wit and conceptual playfulness characteristic of mature Stoppard comedy. Located in Penelope's bedroom, the television set broadcasts the parade welcoming home the lunanauts, foregrounding the medium's role as a mirror of the present moment. And the focus on the here and now helps, in turn, to underscore Bone's absurd obliviousness to history-in-the-making as well as his escapist immersion in the ancient past. The documentary function of television comes humorously into play when Bone turns off the set the better to hear his wife's accusations of his indifference toward her, only to find the parade music continuing "*fainter but more real*" (92) from the street below. As Penelope's window on history, the television broadcast of the parade signifies the destruction of mankind's ability to imagine itself as a meaningful event in cosmic history, governed by absolute rules of good and evil with universal and permanent significance. According to Penelope, the lunanaut "doesn't smile because he has seen the whole thing for what it is—not the be-all and the end-all any more, but just another moon called Earth . . ." (108). The awareness of this has yet to "trickle down" to the celebrants, naively elated over another technological breakthrough. The celebratory reception of the landing, a media-planned event, suggests the wide gap between achievement and understanding that will, in *Jumpers,* open the door to Archie's farcical fascists. Television mirrors both the present moment and its interpretation, here compromised by the show business hype of the parade and celebration.[6]

Stoppard foregrounds TV's documentary function in the newscast scenes to create the sense of a contemporary crisis, but he relies on a stage genre to create the characters and action responding to that crisis. The comedy of manners brilliantly created on the English stage by such Stoppard heroes as Oscar Wilde and Noël Coward sets fashionable characters of the upper classes against one another to see whose social manners will prove the least compromised. The central action of a manners comedy lies in the attempt of the blocking or "humours" character to enforce on others his or her private obsessions (Frye 1957, 168–69). *Moon*'s husband, Bone, suffering from Stoppard's by now familiar obsession with order and predictability, struggles to make rational sense of the modern world by analyzing the pattern of western history from the Greeks to the present. Bone's obsession blinds him to the truth not only about the society in which he is living but also about his marriage: there is no objective historical pattern nor is there much of a relation between himself and Penelope.

Penelope, too, is obsessed, but Stoppard privileges her preoccupation with the moon landing by characterizing it as based in reality rather than illusion. Penelope stands outside of her society in being the only one to see the danger posed by the lunar event. While regarded by her husband and doctor as a troubled (and dangerous) child, the audience recognizes her as a person with valuable insight. We sympathize with Penelope's withdrawal from the world into her bedroom much as we sympathize with the outsider in the manners comedies exposing a society devoted to snobbery and ridicule (Frye, 48).

Albert Pearce, the play's other young, attractive and fashionable character, and therefore Penelope's logical mate in the world of manners comedy, may very well be cuckolding Bone, but the question remains unanswered, again parodying the expectation of illicit sexuality usually featured in the genre (Hirst 1979, 1, 55). Albert assures Bone that his interest in Penelope is purely scientific:

> *Albert*: You think that when I'm examining Penelope I see her eyes as corn-
> flowers, her lips as rubies, her skin so soft and warm as milk [. . . .]
> But . . . to us medical men the human body is an imperfect machine con-
> structed from cells, tissues, organs.
>
> (102)

Albert, whose mock sinister nature comes more sharply into focus in *Jumpers,* here functions simply as the probable usurper of Bone's bed and the apparent winner in the contest for Penelope's affections. Albert has style, wit, and a taste for intrigue, all of which mark him as the victor. Bone loses the implied contest by virtue of his ineffectual attempt to thwart Albert's flirtation.

At the conclusion of the play, Penelope classifies the men in her life in terms of their understanding of the moon landing's implications. As she watches the unsmiling lunanaut leading the parade, she tells her befuddled husband: "Nobody knows except me, and him; so far. Albert almost knows.

You'll never know" (108). What they don't "know" has nothing to do with social decorum, the usual provenance of manners characters, but with a far reaching change in society's view of itself.

While modest by all measures, *Moon* nevertheless predicts what will become Stoppard's characteristic comic method of combining genres—in this case, manners comedy and television documentary—to achieve the blend of wit and broad humor characteristic of his mature style. Stoppard will develop the hybrid more fully in *Jumpers* where the manners comedy and the impending social chaos following the moon landing are tied to the broader problem of moral relativism in a materialist age.

When commissioned by Granada TV in 1965 to write a play for a series on myths and legends, Stoppard produced a spy thriller, *Neutral Ground*. As a screenplay, it takes full advantage of technical innovations in the television industry that had long since moved out of the studio in pursuit of the observational freedom of movement formerly confined to cinema. Locations in this play shift between interior and exterior scenes as well as between towns and cities ostensibly in both Eastern and Western Europe. Of the plot's two major sources, Sophocles's Philoctetes myth, as described in Edmund Wilson's *The Wound and the Bow,* provided the mythic story and characters required by the series' emphasis. (As Stoppard has reported, the series never materialized. Granada broadcast *Neutral Ground* three years later, in 1968, as a single play [*Dog It Was,* 8].) Stoppard adapts what Wilson describes as Sophocles's version of the myth, singular for its contribution of Neoptolemus ("Acherson" in Stoppard's play), a third major character sent by the myth's cunning Odysseus (Stoppard's Otis) to deceive Philoctetes into returning with his magical bow necessary to the Greeks' victory at Troy. Stoppard's use of Acherson closely follows Sophocles, although he adds a female character, posing as Acherson's wife, and several incidental characters, including a small boy, absent in the all-male Greek original.

Sophocles's play opens with an expository scene in which Odysseus tells the youth Neoptolemus why they have arrived at the island of Lemnos. They have come for Philoctetes who, together with his magical bow, was abandoned there ten years earlier after the wound from a snakebite had made him repugnant to men. An oracle has told the Greeks that they will not win the Trojan War without Philoctetes's aid; thus, Odysseus, hated by the exiled hero for having abandoned him, persuades the reluctant Neoptolemus to trick Philoctetes into returning with him to Troy. But when the boy meets the ailing hero in his filthy cave, he is overcome with shame and confesses Odysseus's scheme. The two take sides against the cunning Greek, who prudently leaves, while Neoptolemus attempts to convince Philoctetes that he should come to the Greeks' aid. The hero consents to return only when Heracles appears as a *deus ex machina*, assuring him that he can take Neoptolemus's word as truth.

It is not difficult to guess the appeal of Sophocles's version of the myth for Stoppard, whose outsider figures had long been uncertain of the positive truth of their own and others' statements and beliefs. But the myth strikes another, more personal chord, provoking an oblique reference to Stoppard's own exile from Eastern Europe while an infant and his eventual settlement in England as an adopted land. That John Le Carré's novels should have drawn from Stoppard this uncharacteristically personal reference suggests his sense of kinship with the spy. Spies and writers share an anonymity, a trading of identities, a keen observational intelligence, a talent for unobtrusive eavesdropping, and a reluctance to believe the information they gather by these means (Homberger 1986, 29).

Stoppard's aging Philo, a one-time spy for the British in his native Eastern European country since overrun by the Russians, has lost his incentive to gather intelligence, preferring to return to the West to claim English nationality. But British intelligence chief Otis, falsely believing his cover to have been blown and his intelligence to have been bogus, refuses him entry. Otis later discovers his error. Now homeless and hunted by the Russians, having spent two embittered years hiding in "Montebianca" near Yugoslavia, he is about to be visited by British agent Acherson who is to trick him into returning with him to Britain. As in the Sophocles version, Acherson takes a risk by revealing the trick at a crucial moment, won over by pity for Philo's exile and respect for his stubborn indignation. While moved by Acherson's confession, Philo cannot be certain that it was not part of a performance staged to get him on the departing train. He needs to be able to take someone's word in a world saturated with lies:

> *Philo*: They'll break you for this.
> *Acherson*: One of those things.
> *Philo*: (*Bursts out*) You think I'll go with you, don't you?—to save your neck?
> *Acherson*: No. Goodbye.
> *Philo*: You're blackmailing me! (*Desperate*) Otis set this up, didn't he?
> *Acherson*: No.
> *Philo*: Tell me he set it up!
> *Acherson*: (*Rounds on him.*) That's what you want to think so you can forget all about it. Well, think it.
> *Philo*: No—just tell me the truth.

Acherson: Otis didn't set it up. (ACHERSON *starts running towards the train.*
PHILO *stands still for a moment.*)
Philo: (*Screams*) Acherson!
(PHILO *runs after* ACHERSON *as the train starts to move.*)

(163)

Philo chooses to believe and, in believing, to protect Acherson by boarding the train under Otis's cynical eye. The ethical problem is familiar to readers of Le Carré's *Tinker, Tailor, Soldier, Spy:* Philo, a "non-professional" officer works from a personal sense of conviction, initially, and later refuses to work from a personal sense of hatred. But he is enmeshed in an intelligence organization lately run by "professionals" for whom only impersonal or careerist motives count. An anachronism, he loses whether or not he cooperates with Otis. This Stoppardian twist on the Sophoclean situation adds depth and subtlety to Philo's character, a subtlety occasionally lost in melodramatic dialogue. Philo must choose between his old hatred for Otis and his new friendship with Acherson, with only Otis and perhaps Britain to gain by his choice. Sophocles's hero has the benefit of Heracles's direct intervention, or so it is signified in the play, ensuring him that Neoptolemus is telling him the truth. But for Stoppard, the drama lies in the uncertainty of the characters' motives and, more profoundly, in the uncertainty of their sense of self. Having traded countries, secrets, and allegiances during his lifetime as a spy, Philo fears he will lose his sense of self as well. In a poignant moment, he describes to Acherson a memory that has come to signify the permanence or "reality" of home:

> The things I remember don't change. I was born in a small town. I lived in a street which led into a small square and twice a week there was a market in the square. . . . I particularly remember the peppers lying around the edges of the square—red, orange, yellow, green, and all shades in between. . . . What mattered to us was that they were edible, and free, but what I remember now is the way the square looked on a summer evening after the market. (159)

Stoppard returned to the problem of multiple identities and the loss of self in a more recent radio play, *The Dog It Was That Died* (1982), in which double agent Rupert Purvis finally commits suicide when no longer able to sort out his imagined and his actual loyalties. Again, in 1988, he returned to the spy thriller, but this time in the form of a full-length stage play. *Hapgood* features a triple (or even quadruple) agent who solves Purvis's dilemma by admitting and accepting the reality of complex and contradictory commitments.

In spite of occasional overwriting, *Neutral Ground* powerfully exploits the suspense and melancholy of its second and equally important source, John Le Carré's spy thrillers, written in a spare narrative style diced with spy jargon, and featuring George Smiley, an intensely individualistic loner in conflict with the intelligence system. Le Carré's idiom is suited to television, not only because of its proven popular appeal but also for its psychological credibility. But Stoppard's most striking manipulation of that idiom is his creation of a two-layered dialogue encoding operators' secret stratagems. As the viewer begins to suspect early on, the operators' apparently realistic surface dialogue amounts to a clandestine code for their secret intelligence war—a very precise form of the two-layered dialogue developed in the early radio plays. Stoppard's deliberate heightening of the contrast between surface comedy and hidden menace will become a feature of his later satiric works *Professional Foul*, *Every Good Boy Deserves Favour*, and *Dogg's Hamlet, Cahoot's Macbeth*.

When we first see Philo, he barely escapes assassination. Following this, he speaks on a telephone in the Vienna train station, asking for "Toytown International," which we later learn to be the film's code name for the British intelligence agency. And when the pair of assassins known as "Laurel and Hardy" begin their search for Philo in Montebiancan bars, their dialogue and gestures parody the tough-talking gangsters of American films Stoppard had ridiculed in his 1960 review of a "cops and robbers thriller" ("Its a Joy," 1960). They force their way into a veterinarian's operating room, hoping to trace Philo through his pet monkey. Hardy casually takes out his gun and examines it while asking a series of barely disguised questions:

> *Hardy* (holding a gun): This friend of mine has a monkey.
> *Wolensk*: What's his name?
> *Hardy*: I don't know.
> *Wolensk*: You don't know your friend's name?
> *Hardy*: Oh—I thought you meant the monkey.
> *Wolensk*: Look—what is this?
> *Hardy*: Where do monkeys come from?

(117)

The menace of the interrogation coincides with the looney nonsequiturs, calling to mind Harold Pinter's *The Dumb Waiter*, with its two clown gangsters Ben and Gus struggling with language and matches while waiting to receive "instructions." As in Pinter's comedy, the characters in *Neutral Ground* do not know how much the other knows of the true reason for Acherson's visit to Montebianca. In a drunken moment, Acherson partially drops his mask, telling Philo why "Toytown" is throwing him out:

> I stopped a few black marks, that's all. That's what the factory is all about. The actual job is merely the surface activity. Underneath that runs the main current of preoccupation, which is keeping one's nose clean at all times. (144)

The subtext of the agents' maneuvering, says Acherson, is not even the intelligence war between Britain and Russia but Otis's moves to protect his career. Acherson's story, following both Sophocles and Le Carre, may also be a lie he was instructed to tell Philo to convince him that he is his ally in hating Otis. Again, Stoppard adds a twist to his sources. Where in the myth, Odysseus instructs Neoptolemus to lie to Philoctetes about his own grudge against the Greeks, in Stoppard's play, truth and falsehood are indistinguishable. We do not know whether Otis told Acherson to lie about his bleak future in Toytown, but we discover that Acherson genuinely dislikes Otis's methods and motives. So that while Acherson may have told the story for his own reasons, its effect on Philo plays into Otis's hands.

The action concludes, as it began, on a train, the film's signifier for the tentative, shifting condition of Philo's, and now Acherson's, moral and psychological state. Although written on a small scale and for a director's medium that Stoppard did not fully trust,[7] the screenplay is both more provocative and more moving than Stoppard himself appears to have realized in his apologetic introduction to the published text — "the hand itches for the blue pencil. . . " (8). It concludes with a Le Carré sense of disillusionment and betrayal, a tone typical of Stoppard only when working in the spy genre.

Part II: Mastering the Media, 1982–84

Back to Radio

Stoppard returned to radio and television in the early and mid-1980s with several major stage successes behind him. With his career as a stage playwright firmly established, what prompted him to seek out again what he had earlier judged to be secondary or minor media? Stoppard, of course, had little to do with the fact that the BBC commissioned *The Dog It Was That Died* to help celebrate its sixtieth anniversary. But his acceptance of the commission suggests that he may have looked to it as a chance to surpass his previous work for radio both by drawing in a new way upon the auditor's visual memory and by weaving a new pattern around his familiar theme of dislocation.

The Dog It Was That Died (1982)

Almost exactly ten years after *Artist Descending a Staircase*, Stoppard's seventh radio play, *The Dog It Was That Died,* aired on the BBC's Radio 3 in December of 1982. A superbly crafted small-scale comedy, it continues Stoppard's preoccupation with uncertainty fitted to the idiom of light comedy. His interest in exploiting the purely auditory riches of the radio resulted in another presumably "unstageable" play. *Dog* opens with a distraught man (double agent Rupert Purvis) falling from heights. When Purvis jumps off Chelsea Bridge, he breaks the back of a dog on a barge passing underneath, and this saves his life. According to Stoppard, the image parodies at least two sources: a conventional cinema scene (Eisenstein's *October* with its famous drawbridge sequence?) in which dogs jump off bridges onto barges, and Goldsmith's satirical "Elegy on the Death of a Mad Dog."[8] In the "Elegy," a mad dog severely bites his kind master who, presumed to be dying, recovers and bites the dog, who dies as a result. Without leaning heavily on his source, Stoppard duplicates its dry satirical tone while turning, for the first time, to architecture for inspiration. Purvis's superior, Blair, contemplates his folly during several scenes, an unimaginable hodgepodge of Gothic and classical features that appeals to Blair's fondness for the eclectic:

> I *do* like the mullioned window between the Doric columns—that has a quality of coy desperation, like a spinster gatecrashing a costume ball in a flowered frock . . . and the pyramid on the portico is sheer dumb insolence. (18–19)

In the folly, Stoppard has suggested an object—richer even than Albert's Bridge—to signify his preoccupation with the relativity of perspective. This carries over to two outdoor scenes in which Blair enjoys the vista as he gazes north from St. James's Park. But unlike his younger counterparts from the earlier radio plays, Blair recognizes the tricks the mind can play as it contemplates a removed tableau:

> Domes and cupolas, strange pinnacles and spires. A distant prospect of St. Petersburg, one imagines. . . . Where does it all go when one is in the middle of it, standing in Trafalgar Square with Englishness on every side? (13)

St. Petersburg and London can be conceived as interchangeable only at a spatial and historical distance. Again, briefly at the close of scene 6, Blair paints a picture for the auditor, humorously conflating scenery with his own garden creation: "What a skyline! All the way up Whitehall from Parliament Square, Trafalgar Square, St. James's. . . . It's like one enormous folly" (24). In the visual image and Blair's commentary upon it, Stoppard neatly clinches the connection between England and his British eccentric—both of them equated with architectural oddity.

Purvis, genuinely confused about whether he works for England or Russia, would appreciate Blair's equation between the two skylines. We learn in scene 7—the delay underscores its significance—that Purvis's unsuccessful suicide attempt occurred in response to a problem of perspective. Working for over thirty-five years as a double agent, he eventually lost track of which government he worked for: "Both sides were often giving me genuine stuff to pass on to the other side . . . so the side I was actually working for became . . . lost" (33). Stoppard plays his suffering in a minor key, to be sure. His second suicide letter begins, "Dear Blair. Well, goodbye again, assuming that I don't fall into a fishing boat" (41). And Purvis, like the playwright, mixes the most essential with the least essential matters of his life, announcing his intent to kill himself and his innocence of the theft of a piece of cheese with the same conviction. Considering himself a normally insane Englishman, he finally remains true to his English employer out of respect for his individual countryman. His suicide note alludes to British agent Gell, another eccentric who wore hunting pink to the office in the season. "I thought," wrote Purvis, "I *couldn't* have lied to Gell, . . . not for a mere conviction. The man was so much himself that one would have been betraying him instead of the system" (42).

Stoppard's tribute to his source, John Le Carré's spy novels, particularly *The Spy Who Came in from the Cold,* hints at his affinity for Le Carré's lonely heroes, the last of the individualists, already featured as Philo and Acherson in the 1968 television play *Neutral Ground.* But unlike Le Carré's morose outsiders, Stoppard's Purvis responds to his alienation by seeing the absurd humor in it. Reflecting upon his stay in "Clifftops" (another—this time—humorous reference to height as the precariousness of aesthetic distance), a homey mental hospital, Purvis writes Blair,

> I realize I am where I belong, at last, even though, in common with all the other inmates, I have the impression that I am here by mistake while understanding perfectly why everybody else should be here. In this respect Clifftops has an effect precisely opposite to being in a Marxist discussion group.(42)

Purvis's distress occurs in response to the peculiarly bizarre logic of the intelligence community—a system of double and triple bluffs that attempts to lure genuine intelligence out of the enemy by convincing him that his source is only sporadically trustworthy. Appearance is falsified in such a way that it occasionally corresponds to reality. Two suggestions made in Purvis's opening suicide letter—to wit, that the British intelligence chief runs an opium den in his Eaton Square house and that he sees Blair's wife on the sly—are revealed, at the conclusion of the play, to have been lies planted by the British chief himself who intended that Purvis should pass them on to his Russian contact. He assumed that if the British thought that the Russians thought that they could blackmail the chief, he might be chosen to succeed the nearly retired Purvis. The apparent comedy of intrigue conceals a farcical mid-life crisis.

As auditors in the dark, we share Purvis's dilemma: we can believe what we hear, but what is it exactly that we are believing? Whose point of view is the true one, the sane or the mad? Is morbidly suspicious agent Hogbin actually sane? Has the chief reached the top position by virtue of his relative lunacy? Purvis has lost track of the basic distinctions that make existence a worthwhile proposition. In his last interview with Blair, Purvis quietly expresses his sense of unreality in a brief speech that recapitulates and surpasses some of Stoppard's best writing:

> It *is* extremely depressing to find that one has turned into a canister. A hollow man. . . . I'm like one of those sets of wooden dolls which fit into one another as they get smaller. Somewhere deep inside is the last doll, the only one which isn't hollow. . . . perhaps I'm an onion. My idealism and my patriotism, folded on each other, have been peeled away leaving nothing in the middle except the lingering smell of onion. (34)

The speech recalls several Stoppard plays and sources: Eliot's "The Hollow Men"; Ibsen's Peer Gynt peeling an onion to its empty core; *Night and Day*'s Ruth recollecting her grandmother's packet of salt with its picture of a girl holding a packet of salt; and Guildenstern's becalmed reflection: "We cross our bridges when we come to them and burn them behind us, with nothing to show for our progress except a memory of the smell of smoke, and a presumption that once our eyes watered" (*Rosencrantz and Guildenstern Are Dead,* 61). The speech marks an essential dramatic moment, perhaps the essential moment in Stoppard's plays, when his characters speak of themselves as characters, aware of their own fictionality and yet disappointed by it, since they are searching for an elusive authenticity. The sureness of Stoppard's comic touch lies not so much in the speech itself as in its immediate deflation:

> *Blair*: Please don't cry.
> *Purvis*: I'm sorry. It's the onion. Oh stuff it, Blair!
> *Blair*: That's the spirit. To the taxidermist with the lot of it.

(34)

This is no longer the joking of an anxious young playwright who needs to hear the sound of an audience laughing, but an overriding of sentiment by the comic impulse toward distance or perspective.

Dog does not break new ground in Stoppard's use of the radio medium, but it exploits its suggestive possibilities more fully than any previous play, with the possible exception of *Artist Descending a Staircase*. All of the elements developed in the earlier plays—the interior voice, presented here in epistolary form; the preoccupation with falling; the posing of a primary mystery crossed with a secondary mystery; the teasing evocation of bizarre visual images; and the auditor's collaboration in the protagonist's attempt to see with his mind's eye—are orchestrated to express the position of the Stoppardian hero, inside and outside society.

While radio ranks well below the stage in Stoppard's writing hierarchy, it has helped the playwright learn to write for the theater. Radio taught him to distinguish characters through voice and dialogue; to exploit the dramatic possibilities of narration as recollection; and to involve the auditor in the fiction through the precise use of aural suggestion. The brevity of radio pieces encouraged Stoppard to write with maximum economy, choosing simple situations or gags sufficiently rich in comic potential to hold the auditor's active attention. In his search for the "pure" radio play, Stoppard has turned to painting and architecture as rich sources of comic suggestion. Giving the auditor free rein, Stoppard invites him to complete the picture. Blair's folly is custom built in each listener's imagination guided by one principle: "I admit it looks odd," prompts Blair. "The question is, does it look odd enough?" (18).

Recent Work for Television: *Squaring the Circle, 1984*

While Stoppard's earliest television plays lack the power and intensity of his novice work for radio and the stage, his more recent TV dramas are among the best of his secondary works. In the nearly twenty-year span separating the first and most recent pieces in this medium, Stoppard not only improved as a writer generally but also discovered a reason to write for television rather than for live theater. Recognizing in a mass audience witnesses to political repression and upheaval in contemporary Eastern Europe, he seized on television in the late 1970s as a tool for documenting human rights violations in Russia and Czechoslovakia and for presenting a fictionalized account of the birth and struggle of Poland's Solidarity movement.

In 1977 he wrote his next original play for television, *Professional Foul,* not to gain exposure and recognition in a secondary medium, but to reach millions of viewers. The choice of medium for this piece is overtly ideological (television being associated with documentary truth-telling) and its treatment is informed by the "militant irony" characteristic of satire. For these reasons, *Professional Foul* will be discussed with Stoppard's other satires of the 1970s in chapter 4.

In a long introduction to the printed version[9] of his most recent TV work to date, the 1984 made-for-television film *Squaring the Circle,* Stoppard narrates the history of the film's creation, a troubled collaboration between British art and American money that parallels the dramatized conflict between Solidarity and Polish Communist Party officials. The introduction informs us that Stoppard and director Mike Hodges learned, when it was almost too late, that American Metromedia thought its dollars had given it the right to ultimate control over the film. After long negotiations, Stoppard relates how he won back, piece by piece, original (and crucially nonillusionist) features of the film nearly lost, much as the film's Walesa learns how to win concessions from Party officials. But unlike the fate of Solidarity at the film's end, the script as published seems to represent a victory—something very like Stoppard's original intention.

Squaring the Circle both approximates and parodies the documentary conventions associated with "faction," a term usually applied to television plays, but equally suited to television films combining fiction and historical fact. Stoppard felt a journalist's uneasiness over the quasi-documentary nature of the project, an anxiety with roots in a fairly recent British debate over the potential dangers of "faction." Stoppard's friend, distinguished journalist Paul Johnson, expressed what seems to have been their shared position on the issue:

> The producer of the television "faction" does all in his power to prevent the viewer distinguishing between the two types of "evidence" and to persuade him that all is authentic. The introduction of genuine material makes the programme

more, not less, dishonest, for the mingling of truth and fiction is of the very essence of propaganda. (1981, 363)

Having begun the project at the suggestion of a film producer, Stoppard soon recognized that he lacked the information sufficient to write a factual history of Solidarity. He therefore meticulously dissociated the film from pure documentary with a number of devices, most of them familiar from the stage play *Travesties*. Fearing that whatever he presented would be taken as fact, he created a Narrator with "acknowledged fallibility" (a device used earlier in the radio drama *Where Are They Now?* and in the stage play, *Travesties*) originally conceived to represent and even to be played by Stoppard himself as "Author." The Narrator/Author's fallibility emerges both through his own admissions ("Everything is true," he tells us, "except the words and the pictures") and through his interaction with an editorializing second character known as the "Witness." The Witness exposes the uncertainty of the Narrator's reconstruction of the past, sometimes revealing the Narrator's bias, sometimes providing "factual" knowledge of Poland's past, always criticizing the Narrator's melodramatic tendencies, and, occasionally, overriding his analysis of the events being described. When the Narrator confidently proclaims the disruptive influence of intellectual mavericks to be "the single most important factor underlying the Polish crisis," the Witness dismisses him with characteristic panache: "Horse manure." Chastened, the Narrator follows the Witness's lead and tries a second time, "Meanwhile, the economic situation was the single most important factor underlying—" (41). Keeping two interpreters before the viewers reminds them of the tenuousness of the "facts" in this "faction."

The Witness has little patience with the film's conscious artistry. As Scene 41 opens on the Witness and Narrator playing chess while discussing Gierek's successor, the Witness snorts, "Why is it always *chess*?" He continues to demolish the metaphor by overexposing it: "These ones with the horse's heads, are they the ones which can jump over things?" The Narrator objects, "You're ruining it" (57). But ruining the precious metaphor is exactly the point. Artsiness in the "faction" is suspect if it disguises weak facts. The Witness conditions our credibility through his ironical detachment from the film's content and style.

But the Witness is not the only device through which Stoppard disclaims documentary authority. Portions of the film draw direct attention to the tentative nature of the narrative. The card game scene between Walesa, Archbishop Glemp, and Jaruzelski, a crucial but undocumented event, is filmed in three different versions to underscore its fictionality. The first version shows Glemp hostile to Solidarity and friendly to Jaruzelski; the second version shows Glemp attacking Jaruzelski; and the third presents an acute Glemp seeing through Jaruzelski's "Russian threat." "Everything is true," the Narrator reminds us, "except the words and the pictures" (90). In another scene, we see Gierek's television "news" address to the Polish people filmed in what is supposed to represent his actual office and bookcase but at the conclusion of the scene is revealed to be a fake flat. Two scenes later, Stoppard plays a visual joke, showing us

> what is apparently the studio bookcase but the middle of it is a concealed door which now opens. GIEREK comes through the bookcase to his desk and we see that behind him there is another office with a SECRETARY at a desk. (40)

Not only is the apparently real office with bookcase actually fake but the fake conceals a hidden real office. There is an analogy to the government's deliberate confusing of the real and the unreal and also a caution to the film's viewers watching a fiction occasionally attempting to approximate the truth.

Having recognized the impossibility of accurately documenting the eighteen-month history of Solidarity's fortunes, Stoppard's avowed intention in producing *Squaring the Circle* was to write a "personal dramatized essay" addressing the question whether "freedom as defined by the free trade union Solidarity [was] reconcilable with socialism as defined by the Eastern European Communist bloc" (Introduction, 10). Stoppard's (and thus the Narrator's) position was that they were fundamentally contradictory. The strongest evidence of Stoppard's polemic in the film is the repeated suggestion that the Polish Communist Party never intended to tolerate independent unions and that party members who thought it did, such as Jacek Kuron, were badly misled. Stoppard gives Colonel Jaruzelski a prophetic speech at the conclusion of Part 1. The government will respond with troops, he says, "when there is no alternative." "They [Solidarity] will bring us to it, slowly or quickly, but we'll get there, you have my guarantee" (48). Jaruzelski's prophecy of a military solution to the crisis also implies a belief in the incompatibility of independent unions and Soviet-style socialism, a belief Stoppard may be re-examining in the wake of anti-communist reforms.

While the implied author's point of view is obvious in the film, the same devices foregrounding its fictionality, particularly the Witness's efforts at exposing the Narrator's bias, prevent a narrowly polemical reading of the script. When the Narrator satirizes Polish officials Gierek and Babiuch as defenders of the working people's interests, the Witness dismisses the Narrator's mention of limousines and caviar as "a cheap shot, in my opinion. . . . It's not a factor. I never saw the President of France arrive anywhere on a bicycle eating a salami sandwich" (31). And later, when the Narrator gives party bosses gangster dialogue to speak as a "metaphor," the Witness reacts with predictable disgust: "Wrong. You people—" (60). The tension between art and fact, informed opinion and prejudice, is brought so consciously before the viewer as to prevent the film from being taken either as pure polemic or as straight documentary.

The script's treatment of Jacek Kuron, an intellectual iconoclast advocating a genuine revolutionary workers' state, shows Stoppard attempting to mediate opinion and prejudice without disguising the mediation. Clearly drawn to Kuron as a spokesman for the intellectuals who saw in Solidarity the potential for workers to seize power, Stoppard presents him as a compelling character with a Stoppardian respect for language and ideas. But he also implicitly opposes Kuron's dogmatism, his insistence on Marxist theory as the key to social justice. His Narrator and Witness present Kuron as the product of this complex attitude. Scene 100 shows Walesa's children playing ball while reciting the following lines: "Poor Mr Kuron . . . He thinks if he leaves the Party alone . . . the Party will leave him alone. . . . Poor Mr Kuron." The Witness intrudes at this point: "A cheap trick, in my opinion. . . . Out of the mouths of children . . . " (84). Having rejected the Narrator's cliché use of children's wisdom in exposing Kuron's naiveté, the Witness in the following scene offers his own analysis of Kuron's error:

> He's got it upside down, in my opinion. Theories don't guarantee social justice, social justice tells you if a theory is any good. Right and wrong are not complicated. (84)

In response to the Witness's expression of opinion, the Narrator replays a previous scene, revising his decision to show Kuron criticizing Solidarity's failure to analyze its actions. The Witness has convinced the Narrator to avoid prejudicial treatment of Kuron. If right and wrong are not complicated, the viewers should be able to see for themselves who is "right" and why. As we observe Kuron being made and remade, we recognize the influence of the Narrator's and Witness's own opinions—as well as their revisions to those opinions—on the construction of his character.

The film ends as it began, with the Polish and Russian leaders meeting at the Black Sea in a parodic exchange of small talk. While clearly in the realm of fiction, we identify a foundation of facts informing the events presented in the script. The result expresses the "qualified reality" that Stoppard had hoped for when beginning the project. In spite of misgivings and conflicts with his American backers, Stoppard's written script succeeds as a "personalized essay" about Solidarity, but more importantly, it succeeds as "faction" because it asks the viewers to recognize their role in sorting out fact from fiction, opinion from fact.

Stoppard solved the problem of writing fiction for a medium dominated by documentaries and serials by drawing attention to the artificiality of his fictions. John Brown's exile to his self-styled pastoral retreat depends for its humor on his awareness of withdrawal as an artificial gesture. What in a realistic style of telling could be a play about a nervous breakdown is, in Stoppard's telling, a play about Brown's attempt to substitute art for life. Stoppard's *Teeth* exaggerates fear of the dentist's chair, the sort of mundane emotion celebrated in serials, removing it from the range of domestic detail and placing it more squarely in the realm of farce. In *Another Moon Called Earth,* we watch a viewer watching a TV news broadcast that obscures rather than reveals the significance of the event being transmitted. The live broadcast of the parade welcoming home the lunanauts lulls the public (but not Penelope) into celebrating what she recognizes to be a catastrophe. When Stoppard turns to the Le Carré thriller for his screenplay *Neutral Ground,* he pushes the gangster clichés to a level of surreal comedy and builds the convention of secrecy into a metaphor for the displacement of self. We recognize the Le Carré formula doubled and tripled by levels upon levels of disguise and subterfuge. Similarly, the dialectical play between fact and fiction, pathos and irony, reminds the viewer of *Squaring the Circle* that "faction" is part fact, part fiction.

It is perhaps no surprise that Stoppard drew on many of the non-illusionary devices of his stage plays to alert the viewer of his television plays to his manipulation of the medium. Rather than a seamless portrayal of reality, Stoppard's works for television insist upon their unreality, offering viewers the pleasures of conscious fiction in lieu of the illusions of real talk and image. The stage offered Stoppard the ideal vehicle for his kind of conscious comedy, and it is to his early stage works that we will now turn to trace the fullest development of his comic range.

Chapter 3

On Stage: Re-Playing, Re-Vising, Re-Presenting

Part 1: Pastiche, Parody, Farce

Enter a Free Man: A Look Back at Osborne's *Anger*

Stoppard's writing of plays grew out of his experience as an observer and judge of live and film drama. The ten years spent in Bristol and London theaters, from 1954 to 1964, exposed him to the gamut of contemporary and classical drama—native and imported, traditional and experimental, epic and minimalist. When he decided to try his hand at writing, he attempted drama as well as fiction, drawn to the theater not only through his first-hand acquaintance with plays, actors, and directors but also by the general climate of excitement that grew up around the Renaissance of postwar British theater and drama. As Stoppard told the *Sunday Times* in 1968,

> "After 'Look Back in Anger' young writers tended to be young playwrights . . . because the theatre was clearly the most interesting and dynamic medium. . . . It seemed clear . . . that you could do a lot more in the theatre than had been previously demonstrated." ("Something to Declare," 47)

Having resigned his steady job for the *Bristol Evening World* in 1960, Stoppard

> contracted to write two weekly columns for a total of six guineas [and] started writing a stage play, *A Walk on the Water*. My first play petered out after a dozen pages that were not unlike *Look Back in Anger*. This one was not unlike *Flowering Cherry*. I took it round to the Bristol Old Vic. Nothing happened for nine

months. I wrote 72 more columns, and a one-acter not unlike *Waiting for Godot*. ("The Definite Maybe," 1967, 18)

At the end of nine months, Stoppard sent *Walk on the Water* to Kenneth Ewing, who has since become his permanent agent and supporter. When an option bought on the play was allowed to expire without production, Stoppard and Ewing next tried television, this time with success. Transmitted by Independent Television (ITV) in 1963, Stoppard's first stage play premiered on television, a fact attributable to its domestic themes and relatively realistic surface action, both long identified with the norms of TV drama (see chap. 2). First staged in Hamburg in 1964, the play was revised and retitled *Enter a Free Man* for its 1968 London premiere. Revised at each of its successive performances, *Free Man* was effectively "in process" from 1960 to 1968, overlapping with the writing of several radio plays, a television play, the stories and novel, an adaptation of Slawomir Mrozek's *Tango,* and the decisive stage play, *Rosencrantz and Guildenstern Are Dead.* What I shall nevertheless refer to as the earliest of Stoppard's published plays represents his contribution to the postwar theatrical Renaissance. An Osborne-inspired look at 1950s Britain, *Free Man* looks back at Osborne and at Stoppard's unknown and unpublished "first" play.

The new drama was being written by young provincial and working-class playwrights attempting to revitalize theater by shifting its center from London drawing rooms to middle- and working-class provincial homes where characters spoke a new, authentic-sounding prose. The new playwrights wanted, in the words of John Osborne, "to make people feel, to give them lessons in feeling" (quoted in Styan 1981, 149). They were to feel what it meant to be alive in a postwar British theater registering the shocks of change in Britain's class, economic, and military systems. The fact essential to Stoppard's career was that, thanks largely to George Devine's English Stage Company at the Royal Court Theatre and Joan Littlewood's Theatre Workshop in the East End, artists were choosing stage drama as the medium for "making people feel," that the stage, rather than the printed page or the cinema screen, held first place as a springboard for invention and innovation.

Stoppard entered the Renaissance with his play about a modest British family attempting to salvage its unity, its dignity, and its dreams in a demoralized Britain lost in escapist fantasies. This would be Stoppard's first and only sustained stage treatment of family life until his later success, *The Real Thing,* a more complex questioning of the virtues of marital fidelity and family interdependence. Atypically for Stoppard and a sign of his allying this play with the new drama's interest in the margins of British society, the George Riley family, wife Constance and daughter Linda, are working class, albeit at its upper end: "They had to be a bit upper," he told Ronald Hayman, "because I kept giving them extremely well-constructed speeches to speak at a high speed of knots" (1979, 6). This has remained true of subsequent Stoppard characters, most of whom have been conceived as extraordinarily articulate members of the middle and upper-middle classes. While living modest but stymied lives on meager shop wages earned by Riley's wife and daughter, the Riley family develops "life lies" as elaborate and essential as those propping up the Werle family in Ibsen's *Wild Duck* and the drunkards in O'Neill's *The Iceman Cometh* to compensate for the disappointments of reality. George, the type of the Stoppardian artist, both "inside and outside" society, both loafer and "inventor," plays a double role, a failed inventor at home and a wild adventurer in his local pub. Daughter Linda, a frustrated supporter of her unemployed father, imagines her casual dates to be exotic lovers who will rescue her from her routine life as a sales clerk. The somewhat disappointing character of Riley's wife, Constance, offers encouragement, stability, and maid service to her half-loony husband and daughter.

Stoppard identifies Riley's crackpot creativity with a resilient Britain through the image of his tape-playing clock:

> I have a tape-recorder connected to my grandfather clock! . . . . it appeals to British character . . . twice a day, noon and midnight— Rule Brittania!—And we need it—Did I go through the war to witness the decline of Britain as a maritime power? (26)

In fact, as we later learn, Riley did not serve during the war at all, but like O'Neill's drunken storytellers, Riley refuses to let truth ruin a good tale. In contrast to his source characters, Willy Loman and Jim Cherry, Riley represents Stoppard's vision of the best of the British heritage to survive postwar decline— the individual stubbornly resisting conformity, bureaucracy, and humiliation, but overwhelmed by the inhuman vastness of modern society. Where we pity Loman and Cherry, we are entertained by the Riley we meet in the pub and are invited to sympathize with his belief in his creative vocation. Daughter Linda, a spunkier, younger version of her father, is caught up in a youthful struggle to escape and transcend her limits. Constance appears to signify the quiet stability of the British mother and wife, determinedly married to routine and monotony as the safeguards of her family's well being. The representativeness of the characters hints at the allegorical quality of Stoppard's drama.

Following the spirit if not the style of Osborne's *Look Back in Anger*, *Enter a Free Man* anatomizes postwar British society while exposing the individual's vulnerability in a depersonalized modern world. But it is also a uniquely Stoppardian comedy, not at all declamatory in the Osborne style nor realistically detailed and somber like the Wesker *Roots* trilogy. Buoyant and witty, *Enter a Free Man* declares its theatrical origins in a series of speeches and structural devices foregrounding its artifice. The most obvious of these self-reflexive devices, the split stage signifying pub (stage left) and home (stage right), may have been adapted from the composite interior/exterior sets of its two principal sources, Arthur Miller's *Death of a Salesman* and Robert Bolt's *Flowering Cherry* (influenced in its turn by Miller). The set objectifies Stoppard's examination of the double lives led by his characters, casting them in theatrical terms as roles played in different settings. Accordingly, the action and dialogue on the "pub" side of the stage project an explicitly theatrical vitality and wit, while the domestic melodrama on the "home" side of the stage creates the illusion of an unremarkable reality. The pub Riley demonstrates the linguistic ingenuity of the mature Stoppard hero, while spoofing standard Stoppardian themes:

> Dreams! The illusion of something for nothing. No wonder the country is going to the dogs. Personal enterprise sacrificed to bureaucracy. No pride, no patriotism. The erosion of standards, the spread of mediocrity, the decline of craftsmanship and the betrayal of the small inventor. (15)

Woven in and out of Riley's list of failings are a series of issues that Stoppard has taken or will come to take seriously (even while treating them comically) in other contexts, such as the growth of bureaucracy in *Albert's Bridge* and *If You're Glad I'll Be Frank*, the decline of craftsmanship in *Artist Descending a Staircase* and the erosion of patriotism in *Travesties*.

The *Godot*-style music hall duologue immediately following George's outburst erupts in the same spirit of parodic play, but this time at George's expense:

> *Harry*: It's terrible really. I blame youth.
> *Carmen*: Education.
> *Harry*: The Church is out of touch.
> *Carmen*: The family is not what it was.
> *Harry*: It's the power of the unions.

Carmen: The betrayal of the navy.
Harry: Ban the bomb.
Carmen: Spare the rod.

(15)

The humor in the pub scenes depends in part upon George's playacting, spiraling to heights of farcical excess when he ad-libs his role as cerebral man, egged on by Harry's mock admiration. In spite of being made a buffoon by the blustering Harry, George emerges as the play's comic-pathetic hero capable of endless poses and scenes improvised around his inventions. After seriously accepting Harry's joking offer to become his partner in marketing his double-gummed envelopes, George stalks about the barroom looking for industrial spies. He hits upon an innocent patron by the name of Brown and takes off on a flight of absurdity:

Riley: You're from Imperial Stationery.
Brown: From where?
Riley: I see. Well, we have ways of making you people talk.
(*Barks*.) What's your name?
Brown: (*jumps*) Brown.
Riley: (*hollow laugh*): Brown! Oh dear, oh dear! An amateur!

(23)

Lost in his interrogation, Riley jumps track from fantasy to fantasy until patron Brown exits the bar for safer ground.

The play's less successful "home" scenes shift gears from the histrionic gags of the pub to the muted realistic dialogue of domestic melodrama as translated by its contemporary form, the soap opera (Cantor and Pingree 1983, 20). At home, Riley relinquishes his pub role as hero-buffoon to take up the pose of gentleman buffoon. The hero of the home scenes—the character with the greatest creative energy—is his daughter, Linda, the primary breadwinner and caustic critic of her father, George. From Linda's vantage point, George's perverse refusal to take money from the Labour Exchange has enslaved her to her job selling fancy goods. But to Constance, George's relatively dignified failure as an inventor represents a victory over what would have been his failure as a businessman. In playing these domestic roles, the family acts out the ills of modern living as portrayed in the soaps—monotony, misunderstanding, petty quarrels, frustrated attempts at happiness. Their memories, hopes, and humiliations fuel the dialogue and dominate the action. As in the soaps, their domestic roles, like their routine, have always been and always will be the same, which drives father and daughter to seek escape through fantasy.

But even in the domestic realm, these characters are capable of recognizing the rigidity of each other's parts. Linda and Riley recognize the foolishness in one another, if not in themselves. Bland Constance, the most objective of the family members, emerges as a startlingly reliable reader of character, informing a surprised Linda that she hasn't got what it would take to be an inventor like her father. Her surprise revelations about George—his gentleness, his uniqueness—parallel those of Arthur Miller's Linda and Bolt's Isobel defending their husbands against their sons' attacks. But Stoppard's play, set firmly in a comic milieu, avoids the intense emotions of Miller's and Bolt's, even when borrowing elements of their plots and structure. When both Riley and Linda return home crushed and humiliated (again) at the close of the second act, they discover in one another a source of inspiration to carry on in spite of the fact that they still do not understand one another. Unlike Bolt and Miller, Stoppard does not explore the psychological interest of one character's failure to understand another. He shows his characters finally willing to tolerate one another's roles without claiming to understand them. Accordingly, his melodrama concludes with a happy truce, father and daughter once again reconciled to carrying on with the daily routines and clichés that had earlier become intolerable. As Riley attempts to explain to Linda his resistance to accepting a handout from the Labour Exchange, he affirms his role as creator: "The trouble is, I think I was *meant* to be an inventor" (84). Where Willy Loman and Jim Cherry deflate like punctured dolls when their sales fall off, Stoppard's Riley persists in his inventions, in spite of their flaws.

Enter a Free Man may be in part a transparent pastiche of Bolt and Miller, as Stoppard jokingly called it, "The Flowering Death of a Salesman," ("Withdrawing," 60), but it also tentatively investigates the problem of the artist—the recurrent, nearly obsessive theme of his early work through *Travesties*—questioning the artist's right to withdraw and invent, especially as his inventions, by definition, fail to be useful. Perhaps hampered by his sources, Stoppard fails to work out the problem with the rigor characteristic of his more mature plays. Riley's license to sponge (ungratefully) off of his wife and daughter is not justified by the action or dialogue. We find the pub Riley inventive and amusing, but the domestic Riley too close to Jim Cherry, unworthy of his family's propping up, particularly as they receive so little thanks for their support. In short, domestic Riley comes off as one of the first of Stoppard's narcissistic artists—an early study for Albert of *Albert's Bridge,* of George Moore, Henry Carr, and the more recent playwright Henry. So that while the problem of the artist as parasite appears to have been discounted by the father and daughter reconciliation at the play's close, it has merely been circumvented, as it is in the other "artist" plays.

In spite of its muddle of motives, *Enter a Free Man* hints at Stoppard's deep concern for the artist's rights and responsibilities as an actor on the public and domestic stages, a concern that will resurface later with greater success. On balance, his domestic comedy fits uneasily into the postwar Renaissance, offering comic analysis in the place of serious social criticism, tolerance in the place of anger, and a stubborn, if untested, optimism in the place of cynicism. By the time of his next major stage play, begun in 1964 and staged in 1966, he had found his inspiration not in the quasi-realistic 1950s theater of social criticism but in a theater of reflexive echo and re-play.

At the Boundary: *Rosencrantz and Guildenstern Are Dead*

In his review of the National Theatre Company's 1967 production of Stoppard's first major stage success, Charles Marowitz located the accomplishment of *R&GAD* "not . . . in its thought, but in its craft." Stoppard's "second-hand Beckett" is redeemed, wrote Marowitz, by his careful joining of *Godot* and *Hamlet,* revealed at the moment when "Rosencrantz and Guildenstern, discussing the switched letter which dooms them to death, accept their fate. . . . Suddenly the play becomes a blinding metaphor about the absurdity of life" (1973, 124–25). While I will argue that this moment of discovery is both more particular and more complex than the vague term "absurdity" would suggest, Marowitz's praise of craftsmanship echoes the argument of this book: that Stoppard's sustained commitment to re-present texts, genres, and styles disturbs our assumptions about the place, the prominence, and the significance of those models. *R&GAD* is the first major stage play in which Stoppard ventures a series of overlapping misreadings of major works in the formalist spirit of disrupting the canon.

Thomas Whitaker's brilliant description of the ancestry of *R&GAD*'s playfulness documents how fully Stoppard attempts to engage his audience's participation in the intersecting of multiple texts and frames (1983, 46–54). And while the complex layering of *R&GAD*'s sources and styles can be read as finally pointing toward what Whitaker calls the Courtiers' virtual failure to "be there" as the "already written" artifacts of *Hamlet,* it also points up their stage presence grounded in Shakespeare and Beckett, among others. It points, that is, toward Stoppard's attempt to make theatrical a renewing of the idiom and stage style of British literary theater after Beckett. He attempts this renewal not by erasing the past—as if such a thing were possible—but by repeating fragments of masterworks in a new context that might nudge the spectator to see them in a new way.[1]

R&GAD parodies *Hamlet* locally and globally, copying with difference individual lines as well as broad actions. The most specific parodic procedure Stoppard uses is to repeat *Hamlet's* dialogue intact but out of context for laughs.[2] Some of the repetitions amount to simple comic inversion—a scene narrated in the Shakespeare original is performed in the Stoppard copy. Other of the repetitions point up comic events implicit in the text but usually overlooked in reverent productions of Shakespeare, such as the apparent confusing of Rosencrantz and Guildenstern. But the global pattern of Stoppard's selection and distorted repetition of *Hamlet* reveals his overriding concern with the question of power, obligation, and choice implied by the deaths of the minor Courtiers. Working, like Prince Hamlet, through a metaphor of the theater, Stoppard re-presents the Courtiers' deaths in order to pose the question whether theater can offer light to spectators, can disturb our assumptions about our own roles and plots, or whether it can only reproduce what we thought we already knew about how we play at life.

Even before seeing Rosencrantz and Guildenstern in act 1, most spectators will recognize them as the fictional minor victims from Shakespeare's play, although they fail to recognize themselves as such. Stoppard mediates the fictionality of Rosencrantz and Guildenstern through a primarily Beckettian dialogue and milieu to give them a theatrical identity and significance pointedly missing in Shakespeare's play. The opening scene presents the two Courtiers spinning coins, improvising patter, and reaching for a logical explanation for their situation in what could be a rewrite of *Godot*, particularly if we overlook Guildenstern's references to theories of probability. In an echo of Beckett's clowns whiling away the time, the travelers attempt to size up their situation:

> *GUIL*: Then what are we doing here, I ask myself.
> *ROS*: You might well ask.
> *GUIL*: We better get on.
> *ROS*: You might well think.
> *GUIL*: We better get on.
> *ROS*: (*actively*): Right! (*Pause.*) On where?
> *GUIL*: Forward.

ROS: *(forward to footlights)*: Ah. *(Hesitates.)* Which way do we — *(He turns round.)* Which way did we — ?

(20)

As with Didi and Gogo, the essential dramatic fact of Stoppard's Shakespearean couple is that they did not know and were never clearly told what they were supposed to be doing at Elsinore and why they were supposed to be doing it. Both Beckett's and Stoppard's clowns founder in uncertainty, passing the time with music hall turns and farce gags. One of them thinks, the other feels, with rational Guildenstern and intuitive Rosencrantz doubling for Vladimir and Estragon, respectively. At one moment in the play, Stoppard quotes the trouser gag from *Godot* as Rosencrantz and Guildenstern attempt to block Hamlet's exit:

GUIL *positions himself next to* ROS, *a few feet away, so that they are covering one side of the stage, facing the opposite side.* GUIL *unfastens his belt.* ROS *does the same. They join the two belts, and hold them taut between them.* ROS's *trousers slide slowly down.* (89)

But this is *Godot* with a difference. Acutely aware of writing under what Harold Bloom has called "Beckett's giant shadow" (1986, 2), Stoppard first places and then displaces Beckett by writing against his minimalist style. *The Gamblers* had been his "serious" attempt at a Beckettian play, which he later dismissed after being told by a patron that "all young writers seemed to be writing first plays about people in condemned cells" (Interview with Editors of *Theatre Quarterly*, 4). Even while echoing Beckett's clowns, Guildenstern embellishes his brief exchanges with Rosencrantz by spinning out his reflections in rapid-fire, hyper-articulate set pieces. Some of Guildenstern's most striking dialogue requires a delivery in the style of Shaw's elevated stage talk rather than Beckett's stripped fragments. Embellishing the spare *Godot* idiom and set with rhetorical color, Stoppard marks his preference for the Beckett who came before the severe minimalism of *Happy Days,* censured in his *Scene* review of November 1962 (see chap. 1).

Stoppard was one of many playwrights wrestling with the appearance of *Godot* on the London stage. Another *Godot*-like play, written by Stoppard's friend James Saunders, echoes distantly throughout *R&GAD*, offering an additional example of the British response to Beckett. As several commentators have noted (Sammells 1988, 37; Whitaker 1983, 45; Corballis 1984, 46),

Stoppard borrowed a series of images and rhetorical devices from Saunders's *Next Time I'll Sing to You,* a 1963 West End success. But it was less the language of Saunders's play than its offhanded acknowledgment of Beckett that seems to have set a precedent for later treatments of *Godot,* among them Pinter's *The Caretaker. Next Time* opens with a young man, Meff, reading from a sheet of paper a turgid speech that simultaneously declares and laughs at its Beckettian origins:

> There is pretense, and there is the pretense behind pretense. Through the ages of the groping of man from the dark chaos of his beginnings when shrouded by ignorance of his ignorance, he stared first blankly at a sky devoid yet even of mystery and clawed himself awkwardly and for reasons unknown to stand unsteadily on his two back feet— (1)

This tongue-in-cheek Beckettian angst is relieved occasionally by jokes and music hall turns, but for the most part it occupies long stretches of the play, suggesting that West End audiences must have been hungry indeed for mock-Beckett. Arriving in a theatrical scene defined as post-Beckettian, Stoppard was likely to be not only self-conscious but also light-handed in his references to Beckett's work, which may explain why his choice of lines from *Godot* tends to favor the lighter parts—the music hall exchanges and farce gags—to convey the comic feel of Beckett's trapped couple.

But the repeated tossing of coins, the most distinctive action in Stoppard's opening scene, is not Beckettian at all. In asking Rosencrantz to attend to the bizarre run of eighty-five heads tossed consecutively, Guildenstern invites him to join the spectators in probing for the significance of the suspension of probability. The oddity of the event we are witnessing is Stoppard's equivalent to the ghost opening *Hamlet:* both events signal the suspension of the ordinary and the entry into art. My own guess at the origin of the coin-tossing business points to logical positivist Richard von Mises's definition of probability as "the limiting value of the . . . frequency of a given attribute . . . within a given collective."[3]

Mises used the event of coin tossing to illustrate a "collective" within which the probability of an event (heads) can be meaningfully determined. If my guess is correct, the coin tossing is the first example of Stoppard's sustained interest in illustrating philosophical and mathematical principles in precise stage terms (among later examples are Cantor's proof and Zeno's paradox in *Jumpers,* Wittgenstein's language game in *Dogg's Our Pet;* and particle physics in *Hapgood)*. In Guildenstern's talk, "probability" is the technocratic jargon for post-Beckettian "reality," and as such identifies Stoppard's Courtiers as members of contemporary culture for whom the "real" can be defined only as the probable and for whom the probable has been mysteriously suspended. This layer of scientific metaphor distinguishes Rosencrantz and Guildenstern from both their Shakespearean and their Beckettian models.

In subsequently listing possible explanations for interpreting the run of heads, Guildenstern not only mocks our own efforts to interpret what we see but also announces the larger comic strategy of declaring and resisting the texts at play.

> List of possible explanations. One: I'm willing it. . . . I am the essence of a man spinning double-headed coins, and betting against himself in private atonement for an unremembered past. . . . Two: time has stopped dead, and the single experience of one coin being spun once has been repeated ninety times. . . . Three: divine intervention. . . . Four: a spectacular vindication of the principle that each individual coin spun individually is as likely to come down heads as tails . . . (16)

In listing all of these potential reasons for the unreality of their situation, Guildenstern pointedly refuses to adopt any one of them as more true than any other. While logically possible, they sound equally farfetched. Poised at what William Gruber has called "the boundary situation" between life and art, we look with Guildenstern both ways at once but recognize that we are in neither realm exclusively (in Bloom 1986, 111).

The arrival of the Players would seem to move the action out of the boundary and fully into the fiction of *Hamlet*, but it does not. Instead, it more completely defines the boundary as the fictional space between the two primary source texts, underscoring not only Rosencrantz and Guildenstern's preexistence[4] as Beckettian and Shakespearean clowns but also their resistance to their source characters. When the Players arrive on Stoppard's stage, we recall both their promising arrival at Elsinore in *Hamlet* and the anti-climactic entrance of Pozzo and Lucky in *Godot*. Guildenstern is disappointed by the Players who he hoped would be something completely fantastical, like a unicorn. He was prepared to be transported ("saved" in the *Godot* idiom) out of the real into the surreal by means of an extraordinary sign. For this, the Players are a poor substitute: "No enigma, no dignity, nothing classical, portentous, only . . . a comic pornographer and a rabble of prostitutes . . . " (27). The Players' pathetic offering of *flagrante delicto* is the literal remnant of a once grand metaphorical art, shrunk, like Lucky's intellect, to a puny and inconsequential dimension in a fallen age ("The very *air* stinks").

In addition to shadowing Pozzo and Lucky, Stoppard's Tragedians recollect the adult Players in Shakespeare's play who promise not only to lift Hamlet out of his gloom but to serve his turn by triggering Claudius's guilt. From Hamlet's point of view, the Players' arrival brings with it freshness and hope: not only does he enjoy watching them perform but he learns from their performance how he might perform in turn. The Players are marvelous (and malleable) because entirely empty of anything but their parts; or, put another way, they are completely constituted by their parts which seem to infuse even their bodies: "Tears in his eyes, distraction in his aspect, / A broken voice, an' his whole function suiting / With forms to his conceit? And all for nothing, / For Hecuba!" (2.2.555–58). In reflecting on the monstrous difference between his own real but as yet unrepresented passion and the Players' entirely unreal but fully represented sorrow, Hamlet strikes upon the idea of tricking Claudius by mimicking his hidden crime with a fictional crime. Hamlet's trap works: the unexpected congruence between the hidden and the represented fools his uncle into revealing his secret guilt. Claudius is tricked into conflating the fictional with the actual.

From the point of view of Stoppard's Courtiers, however, the Players are neither inspirational nor fresh, but quite the opposite—they do not create but recreate what has already been written for them in a style already anticipated by the spectators. Later in act 2, when Guildenstern naively tells the Player that people don't believe in their staged deaths, the Player retorts, "On the contrary, it's the only kind they do believe. They're conditioned to it" (83–84). The Tragedians trade on the conditioned response. In this sense, they are the agents of theatrical convention and the Courtiers' literary and theatrical enemies.

Our act 1 acquaintance with the Players shows them hungry for an audience, as they require witnesses to play at all. In the absence of observers, they are incomplete and must suspend performing until new spectators come along. Further, they are entirely dependent upon tradition and authority for what they do and where they do it: "We have no control. Tonight we play to the court. Or the night after. Or to the tavern. Or not" (25). Their radical contingency is like that of puppets: nearly emptied of human being and filled by their parts, they are the direct descendants of Hamlet's troupe. At two significant moments in the action, however, Stoppard suggests that the Tragedians may not be unanimous in consenting to their enslavement—that they are vestigially "human" after all. When the Player offers young Alfred as payment for having lost their bet on the coin throw, Guildenstern asks the boy, "Do you like being an actor?" When Alfred answers, "No, sir," Guildenstern appears to agree with him and, for a moment, contemplates abandoning the stage: "GUIL *looks around, at the audience.* You and I, Alfred—we could create a dramatic precedent here" (32). Alfred's sniffling suggests that he has misread Guildenstern's intention, undercutting the potential seriousness of the moment. But Stoppard returns to the issue later in act 2 when the Player tells a story of one of his actors who confused himself with humanity:

> I had an actor once who was condemned to hang for stealing a sheep—or a lamb, I forget which—so I got permission to have him hanged in the middle of a play. . . . and you wouldn't believe it, he just *wasn't* convincing! It was impossible to suspend one's disbelief. . . . he did nothing but cry all the time—right out of character. (84)

The Player describes the difference between actors and non-actors as the difference between "seeming" and "being"—"we're the opposite of people!" (63). As the executors of tragic design, the Tragedians are indifferent to its meaning. They thus have little in common either with Rosencrantz and Guildenstern, who vainly seek meaning, or with Pirandello's Actors with whom they have frequently been compared. Pirandello's six characters searching for an author, to cite one example, claim a greater value for their fictionality than for that of the professional actors who would play their parts. The parallel to Pirandello's "characters" would have to be Rosencrantz and Guildenstern, who, in spite of their (unacknowledged) fictionality, consider themselves more "real" than the actors. On balance, the differences between the two plays are more instructive than their similarities. If he is specifically indebted to Pirandello, which I doubt, Stoppard's debt lies less in his use of actors as characters than in his broad exploration of the mutually penetrating realms of art and life.

With unfortunately little apparent interest in the theater or in acting, Rosencrantz and Guildenstern abandon the Tragedians preparing for "no. 38" and find themselves abruptly at Elsinore observing a mute scene between Ophelia and Hamlet. We are now in *Hamlet,* but with a difference. The difference significantly does not lie in a rewriting of Shakespeare's dialogue—that remains intact as an instrument of the text's power—but in an inversion of the spoken and the acted. Stoppard wittily implies that Rosencrantz and Guildenstern literally as well as figuratively play behind the scenes. When the Courtiers, now speaking fluent Elizabethan, briefly take up their preexisting roles, they are no longer naturalized to them, having demonstrated their fluency in

Beckettian speech and action. This is made especially clear in their dialogue following the exit of Shakespeare's characters, as they rehearse how they might interrogate the prince:

> *ROS*: To sum up: your father, whom you love, dies, you are his heir, you come back to find that hardly was the corpse cold before his young brother popped onto his throne and into his sheets, thereby offending both legal and natural practice. Now why exactly are you behaving in this extraordinary manner?
> *GUIL*: I can't imagine! (*Pause.*) But all that is well known, common property. Yet he sent for us. And we did come.
>
> (51)

While the *Hamlet* fable is so commonly known as to appear trite, Rosencrantz and Guildenstern's particular role within it remains a mystery. Their sole instruction—to glean what afflicts the prince—could have been carried out by anyone. But they alone were sent for, just as Didi and Gogo were singled out by Godot to wait. As particular people, the two couples are at once flattered and baffled by the special attention given them by those in power. They can interpret their instructions as the Tragedians do their parts—as a happy release from the evaluating, judging, and choosing necessary to the exercise of improvisation. But both recognize the threat implicit in this release: if they are not directing their parts, they are being directed by someone else.

By the close of act 1, the Courtiers describe themselves as marked men. Thus, while completely ignorant of their role in Shakespeare's play, they are nonetheless granted a vague awareness of its imminence denied their literary predecessors. The effect of this vague awareness is to spur them on to new heights of ingenuity in a frantic attempt to decipher what they are expected to do and how they might do it. The spectators join in this effort which is not simply an attempt to recover Shakespeare's plot (most of them know it already) but to play along with the couple's attempts to justify it.

Act 2 carries forward the multiple texts informing act 1, but interrupts them frequently with abrupt and brief incursions from *Hamlet*. As striking as the textual interplay is the crossing of performance styles. Three kinds of playing cross and re-cross in this act: the highly charged and stylized presenting of *Hamlet*; the intimate bantering of Rosencrantz and Guildenstern; and the melodramatic rehearsing of the Tragedians. The Courtiers' private game of mapping the rhetorical exchange between themselves and Hamlet brings us closer to them than we are brought to the other sets of players, who remain aloof and guarded. When Guildenstern appeals to the Player for help in approaching the prince, the Tragedian parodically echoes Hamlet's advice to the Players, suggesting that they "act natural." And this is how Rosencrantz and Guildenstern do "act" relative to the stylized Shakespearean performers and the melodramatic Tragedians.

The question of the purpose of playing is sparked by the interplay of styles enacted in the crucial dumb show rehearsal at the center of act 2. Rosencrantz wants "a good story, with a beginning, middle and end," while Guildenstern prefers "art to mirror life" (81). Art mirrors art in the following dumb show narrated by the Player, culminating in the deaths of two actors dressed to look like Rosencrantz and Guildenstern. In this ingenious extension of the dumb show from *Hamlet*, Stoppard's characters simultaneously demonstrate and comment upon the theater's potential to place the spectators at the boundary, nudging them out of their customary viewing of their own actions. The Tragedians' gesture and commentary repeat and reinforce the question as the Player prepares to "show" how well his troupe can die. A consummate professional, the Player explains his role as extracting a

> significance from melodrama . . . which it does not in fact contain; but occasionally, . . . there escapes a thin beam of light that, seen at the right angle, can crack the shell of mortality (83)

A relative amateur, Guildenstern discounts the efficacy of theatrical convention altogether, implying that its very conventionality prevents it from imitating authentically "real" death, which eludes mimesis:

> You scream and choke and sink to your knees, but it doesn't bring death home to anyone—it doesn't catch them unawares and start the whisper in their skulls that says—"One day you are going to die." . . .
>
> . . . you can't act death. The *fact* of it is nothing to do with seeing it happen. . . . It's just a man failing to reappear, that's all—now you see him, now you don't. (83, 84)

Telling the story of his condemned actor, the Player informs him that "real" life is completely unconvincing on stage. Stoppard's own procedures suggest that neither view alone is correct, but that together they describe how art can work at its most powerful. Art must both copy and distort its models if it is to have any effect at all. The scene demonstrates the parodic method itself: both the familiar and a departure from the familiar are required to penetrate the spectators' habitual modes of perception. And in case we did not catch the point, the following scene opens on an empty stage "*with two cloaked figures sprawled on the ground in the approximate positions last held by the dead SPIES. As the light grows, they are seen to be* ROS *and* GUIL" (85). Fictional layers overlap, separate, and intersect again as the exiles from Shakespeare's play imitate the actors imitating them in Stoppard's play.

By the close of the second act, Rosencrantz and Guildenstern know the story of the two spies as performed by the Tragedians, but refuse to repeat Claudius's error of conflating the actual and the fictional. In their case, of course, there is no "actuality" to be confused with "fictionality," but they do not admit to this. Their stubborn resistance to their Shakespearean role is both ludicrous and admirable. In rejecting the Player's "cheap tricks," they are also rejecting the unquestioned authority of Shakespeare's tragedy as it has been culturally deployed—to serve the great at the expense of the weak. But in refusing to see that they, too, have parts in some kind of play, in insisting that they are spectators of rather than agents in the action, Rosencrantz and Guildenstern default to the role prescribed for them by tradition.

Stoppard gives them one moment of choice in the play when they are empowered, as it were, not only to resist but to change Shakespeare's script. But at this moment they choose to reproduce it. Having read the letter addressed to the English king calling for Hamlet's instant death, they debate whether, out of compassion or human decency, they should show it to him. If left alone, the intuitive Rosencrantz probably would show it to Hamlet: "He's done nothing to us" (111). But the cerebral Guildenstern still insists that they are merely spectators of the action, and can avoid entanglement by remaining so. In his rehearsal of platitudes intended to justify their inaction, he concludes:

> We are little men, we don't know the ins and outs of the matter, there are wheels within wheels, etcetera—it would be presumptuous of us to interfere with the designs of fate or even of kings. (110)

In fearing involvement, in taking the perspective of the Stoppardian artist "both inside and outside" society, Guildenstern unwittingly reproduces the moral standard of the *Hamlet* text that will be used to write them out of existence. Embracing their Shakespearean role as "little men," Guildenstern collapses his resistance to their Elizabethan predecessors, defaulting to their prescribed roles. In showing the couple repeating Shakespeare's rationale for their deaths, Stoppard is neither vindicating the moral authority of the *Hamlet* text nor declaiming the "absurdity" of human life.[5] The point is finally a moral one to be pondered by the offstage spectators: in refusing to become involved at this particular moment in the action, and in justifying their hesitation by claiming to be powerless, Guildenstern implicitly grants hegemony to Shakespeare's play and consents to its power over them. While he does not recognize the implications of his choice to remain an observer, Guildenstern nevertheless signals a lowering of his resistance that eventually proves fatal.

Stoppard's attitude toward Rosencrantz and Guildenstern's demise is complexly presented: on the one hand, he implies that they failed a test of courage, but on the other hand, he justifies their failure, for they could *never be sure* whether their actions were part of someone else's plan. Their manner of dying can be read as a final, if minor, vindication of their resistance to traditional playing. Surrounded on all sides by the Tragedians' professional performing of death, Rosencrantz and Guildenstern's disappearance – "now you see [them], now you don't" (84) – refuses mimesis in a sudden and final gesture of defiance that could, "seen at the right angle . . . crack the shell of mortality" (83). Even at the moment of their disappearance, Rosencrantz and Guildenstern are showing us a *Hamlet* and a *Godot* we have not seen before. And when, at the play's conclusion, we hear the announcement of their deaths, we hear it as we have never heard it before.

The Paradox of Parody: *The Real Inspector Hound*

As he told *Theatre Quarterly* in 1974, Stoppard began a "goon-show version" of *Hound* in Bristol after completing *The Gamblers* in 1960. Although he resists the notion that it is a play "about theatre critics," it would seem that his reviewing experiences figured importantly in his decision to parody the thriller genre. His signed *Bristol Evening World* reviews of plays and films included a number of thrillers, and a later 1962 *Scene* review of an Agatha Christie trilogy, *Rule of Three,* describes an unprecedented boom in the whodunit, with four plays by Christie alone in the West End ("Who Killed Peter Saunders," 1962, 30). Keenly aware both of the popularity and of the predictability of the genre, reviewer Stoppard wrote his *Scene* essay as a farcical dialogue between a "suave" theater critic, "Slurp," and a detective, "Rafferty." Slurp, author of "Whodunits Cluttering Up Social Theatre" and "Complacent Escapism an Insult to My Intelligence," reclines on his chaise longue, reading aloud his review of *Rule of Three,* while Rafferty waits to announce the death of its producer, Mr. Peter Saunders, slain by the quarto hidebound edition of *Agatha Christie: Works.* Once accused of murder, Slurp warns Rafferty, "You'll never take me alive," and abruptly dies after eating the words of his review. Too slapdash and unfunny to serve as a sketch for *Hound,* the review nevertheless predicts the tone and treatment of Stoppard's thriller. He would justify his attempt at yet another mystery by first flaunting and then displacing the genre's clichés.

Completed in 1968, *Hound* parodies a popular genre rather than a single classical text. Commentators have found traces of a number of country-house thrillers in *Hound,* particularly those by Agatha Christie, although other sources have been suggested, among them Ludwig Tieck's *Puss-in-Boots* (Davison 1982, 101–3) and even Pirandello's trilogy of theater plays (Whitaker 1983, 70), mockingly cited by the critics themselves. While all sense the Christie behind *Hound,* none agree on exactly which Christie is being parodied. The explanation seems to lie in the fact that the mockery is general, not particular. Thus, the pleasure of this parody initially lies not in recognizing the differences between a particular Christie and Stoppard's copy but in recognizing in the copy the distorted echoes of multiple source plays united by their use of stock features.

Stoppard's playing on Christie conventions both announces the origins of his play and suggests that it will, as a function of its awareness of its own making, attempt to improve upon those origins. But Stoppard's "improvement," while unusually clever, finally proves to be as thoroughly conventional an example of the genre as any to be found, illustrating what Linda Hutcheon has called the "central paradox of parody: its transgression is always authorized. In imitating, even with critical difference, parody reinforces" (1985, 26). Not content with merely ridiculing a tired genre, Stoppard conspicuously displays the formulaic nature of *Hound* in the first two "acts" of the inner play, then appears to break the formula and rewrite the rules for its third act from which an unexpected, but quite conventional, mystery emerges.

The thriller begins with the housekeeper, Mrs. Drudge, telescoping the narrative details of a plot that declares and ridicules its source simultaneously:

> Mrs. Drudge (*into phone*): Hello, the drawing-room of Lady Muldoon's country residence one morning in early spring?. . . . this is all very mysterious and I'm sure it's leading up to something, I hope nothing is amiss for we, that is Lady Muldoon and her houseguests, are here cut off from the world, including Magnus, the wheelchair-ridden half-brother of her ladyship's husband Lord Albert Muldoon who ten years ago went out for a walk on the cliffs and was never seen again. (15–16)

In *R&GAD,* Stoppard had already found a dramatic structure suited to the doubleness of parody. The play-within-the-play through which we view

Shakespeare from a Beckettian vantage point gave his characters a conventional device for stepping into and out of Shakespeare's text, which in turn helped to define their difference from their source characters. He returned to this device in *Hound,* as he has returned to it in most of his subsequent full-length works to date, opening the action with a pair of theater critics, Moon and Birdboot, already seated in the auditorium waiting for "the play" to begin.

The critics' names derive from the same period during which the thriller preoccupied Stoppard: his early days as a journalist. Originally the name of a character in a Paul Newman western, *Left-Handed Gun,* "Moon" took on a variety of associations in Stoppard's early writing having to do with romance and the individual's struggle for dignity in a mechanized world. The Moon type often represents the cerebral half of Stoppard's persona while the Boot type represents the sensual half. "Boot," a name stolen from the hero of Evelyn Waugh's novel *Scoop* about a bumbling anachronistic reporter, actually served as a pseudonym for Stoppard while he was simultaneously interviewing playwrights and reviewing their plays for *Scene.* But lest the distinction between "Moon" and "Boot" appear too rigid, Stoppard once told an interviewer that, although he is a Moon himself, he used "Boot" as a pseudonym because Waugh's Boot is really a Moon too (quoted in Tynan 1980, 67).

We wait with Moon and Birdboot for the action to begin, but the onstage corpse would suggest that it began some time ago and we are encountering it in medias res. "Has it started yet?" asks Birdboot. And Moon quips, "It's a pause" (9–10). Oblivious to Moon's witty reference to the Pinter pause, Birdboot rejoins, "You can't start with a *pause!*" (10). There are, after all, rules to be followed in the theater, and Birdboot unquestioningly accepts them all until a fatal moment when he breaks the most important (and obvious) one dictating the separation of the actual and the fictional. We gradually learn each critic's private obsession—Moon's jealousy of the first-string critic, Higgs, and Birdboot's lust for the actress playing Felicity—through which Stoppard will motivate their involvement in the thriller's plot.

Throughout its first act, the critics' attention jumps from the mystery's onstage action to their private fantasies and back again, so that the spectators find themselves following at least two tracks simultaneously—the frame play, which is itself divided between the critics' private and public utterances—and the inner play with its overacted mockery of thriller conventions. This juggling of separate, intersecting fictions, particularly of parallel but unconnected dialogue, provides much of the comedy in *Hound*'s opening scenes and prepares us, unwittingly, for the subsequent merging of frame and inner play.

At the close of its first act, the thriller's shape is beginning to emerge but is not yet completed. None of the actors has acknowledged the corpse on stage, conveniently hidden from view by the strategic placement of props. Not until Inspector Hound's act 2 entrance is the corpse discovered, and then no one recognizes it. When Simon enters and turns it over, he is "shot." The curtain rings down on Hound's question, "Who killed Simon Gascoyne? And why?" (41). At the end of act 2, then, we have a real thriller: two corpses and a nameless killer on the loose whom the characters are trying to identify.

Immediately following this scene, we overhear Moon's daydream of murdering the first-string critic, Higgs, and recognize that the inner and frame plays are beginning to resemble one another. Birdboot announces in his "public" voice that "It is at this point that the play, for me, comes alive" (42). Soon after, when Birdboot's wife, Myrtle, calls on the stage phone to ask who was the woman he was with last night, a woman we know to have been the actress playing Felicity, the play literally comes alive for Birdboot. The inner drama restarts with Birdboot still on stage. Felicity enters as before, only now she addresses Birdboot as she had earlier addressed Simon Gascoyne. We recognize the device from *R&GAD:* the critics are becoming entrapped in a text. But in the case of *Hound,* the spectators do not know where the text is taking them. Thus, our role in *Hound,* unlike in *R&GAD,* becomes identical to that of Moon, as we attempt to decipher clues to explain the corpses before us.

Moon attempts to lure his colleague off the stage, but the promise of meeting Cynthia (an actress who encourages Birdboot's confusion by kissing the actor playing Simon with her mouth open) traps him into staying. At this moment, the dialogue and gesture of the inner and frame plays begin to cross:

> *Birdboot*: No, Cynthia—now that I have found you—
> *Cynthia*: You're ruthless—so strong—so cruel—
> *Moon*: Have you taken leave of your tiny mind?
> *Cynthia*: Stop—can't you see you're making a fool of yourself!
> *Moon*: She's right.
> *Birdboot (to Moon)*: You keep out of this.

> (47)

Act 3 repeats the language and gesture of act 1 with a significant difference: Birdboot and Moon take the places of the actors playing Simon and Hound, compounding the parodied text of the Christie original with the critics' private dramas of sex and ambition. Now the humor lies not in detecting the difference between the Christie thriller and Stoppard's distorted imitation but in recognizing the coincidental (and farcically improbable) similarity between a private fantasy and a public play. In shifting the spectators' attention from detecting difference to expecting similarity, Stoppard invites our involvement in the action as we follow Moon's ill-fated attempt to interpret his way out of danger.

During this act, at least three kinds of address intermingle: Moon and Birdboot address one another as "real" people, with Moon exhorting Birdboot to return to his seat; the actors address one another as actors; and Birdboot addresses the actors as if he were addressing "real" people. In this way, Stoppard is conditioning the spectator to accept as credible (albeit implausible) the intersection of the two distinct fictions. The dramatic turn comes when Birdboot discovers the corpse to be Higgs, the first-string critic of Moon's newspaper. At that moment a shot rings out and Birdboot falls dead. Moon runs onto the stage to Birdboot's body. Almost immediately, sensing himself trapped, he attempts to return to his seat. But the actors who had earlier played the roles of Simon and Hound have taken his place. Their motive for doing so, as Richard Corballis has pointed out (1984, 54), is never established, but one infers from their harsh criticism of the play that they are seeking revenge against the entire tribe of critics that lives by preying upon the work of artists.

Distraught and agitated, Moon then takes on the role of Inspector Hound, determined to solve Birdboot's murder. He accuses Magnus, whom we eventually learn to be third-string critic Puckeridge in disguise, but cannot attribute a motive for the crime that does not implicate himself more fully than Magnus. After all, in "real" life, Moon dreamed of Higgs's death as an opening to his promotion to first-string critic. Guiltily confusing his private fantasies with the "actual" murder, Moon retreats from accusing Magnus, and, to divert suspicion from himself, makes the fatal error of blaming Birdboot, whom he calls by his fictional name, "Simon," for Higgs's murder.

In drawing on the thriller's plot to explain the double murder of Higgs and Birdboot, Moon seeks to divert attention from his motive as second-string critic. In doing so, he betrays not only Birdboot but also himself, choosing to remain a spectator when he is called upon to act. Moon belongs to the tribe of Stoppardian artists, both "inside and outside society," paralyzed by doubt and uncertainty when called upon to act and therefore victimized by those more ruthless than himself. Just as Guildenstern defaulted at a crucial moment to his role in *Hamlet*, dropping his resistance to its tyranny, so Moon surrenders to the Christie play whose author then writes him out of the script. Third-string critic Puckeridge, his equal or better in ambition, is unhampered by Moon's paralyzing conscience.

At the play's conclusion, when Moon realizes that his private fantasy of murdering Higgs has been acted out by Puckeridge, he attempts to run off-

stage, providing his rival with an excuse to shoot him. Within the broad lati-
tude granted by farce, art appears to imitate life as Puckeridge directs and in-
terprets the Christie play to justify his murderous ambition and to satisfy his
lust for the leading lady. Puckeridge's success at posing as the "real" inspector
hound—his greater skill at improvisation—earns him the girl and the place of
first-string critic.

Involving the spectator in Moon's frantic struggle to interpret two
corpses, Stoppard diverts us from the murderer's obvious, although back-
grounded, motive. Ambushed by the sudden appearance of Puckeridge, the
spectator grants him, and implied playwright Stoppard, credit for an ingenious
resolution. The dying Moon says it all, "Puckeridge! . . . You cunning bastard" (59). The conclusion of *Hound* vindicates the thriller, circling back to
the fiction it appeared to have abandoned when the critics entered the inner
play. Surprising us with the familiar, the obvious, the trite, *Hound* celebrates
its careful craftsmanship in the figure of cunning Puckeridge whose ingenuity
might well be the playwright's joke on his own creative temperament: "The
effect of elegant economy is something we all respond to. . . . . I really hate
gratuitousness" (Hayman 1979, 145). Perhaps because of its greater simplic-
ity, *Hound* reveals to us more clearly than *R&GAD* Stoppard's method for
writing well-crafted plays: begin with a formula, expose it, appear to abandon
it, then circle back and pick it up again suddenly, surprising the spectator with
a denouement both familiar and unexpected.

After Magritte: "This Is Not a Magritte Painting"

"*After Magritte* and *The Real Inspector Hound* are short plays . . . attempt-
[ing] to bring off a sort of comic coup in pure mechanistic terms," Stoppard
told *Theatre Quarterly* in 1974 (8). Both plays were conceived as what he calls
"nuts 'n' bolts" comedies, a term reserved for his shorter works, whose interest
lies as fully in their ingenious plotting as it does in any ideas they may juggle
on stage. Written for Ed Berman's Inter-Action theater troupe, *After Magritte*
was first performed at the Ambiance Lunch-House Theatre Club on 9 April
1970. The American-born Berman, a Harvard graduate who went to Oxford
as a Rhodes scholar in the early 1960s, stayed on to found, among other things,
Inter-Action, a charitable trust designed to encourage community involvement
in the arts (Londre 1981, 122). Berman's devotion to the pun, along with his
fanatically energetic involvement in community theater, struck a responsive
chord in Stoppard who has, to date, written four additional plays for him,
Dogg's Our Pet, The 15 Minute Hamlet, The (15 Minute) Dogg's Troupe Ham-

let (a conflation of the two previous plays), and *New-Found-Land,* a short occasional piece embedded somewhat awkwardly in the middle of *Dirty Linen.*

Like *The Real Inspector Hound, After Magritte* imitates a popular genre
(the thriller again) and the works of an avant-garde artist (René Magritte)
rather than a specific model. Magritte's works, many of them parodies, had
recently been exhibited in a retrospective at the Tate Gallery in 1969 where
Stoppard may well have been a visitor. The playwright's attraction to Magritte
appears to have centered on what he called "Magritte labelling," exemplified
by one of the Belgian's paintings "in which there's a picture of a shoe, and underneath it's labelled 'A HORSE' " (Hayman 1979, 3–4). In what is undoubt-
edly his imperfect recollection of the Magritte exhibit, Stoppard may be referring either to Magritte's parodic painting of a pipe labeled "This is not a
pipe"—itself a parody of the medieval and Renaissance tradition of emblem
painting and a specific joke on Le Corbusier's use of the pipe to illustrate plain
functional design (Hutcheon 1985, 2)—or to his series of illustrations, "Words
and Images," in *La Révolution Surréaliste* (1929), in which a series of objects
are labeled in such a way as to appear to illustrate a principle, written above
the drawing. Whichever of these may have provided his model, Stoppard
reproduces Magritte labeling by mismatching banal dialogue with a series of
mock-ominous gestures and bizarre tableaux.

While the original of Stoppard's copy consists of Magritte's oeuvre
rather than a particular painting, virtually all commentators have noted that
Magritte's *L'Assassin Menace* comes close to serving as a particular model for
the play's opening tableau. The bowler hat, the prone (perhaps dead) figure,
the framed torso, the draped chair, the wind-up gramophone with horn—
present a living canvas with its menace in quotation marks. In coming "after"
the Magritte of the Surrealist heyday, Stoppard both reproduces his iconography and domesticates its menace. Crowded with objects too familiar to
threaten, the mise-en-scène includes cliché signs of the mystery thriller (keystone cops cutout) and of surrealist "threat" (ironing board in lieu of surgical
table topped by motionless body in turn topped by Magrittean bowler hat) arranged in illogical relation to one another. The dominant object is the sheeted
corpse and the window behind it framing a helmeted police constable gazing,
like the spectator, upon the scene. Other objects are harmless but arranged in
bizarre configurations: a hemispherical ceiling light and a basket of fruit
balanced on a counterweight system; a stack of furniture piled against the
street door; the wooden chair draped with men's evening clothes; a coiffured,
barefoot Thelma Harris, dressed in a full-length dance gown, gazing on hands
and knees at the floor below her, sniffing at irregular intervals; and, finally,

Reginald standing on the wooden chair bare-torsoed, wearing thigh-high green rubber boots and black dress trousers. Hands at his side, he is blowing slowly into the recess of the shade. Keeping one eye on Constable Holmes, we ask not only what does all of this mean but also what does Holmes think it might mean?

While the visual medium presents us with a series of familiar signs in ambiguous relation to one another, the verbal medium labels the scene with bland domestic platitudes. In reference to Reginald's blowing into the lamp-shade, Thelma opens the dialogue with a tactful reminder,

> *Thelma*: It's electric, dear.
> *Harris*: (*mildly*) I didn't think it was a flaming torch.
> *Thelma*: There's no need to use language. That's what I always say.
>
> (69)

The discrepancy between image and word on the one hand, and between words themselves on the other, becomes a central preoccupation of the narrative in the following scenes as the members of the Harris household, including Reginald's mother, a devotee of the tuba in whose honor they had all attended a Magritte exhibit earlier that day, join with Detective Inspector Foot and Police Constable Holmes to solve what Foot has labeled "the Crippled Minstrel Caper," a series of events observed by each of them and by each of them interpreted differently. The narrative sequence both extends the joke on labeling already established in the opening scene (the "Crippled Minstrel" proves to be Foot himself) and implicates the interpretive process in Stoppard's mockery.

The earliest attempt at a narrative reconstruction of the caper begins with Thelma's musing on the young, one-legged footballer in a West Bromwich Albion uniform, masked in shaving foam, holding a football under one arm and swinging an ivory cane with the other, seen earlier in the day after their visit to the exhibit. Husband Reginald saw an old, blind, one-legged, white-bearded man dressed in pyjamas hopping along with a tortoise under his arm and brandishing a white stick. Mother's description of the apparition includes a man wearing dark glasses and a surgical mask playing hopscotch on the corner in a felon's uniform, carrying a handbag under one arm and waving a cricket bat with the other. Inspector Foot bases his version, the most implausible of them all, upon an eyewitness account of the mystery figure provided by an elderly fan of minstrel shows. Accordingly, Foot is searching for the "talented though handicapped doyen of the Victoria Palace Happy Minstrel Troupe" in blackface carrying a broken crutch in one hand and a crocodile boot in the other

stuffed with money stolen from the box office. When Foot learns that no rob-
bery has occurred, he is forced to reconsider the grounds on which he might
arrest the members of the Harris household whom he has inferred, following
Holmes's eyewitness account of the opening tableau, to have operated upon the
one-legged would-be robber. "The man's quite mad," Mother concludes as she
settles down to practice on the tuba.

While these wildly divergent interpretations are emerging through the
dialogue, the mise-en-scène is undergoing a series of transformations in counterpoint to the narrative. The first contrapuntal sequence occurs in the opening
scene and concludes with the arrival of Holmes and Foot moments after the
characters have reconstructed the bizarre arrangement of props to resemble a
conventional living room. From his vantage at the front window, Holmes
"saw" what the spectators saw, but did not hear what we heard. What we have
learned to "see" as an ordinary domestic situation with an odd decor, Foot infers from Holmes's account to be a criminal melodrama: "Tarted up harpies
staggering about drunk to the wide, naked men in rubber garments hanging
from the lampshade. . . . offering cut-price amputations to immigrants" (90).

The second contrapuntal sequence assembles gradually during the narration of the "Crippled Minstrel Caper." While Foot interrogates the Harrises,
Reginald and Thelma continue to prepare for their dancing engagement;
Mother settles down to the tuba; and Foot himself comes down with a migraine
after discovering his error of deduction. The tableau begins to reconstruct itself again, this time in the apparent image of a surrealist canvas, so that after
a brief blackout, the final scene reveals: Mother standing one-legged on a chair
placed on the table, playing the tuba with a woolen sock on one hand; the light-
shade slowly descending while the basket of fruit ascends; Foot eating a banana in sunglasses with one bare foot; Harris gowned, blindfolded with a cush-
ion over his head, slowly counting with his arms outstretched; Thelma in
underwear inspecting the floor on her hands and knees while sniffing; and
Holmes, paralyzed with shock. Oblivious to the end, Foot turns on Holmes,
"Well, Constable, I think you owe us all an explanation" (105). What might
have been Holmes's exegesis is eclipsed by the final descent of the lampshade.
The scene appears to have the spontaneous quality of an unplanned surrealist
event, while the dialogue has provided us with a logical explanation for every
gesture on stage. Unlike a Magritte painting, therefore, everything we see in
the scene can be explained. We laugh at the incongruity of the pseudo-
Magrittean tableau not only because it looks odd but also because its odd appearance belies its mundane reality.

In what sense, then, does Stoppard's play take after Magritte? Keir Elam argues that the implicit moral judgement by which Foot admits to the folly of his fictional caper—"Bear in mind that my error was merely one of interpretation . . . " (102)—distinguishes Stoppard's play from Magritte's insoluble and amoral ambiguities. The play's characters prove finally to be the victims of "their own logical absolutism" (Elam 1984, 476). Or, to put a slightly different slant on their weakness, they prove to be entrapped by their interpretive logic, by a single view of a situation that fails to account for themselves as the seers. And while such foolishness may seem to differentiate Stoppard's conventional farce from Magritte's mysteries, it can also be viewed as a meeting ground between the two artists. For is not the habitual perception and the habitual response Magritte's target, also?

In his essay on Magritte, Michel Foucault anatomizes Magrittean labeling first as the intertwining and then the separating of object and legend in the manner of the calligram, the poem whose words form a picture of its topic, thereby aspiring to eradicate the opposition between showing and naming, looking and reading. The painting of a pipe identified by the label, "This is not a pipe," is doubly paradoxical, writes Foucault, as "It sets out to name something that evidently does not need to be named. . . . And at the moment when he should reveal the name, Magritte . . . (denies) that the object is what it is" (1982, 23–24). The sense of the paradox lies in its fidelity to the calligram which "never speaks and represents at the same moment. The very thing that is both seen and read is hushed in the vision, hidden in the reading" (25). Stoppard's characters have all seen the same series of events—a white-faced man hopping down the street holding several objects—but they have each used different words to label what they have seen. The spectators undergo a similar experience, but only during the play's opening moments, when they are first confronted with the silent mise-en-scène. Thus, in spite of observing the conventions of what Elam calls "bourgeois farce," Stoppard's parody appropriates Magritte to the Magrittean end of poking fun at the logic of linguistic and visual representations of experience. Magritte's labeling of his painting, "This is not a pipe," might be applied to Stoppard's parody: "This is not a Magritte painting," but it occasionally looks like one.

The significant difference between Stoppard's farce and Magritte's oeuvre would seem to lie in each artist's use of irony. With the exception of the first moments of the opening scene, Stoppard privileges his spectators with full knowledge of the context for his Magrittean mise-en-scène, while Magritte's canvases surprise us with juxtapositions deliberately lacking an orienting frame of reference. While the experience of the Stoppardian spectator will, therefore, be less disorienting than that of Magritte's viewer, the spirit of Stoppard's parody, in its mockery of single vision and hyperrationality, nevertheless pays homage to the Belgian's evocation of the aleatory and the mysterious, an evocation that proceeds by logical appeals to causality, to size and scale, and to trompe l'oeil effects. Not surprisingly, the playwright has claimed an affinity with the painter, telling a Dutch interviewer that Magritte " . . . had a sense of humour which appealed to me . . . but I also like the way he did things very carefully and perfectly" (Interview with Joost Kuurman 1980, 55–56). Magritte, that is, displays a temperament much like Stoppard's own. Stoppard reinforces the Magrittean ethic of subverted logic not only by dint of imitation but also by his rhetorical strategy. Bracketing the spectators' responses with an awareness of themselves as interpreting witnesses, Stoppard shows how we take refuge from doubt and uncertainty in fictional explanations of what we see and hear. The figure of Holmes dominating the opening mise-en-scène presents the audience with a Keystone cops cliché image of itself looking on at a pseudo-Surrealist tableau. We have seen all of this before, but never in quite this combination! Finally, it is not Magrittean menace but Magrittean humor and precision that finds a place in Stoppard's play.

Dirty Linen: A "Knickers Farce"; and *New-Found-Land:* An American Elegy

Commissioned by Stoppard's American friend Ed Berman in 1976 to celebrate simultaneously Berman's British naturalization and the bicentennial of the American Revolution, *Dirty Linen* "went off in a different direction" (quoted in Rusinko 1986, 74), providing an example of one of Stoppard's nearly "pure" farces that had little to do with things American. So Stoppard restarted his Berman play—eventually titled *New-Found-Land*—and then boldly inserted it midway through *Dirty Linen,* to which it bears an indirect but witty relation. The result is a British farce interrupted by a parodic hymn to America, structured playfully upon Berman's bicultural alliances. In recognition of its thematic and generic idiosyncrasies, I will disregard chronology in favor of genre as an organizing principle, and discuss both plays here with other of Stoppard's shorter pieces.

Of course *Dirty Linen,* too, has an argument to make, centering on the conflict between the public's right to know how well its elected officials are performing their jobs and the officials' right to protect the privacy of their personal lives. But Stoppard never fully developed this central question in *Linen,* content to produce it as one of his "nuts 'n' bolts" comedies, a light joking entertainment. And as such, it is admirably economical, plausible if not actually believable, and generally humorous, in spite of turning on a number of stale sexist jokes. The puerile sexuality of the M.P.'s mitigates the triteness of the sex play and sets up Maddie as a free spirit who can enjoy openly what others feel must be hidden.

Dirty Linen's three movements are driven by the intersecting of dialectic forces endemic to farce. As usual in Stoppard, following the tradition of Wilde, the violence associated with the genre has been omitted from the action, and the sex is merely implied. Maddie's promiscuity, an innocent sexuality that has given her entrée to privileged governmental information, is not the lusty sort of Molière's or Feydeau's farces, but it is the cornerstone of Stoppard's farce plot. The surface dialectic in this piece lies in Maddie's simultaneous innocence and outrageousness. Her liaisons, too numerous to count, have given her an influence she never sought. Her promiscuity is driven, ostensibly, by her sheer enjoyment of sex and the expensive gifts that come with it, but the other facet of her spontaneity shows itself in her disdain for cant and hypocrisy. This disdain expresses the deeper dialectic at work in the play contrasting the mask of propriety and dignity worn by members of the parliamentary Committee on Moral Standards in Public Life and the revealing glimpses of childishness beneath that mask shattered by Maddie's innocence.

Each of the three movements in this piece concludes with the surprise triumph of Maddie's values. Movement one, beginning with her entrance and closing with the belated arrival of French, pits the Select Committee's efforts at fabricating a cover-up of their separate affairs with the typist against Maddie's candor, deftly enacted by the gradual, accidental shedding of her skirt and slip as the action progresses. Early on in the scene, each of the four men present attempts secretly to advise Maddie to deny having met with him at a posh French restaurant, whose several names are similar enough to justify her hopeless confusion.

> *McTeazle*: I mean *forget* Charing Cross.
> *Maddie*: Forget Charing Cross—
> *McTeazle*: Plucky girl—
> *Maddie*: Plucky girl—Charing Cross—Olden cocks.
> *McTeazle*: But not with me.
> *Maddie*: Not with Jock at the Old Cock—
>
> (26)

We learn in the course of the scene that the report has already been falsified to cover up their affairs and to satisfy the Prime Minister who "insists . . . he wants a thorough job which he can present to the House the day before the Queen's Silver Jubilee, along with trade figures" (29). While she says very little during the proceedings, it soon becomes apparent that Maddie has nothing but contempt for the committee. The harder they work to contrive a semblance of respectability, the closer she comes to revealing its foundations, losing first her skirt and then her slip, both accidentally pulled off by committee members trying to cover her up. By the end of the opening movement, Maddie is revealing to the committee the actual nature of the so-called investigative press as the product of postadolescent male competition. As such, her speech anticipates Ruth's in *Night and Day* in which the latter bitterly denounces journalists' motives: "You're all doing it to impress each other and be top dog" (108). Maddie's critique is distanced by the mask of the naif:

> They're not writing for the people, they're writing it for the writers writing it on the other papers. "Look what I've got that you haven't got." (42)

Movement two begins with the sudden entrance of French, the ironically named prude, who throws the M.P.'s' delicately balanced plot into abrupt confusion by demanding that the report be produced along conventional lines. As yet unacquainted with the typist's charms, French contributes to Maddie's exposing of the report's falsity, but for the opposite reason. Taking appearances with deadly seriousness, always a dangerous failing in farce, French eventually discovers Maddie's identity as "the mystery woman." But just as he does so, he inadvertently pulls off her blouse, leaving them all — himself excepted — literally and figuratively stripped to their knickers. The redhead defiantly lists all of her conquests as the Chair hastily adjourns the meeting.

As Maddie and French exit, another door opens and two men, characters "in another play" enter. *New-Found-Land* takes up the theme of the Berman series for which *Dirty Linen* was originally commissioned — "The American Connection." Opening on a very young and very old Home Office official meeting to discuss a bearded American's (Berman's) application for naturalization, the interlude begins with the senior official launching into a narrative recollection of having won a £5 note from Lloyd George while an invalid young lieutenant. Apparently unconnected to the preceding action, his story includes a brief episode involving a sexual friendship between his mother and the Prime Minister (the erotic nature of which has escaped him entirely), thus extending the sex-politics link exposed in *Dirty Linen*. His story concludes with a description of Field Marshall Haig whose military rescue by the Americans underscores "The American Connection" and returns the junior official to the subject of the unnamed American's application for naturalization.

But the young man also prefers storytelling to paper pushing, and so, in a second apparently unmotivated outburst, he launches an enthusiastic monologue (or travelogue) of American geography and culture, tracing an imaginary path from New York harbor, through the eastern states, southward, and then westward to the Pacific Ocean. His narrative pastiche of Hollywood regional clichés parodies—in the mocking sense—the young man's romantic infatuation with the new land:

> Blue skies and grass are as one on the azure horizon of Kentucky. Soon thoroughbred stallions race the train on either side. Young girls in gingham dresses wave from whitewood fences . . . hillbilly groups sullenly [look] up from their liquor jugs and washboards. (62)

His enthusiasm for America is apparently no more reliable than is his senior colleague's romanticizing of Britain's past.

Typically for Stoppard, the strongest thematic and structural link binding the farce frame to the parodic interlude lies in another text—the Donne poem that Richard Corballis first identified (1984, 102–4) as the source for Stoppard's title, *New-Found-Land*. Donne's "Elegie XIX. To his Mistris going to Bed," itself a parody of Ovid's *Amores* I.v., echoes erotically while the young official describes the American landscape, and while, simultaneously, we are to imagine Maddie seducing French offstage. The most relevant lines, taken from the poem's second stanza, link erotic with geographical exploration, "License my roaving hands, and let them go, / Behind, before, above, between, below; / O my America! my new-found-land!" (25–27). Thus tied to America, to the erotic, and to innocence ("cast all, yea, this white lynnen hence; / There is no pennance due to innocence" [44–45] through the barely suggested text of Donne's poem, Maddie binds the inner to the outer play.

Following the interlude during which French has been initiated to the typist's charms, he proposes scrapping the Chairman's Report, replacing it with a single paragraph dictated by Miss Gotobed. In the third and final movement of the play, French crowns her sexual and political triumph with his parting exclamation, "Toujours l'amour," uttered while wiping his brow with a pair of lace panties. Maddie has leveled them all, substituting plain speaking for parliamentary nonsense in the process. But can the farce survive her finger-wagging declamation? Maddie's answer to a nosey press is to tell them to mind their own business:

The press. The more you accuse them of malice and inaccuracy, the more you're admitting that they've got a right to poke their noses into your private life. . . . All you need is one paragraph saying that M.P.s have got just as much right to enjoy themselves in their own way as anyone else, and Fleet Street can take a running jump. (41)

When Maddie uses speech, the farce turns toward satire, with her pose of defiant innocence acting as an ironical example for the politicians. Stoppard appoints Maddie spokesperson for his quarrel with the press for the logical reason that only the Mystery Woman herself is unintimidated by its power. She cannot be threatened by exposure, when exposure serves as her raison d'être. She has, for this reason, a contradictory nature and role, both innocent and aggressive, anarchic and commonsensical. With a strong opinion and point of view disguised beneath her cliché pinup pose, she shows a kinship with the female characters of Shaw and Wilde who use their sexuality as weapons against the men who regard them as the weaker sex.

Probably the closest to "pure" farce of his comedies to date, *Dirty Linen* nevertheless eludes classification by treating the traditional subjects of farce — sex and power — in the critical spirit of satire, and by substituting for pratfalls a multilingual dialogue that at moments threatens to steal the show. Stoppard told the BBC's Alastair Lack in 1976, "I intended to write an entire play in foreign phrases, all of which would be comprehensible to an English audience." The opening scene of *Dirty Linen* consists entirely of a pastiche of French and Latin clichés spoken between two stereotypical M.P.s, McTeazle and Cocklebury-Smythe, shortly before the entrance of a stereotypical dumb blonde and the initiation of a bogus committee meeting. The clichés pile up without break: "Après vous," "J'y suis, j'y reste," "Quel dommage," "Le mot juste," "C'est la vie. Che sera sera," etc., setting the screwball tone for the farce and simultaneously ridiculing the speakers as men of cliché culture. Stoppard resurrects the language gag at the conclusion of the last act, as the reformed French, no longer the officious upholder of decency, wipes his brow with Maddie's knickers and salutes her charms, "Toujours l'amour." As Big Ben chimes the quarter hour, Maddie brings down the curtain in Italian: "Finita La Commedia" (73).

Part 2: Gymnastics and Travesty

Stoppard took great time and care composing his second major stage play, recognizing that it would be compared to his earlier success and hoping to match or top that success by pointedly refusing to repeat its close parody of source texts. The successor to *Rosencrantz and Guildenstern Are Dead* was to take the form of a post-Shavian intellectual comedy, *Jumpers*, a title punning on philosophers' verbal juggling and on gymnasts' erratic philosophy. *Jumpers* does repeat source texts, but in a fragmentary and discontinuous fashion, preferring to put at its center problems and events recognizable in the extra-artistic world of contemporary philosophy and science. Stoppard thus opened the second major phase of his stage career by modeling the problematic interchange between art (philosophy) and life not upon previously represented texts but upon genre markers familiar from his earlier plays.

Jumpers: "A Comedy and a Philosophy"

In its attempt to engage spectators in a playful critique of contemporary ideas, *Jumpers* demanded a greater imaginative effort from Stoppard than had any of his previous works, including *R&GAD*. *Jumpers* questions the significance of modern British philosophy (logical positivism) and technology (the moon landing) not by parodying earlier representations of these events but by dramatizing them through two comic genres—George's post-Shavian play of ideas and Dotty's murder mystery. With a few minor exceptions, Stoppard's texts are his own, paraphrased from his reading and rewritten in a mix of idioms and styles of his own devising. As such, they reveal his thematic preoccupations more directly than do the parodied texts of *R&GAD*. In the place of the recycled *Hamlet* and *Godot* through which Rosencrantz and Guildenstern resist tradition, Stoppard's Moores resist the drift of contemporary culture by acting out the moves of the thriller and debate genres. These are finally abandoned at the play's conclusion when Stoppard resorts to the musical device of the Coda to signify the Moores' failure to restore the power of God and the moon as ordering fictions.

The germ of *Jumpers* lay in Stoppard's 1967 comedy of manners TV sketch, *Another Moon Called Earth* (discussed in chap. 2), in which Penelope, the beautiful and neurotic wife of Professor Bone, distraught over man's landing on the moon, receives visits from the dapper Albert Pearce after having pushed her nanny from an upper-story window. Most of the manners comedy types, the befuddled husband, the charming wayward wife, the witty and fashionable wooer, complete with their excesses and obsessions, were already in place when Stoppard returned to his sketch sometime around 1970. Stoppard kept the suggested love triangle—Archie is still a daily visitor—but made its ambiguity more teasingly apparent. Even the most intimate scenes between

Dotty Moore and Archie Jumper, while initially appearing to be sexual in nature, on second glance seem to be clinical, even mildly pornographic in their abstraction.

The neuroses assigned to each character in *Another Moon* have become, in *Jumpers*, firmly rooted in the play of ideas. Archie Jumper, cynical manipulator of language and appearance, has discovered (and suffers from) "Cognomen Syndrome," a disorder in which patients become obsessed with their surname. Accordingly, he calls his political party the "Radical-Liberal Jumpers," and requires that his followers tumble and jump through hoops to earn his favors. Dotty's nervous condition following the moon landing is taken more seriously in the later play, where it foreshadows an impending cultural breakdown. Among the first to recognize the moon landing as a major threat to traditional systems of morality, Dotty turns for solace to her academic husband. When he fails her, she begins to drift toward Archie, whose daily visits bolster her spirits. George's obsession in the later play is no longer the historian's logic of cause and effect but a determination to prove that God exists, from which will follow the existence of moral absolutes and the redemption of modern moral philosophy. George now pursues his obsession in the idiom of academic philosophy, a language Stoppard taught himself in the two years he spent rewriting the play.

In developing the structure of *Another Moon Called Earth*, Stoppard used elements from two primary genres. To begin with, he replaced Pinkerton's murder with the murder of McFee in the opening party scene. The whodunit formula, parodied in *Real Inspector Hound*, is thus introduced early and sustained by a new character, Inspector Bones. A second (also unsolved) murder at the play's close is witnessed but not prevented by George Moore. The two corpses go unexplained as the mysteries in what Alan Rodway has called a "comedy of incertitude" (in Bloom 1986, 10) are never solved. The second genre, the comic debate, probably adapted from Shaw but familiar to comedy since Aristophanes, amounts to a series of monologues in which George Moore attempts to prove the existence of God and of knowledge – or their opposites. But George succeeds in convincing no one, least of all himself. The debates end in stalemate.

Jumpers' comic energy can be felt not only when George and Dotty struggle to resist the diminishing of human value but also when their distinct styles of resistance collide. Act 1 opens with a direct demonstration of Dotty's problem. Attempting a comeback in her musical stage career during her party to celebrate the Rad-Lib's victory at the polls, she tries but fails to sing her way through moon lyrics. Having lost a sense of life's mystery following man's landing on the moon, Dotty now finds life drained of excitement and meaning. The Jumpers' unimpressive gymnastic display reminds her of the stale and unprofitable uses of the world: "Get me someone unbelievable!", at which she finds herself face to face with husband George, lecture notes in hand. Academic George has come to plead for the peace and quiet he needs to finish his lecture: "Man: Good, Bad, or Indifferent." George's talk is essential to his attempt to restore his and others' faith in life by reinventing God through philosophical argument. Dotty, suffering an equivalent loss of mystery, looks for restoration through the theater and music, but she can no longer sustain a single melody.

Dotty becomes implicated in the murder mystery in the following scene when she disappears at the moment of McFee's murder. Following her dismissal of Archie's all-too-believable gymnasts, she strolls behind a line of Jumpers when a shot rings out. Blown out of the human pyramid, "mad Jock McFee" becomes the play's first casualty and adds to Dotty's emotional problem the practical problem of a corpse, now draped in her arms.[6] With the dead McFee over her knees, Dotty watches television in her bedroom where TV shots of a moon landing by (British!) astronauts reveal another murder taking place, this one clearly motivated by self-interest and the need to survive. As the announcer narrates the video image, we learn that the damaged space capsule will permit the return of only one of the two astronauts on board. Captain Scott has knocked Oates to the ground and pulled up the ladder, leaving him to die alone in the lunar desert. Stoppard chose the names Scott and Oates to recall the countervailing example of South Pole explorer, Scott, who sacrificed his life to save the other members of his team. As we later learn, it is the possibility of altruism implied in this earlier example that decides McFee to abandon the Jumpers for the cloistered safety of a monastery. Surrounded by evidence of postlunar chaos, including a corpse, Dotty begins her cries for help.

The bedroom blacks out and George's study takes the stage. Every bit as theatrical as Dotty, but verbal where she is musical, George delivers his Colloquium address to an imaginary audience, first reading and then ad libbing his way through an argument for the existence of God. George has a bit of trouble keeping his argument on track, just as Dotty has had trouble completing a song. Fully absorbed in his thoughts, George seems to be thinking aloud, freely associating bits of argument, instructions to his secretary, and reminiscence, mixing the sublime and the ridiculous with absentminded indifference. His post-Shavian monologues mock his attempt to achieve truth through language deployed in a strictly logical fashion. Where Shaw held out great hope for "the discussion" as a dramatic tool for advancing the spectators' awareness of social issues (Meisel 1984, 292–93), Stoppard uses the idiom of the academic lecture to expose the futility of George's attempt to reason God back into existence. Shaw's mature discussion play is crowded with complementary incident and talk, while talk and action tend to collide in *Jumpers*, as in the apparently gratuitous gestures with which George punctuates his rehearsal — shooting a bow and arrow, drinking pencils from a tumbler, studying his mismatched socks.

George's theatrical style is to appear not to be theatrical, to be unaware of his performing self while delivering exquisitely comic speeches crammed full of puns, epithets, asides, declamations, and narrative summaries. George wants to believe that his struggle with language can redeem the time: "I had hoped to set British philosophy back forty years, which is roughly when it went off the rails, but unfortunately, I can't seem to find the words . . . " (36). His logocentric resistance to the Jumpers' relativism is stylistically antithetical to Dotty's gestural and musical resistance to the death of romance. But they are alike in resisting the Jumpers' mock-positivist reading of human life as nothing more than meaningless transformations of nucleic acids.

The friction between Dotty's sensational displays and George's verbal struggles gives this play the heightened energy of farce, the genre of stark contrasts. Eric Bentley's description of "the farce dialectic" as "a relation . . . of active conflict and development" (1967, 244) between two sharply opposing forces works to describe Stoppard's deliberate shifting between husband and wife, study and bedroom, as George and Dotty struggle against one another and against their shared sense of desolation. When Dotty's cries for help go unanswered, they become increasingly outrageous until George shouts down her "gratuitous acts of lupine delinquency" (18). The dialectic between George and Dotty emerges with brilliant clarity from the merest verbal suggestion:

> *George*: . . . But when we place the existence of God within the discipline of a philosophical inquiry, we find these two independent mysteries: the how and the why of the overwhelming question: ——
> *Dotty (off)*: *Is anybody there?*
>
> (17)

In his Prufrockian absence, George fails to be there for Dotty as God has failed George.

Act 1 closes with another dialectical clash between George's philosophical struggles and Dotty's show-biz displays. Attempting to answer the question, "What, in short, is so good about *good*?" George paraphrases his opponent's position:

> *George*: Professor McFee succeeds only in showing us that . . . the irreducible fact of goodness is not implicit in one kind of action any more than in its opposite, but in the existence of a relationship between the two. It is the sense of comparisons being in order. (*Pause.*) Full stop.
> (*Music! Lights! Dorothy Moore—in person! . . . In fact, a track from* DOTTY's *record, playing in the Bedroom, and* DOTTY *singing and miming to it. . . .* DOTTY *continues to sway and mime.*
>
> (46)

George's implied rebuttal of McFee's "orthodox, mainstream" logical positivism is rendered absurd by his obliviousness to practical morality, namely McFee's murder and its cover-up by the Rad-Libs. Dotty's mime to "Sentimental Journey" immediately following George's monologue, steals its theatrical thunder with the spectacle of the Jumpers bagging McFee's corpse.

In act 2, the murder mystery comes to the fore with the reappearance of Inspector Bones. As Dotty disappears into her bedroom (with Archie) for much of this act, Bones, a fan of show business and a talented mimic in his own right, takes her place as George's stylistic opponent. But unlike Dotty who confines herself to her bedroom, Bones ranges freely over the Moores' flat. A close relative of Stoppard's band of loony detectives, Bones moves through George's study, Dotty's bedroom, and other, unseen rooms in the house while making wisecracks about his suspects, all in the name of enforcing the law. Shortly after Bones's entrance, when George complains that he "can't find the words" in which to express his convictions about God, Bones offers helpful criticism, "Well, 'Are God?' is wrong for a start" (36).

While Bones and Archie discuss Dottie's predicament as a suspect in McFee's murder, Bones assuring Archie that he will treat her with partiality, George, blissfully ignorant, prepares for a new assault on the question of God:

> *Bones*: This is a British murder inquiry and some degree of justice must be seen to be more or less done.
>
> . . . .
>
> (*In the Study,* GEORGE *resumes*.)
> *George*: The study of moral philosophy is an attempt to determine what we mean when we say that something is good and that something else is bad. . . .
>
> (56)

With Bones's help, the farce dialectic also operates as a contest between the informed (the spectators and some of the characters) and the ignorant (principally George). Locked away in his study, oblivious to McFee's murder, George thinks that Bones has come to their home in response to his telephone complaint about the Jumpers' party noise. Bones thinks that George is accepting responsibility for McFee's murder to protect a guilty Dotty. The resulting cross talk is one of Stoppard's favorite farce devices:

> *Bones*: I don't think the burden of being a householder extends to responsibility
> for any crime committed on the premises.
> *George*: Crime? You call that a crime?
> *Bones*: (*With more heat*): Well, what would you call it?
> *George*: It was just a bit of *fun*! Where's your sense of humour, man?
> *Bones*: (*Staggered*): I don't know, you bloody philosophers are all the same, aren't you? A man is dead and you're as cool as you like. . . .
>
> (50)

Active conflict and development occurs within as well as between characters. While George shares his profound ignorance of what goes on in his own house with other farce characters such as Plautus's Brothers Menaechmi and Shakespeare's Antipholus twins, Stoppard prevents us from viewing him as a puppet dangling at the end of a farceur's strings by attributing to him a self-conscious and divided nature. The contradiction between George's ignorance and his ingenuity, his obliviousness and his humanity, enlivens his linguistic struggle to create and justify God and goodness. To the extent that Stoppard foregrounds the contradictions within George's monologues, their serio-comic self-consciousness as linguistic experiments, he gives them a texture, pace, and intensity equal to that of Dotty's most bespangled displays.

In his crucial act 2 monologue, George offers the most lively articulation of his dilemma:

> How does one know what it is one believes when it's so difficult to know what it is one knows. I don't claim to *know* that God exists, I only claim that he does without my knowing it, and while I claim as much I do not claim to know as much; indeed I cannot know and God knows I cannot. (*Pause.*) And yet I tell you that, now and again, not necessarily in the contemplation of rainbows . . . but . . . ambushed by some quite trivial moment . . . then I tell you I *know*—I sound like a joke vicar, new paragraph. (62)

Knowledge is possible not as the result of sustained rational analysis nor as the transfer of biological signals but as the unanticipated byproduct of a surprise momentary perception of shared awareness — like that we can experience at special moments in a theater. Stoppard privileges this moment by fading to a spot on George as he presents his image of the "limiting curve," a metaphorical substitute for mathematics' modeling of a circle. Just as a polygon can be imagined to become a circle, so human life can approach some kind of perfect form through the exercise of a doubting intellect. But the moment of truth is short-lived. No sooner has George achieved his small linguistic triumph than a "delicious" laugh issues from Dotty's darkened bedroom where she is enjoying lunch with her psychiatrist, and George surrenders the scene to a cuckold's indignation. Even the moment of his destruction teeters between pathos and farce as he discovers his pet hare Thumper accidentally impaled with an arrow he had earlier shot himself and seconds later steps on his pet tortoise, Pat, with a fatal "crunch." It is now his turn to scream "Help! Murder!"

As George lies defeated on the floor of his study, holding his dead tortoise and hare, Stoppard borrows a convention from film to suggest what follows. The prone George has a nightmare vision of the long-awaited Symposium on the question, "Man: Good, Bad or Indifferent?" Written in the form of a Coda, a formally distinct section of the play that summarizes with new emphasis elements of the first two acts, the dream sequence surrealistically distorts the characters and idioms we have already seen and heard. The disturbing quality of the distortion lies in its irrational mocking reduction, its burlesque, of the positions presented earlier, now rated by scorecards—9.7, 9.9, and so on.

Archie opens the Symposium speaking a nonsense academese that recapitulates George's theism:

> Indeed, if moon mad herd instinct, is God dad the inference? — to take another point: If goons in mood, by Gad is sin different or banned good, fr'instance? — thirdly: out of the ether, random nucleic acid testes or neither unversa vice, to name but one — (73)

Written in a Joycean dialect (Whitaker compares the entire Coda to the Circe episode in *Ulysses* [1983, 98]), Archie's mockery translates something like: "If moon man has instinct, is the death of God to be inferred from it? To take another point: If good is in the moon [if God can be said to exist on the moon?], then is sin to be defined as a quality different from God or as the absence of good; thirdly, [has the universe arisen] either out of the ether or out of random mixing of gases, or neither [or] vice versa?" Archie follows George's earlier lead in separating the God of goodness from the God of creation, but says nothing coherent about either hypothesis. For logocentric George, such a mockery of philosophical argument is horrifying in prohibiting rebuttal.

Archie's sinister quality is more pronounced in the Coda, which finally serves as a moral lens through which we re-view the central questions of the play. Since qualities like good and bad are, for Archie, anachronistic fictions, he openly dismisses all speculation on the subject of man's moral condition by observing merely that the human race is relatively happy. Archie expects nothing because he assumes nothing; he resists nothing but appears to comprehend everything. Thus his character, while theatrically entertaining in small doses, is finally one-dimensional.

The Coda also magnifies George's characteristic weakness. At a climactic moment, George stands by, refusing to interfere while Archbishop Clegthorpe is shot for failing to repudiate his belief in a supreme being. George's error replicates Guildenstern's: unwilling or unable to apply his humanism to human situations, to connect his belief in God to his judgment of how people should treat one another, George behaves like the "tame believer" of Archie's mockery—he becomes the powerless ivory-tower intellectual of Archie's description. As another of Stoppard's artist figures, George has failed to learn how to negotiate the boundary dividing art (here conceived as philosophical argument), from life (moon landings, distraught wives, power struggles). His attempts to solve his problem amount to ignoring the human ("real") world altogether. Thus he unwittingly proves Archie right: he *is* harmless.

Dotty appears to have done better than her male partners in the Coda, but the appearance is deceiving. In this dream state, she has regained her power of song, but her lyrics show her to be the same Dotty Moore who was broken by the demystifying of the moon. Dotty delivers her "philosophy" in her closing song: two and two make roughly four—generally speaking, we can assume that numbers will behave how we expect them to. However, judging by her own experience of men (both in and out of bed), they can be either good or bad but never neutral (—"Some ain't bad and some are revelations, / Never met indifference"). But how, asks Dorothy, can she be expected to believe in God? "Heaven, . . . Just a lying rhyme for seven! / Scored for violins on multi-track" (77). God is a fictional disguise for chance made attractive by appeals to sentimentality. Firmly rooted in common sense and feeling, Dotty rejects metaphysical fictions as childish lies.

Finally, while Stoppard's sympathy belongs clearly to George and Dotty's struggle to refashion an intellectual and emotional center to contem-

porary life, he closes the play by suggesting that George, at least, has failed
in that struggle not only because he could not find the words but also because
he made his search for them its own justification. The implication of the Coda
is glaringly apparent: art and the artist cannot exist for their own sakes alone.
They are firmly embedded in the world around them and will always be used
to some worldly end, perhaps a vicious end. But where does this conclusion
lead playwright Stoppard? In spite of appearing two years later than *Jumpers*,
Travesties does not resolve the dilemma. In Stoppard's terms, there is no solution, no final resting place for the artist either inside or outside of the public
political world. Artists are always in conflict, always attempting to balance a
view of art as, on the one hand, hermetically self-contained and, on the other,
answerable to the problems of its particular time and place. *Travesties* is Stoppard's fullest expression of resistance to choosing between these two competing claims.

Travesties: Bursting Wilde's Bubble

Richer in literary echo, more various in tone and experimental in structure than
his previous stage works, *Travesties* is widely considered the best Stoppard play
to date.[7] Stoppard himself has recognized in *Travesties'* speeches, if not its
structure, an accomplishment he could not hope to surpass: "A lot of things in
Travesties and *Jumpers* seem to me to be the terminus of the particular kind of
writing which I can do" (Hayman 1979, 138). This kind of writing—
hyperparodic comic echoing—would begin to change after *Travesties,* as Stoppard looked toward "natural-seeming" language for new comic inspiration.

    An uncommissioned work, *Travesties* grew out of an informal request
for a play made by Royal Shakespeare Company (RSC) director Trevor Nunn.
From the start, then, it was an "RSC play," intended for a literate, middle-class
RSC audience, the same audience for whom Stoppard has written the majority
of his stage and radio works, and which he assumes to be composed of people
like himself (Interview with Joost Kuurman 1980, 46). It is the sort of audience
that would be expected to recognize and relish the play's appropriation of Oscar Wilde, James Joyce, Tristan Tzara, Shakespeare, and the Lenins.

    Travesties looks back to the earlier parody plays while surpassing them
in complexity and comic craftsmanship. The Prologue samples the ideological
and stylistic possibilities to be presented during its two acts. Set in the Zurich
Public Library, it is a direct enactment of three writers producing and reciting
their works in several languages virtually exclusive of English. Tzara is cut-

ting and shuffling the words to a poem which, when translated, proves to be an extended cross-lingual pun describing the idea of Dada:

> Eel ate enormous appletzara / He's astonishing, the one called Tzara
> key dairy chef's hat he'lllearn oomparah! / Who rushes headlong once again! Peerless jokester!
> Ill raced alas whispers kill later nut east, / He stays with the Swiss 'cause he's an artist.
> noon avuncular ill day Clara! / "We have only art," he declares to us.[8]

Hardly a chance composition, Stoppard's parodic rewrite of the Dada doctrine punningly insists upon the sacred status of art and the artist. Later in the scene, Tzara will dismantle his poem, imitating his own method of writing as a process of continuous construction and deconstruction. Simultaneous with Tzara's performance, Joyce is dictating to his assistant, Gwen, the three incantations opening the Oxen of the Sun episode in *Ulysses*, the chapter described as an encyclopedic parody (or travesty or pastiche) of western prose.[9] In showing us Joyce compressing reference, combining idioms, and repeating language for magical effect, Stoppard is showing us the artist Joyce whom we will not see again. He will later appear as Joyce the penny-pinching producer and Joyce the critic, but here he is actually doing art.

The Lenin we see speaks only Russian and is, therefore, nearly incomprehensible to most spectators, except when he repeats the noun, "*revolutsia!*" (The only recognizable English sentence in the entire scene is the introduction to "Galway Bay" sung by Joyce as he strolls offstage.) Readers of the play can benefit from Stoppard's English translation of the dialogue, which reveals that Lenin's wife Nadya is reporting the outbreak of revolution in St. Petersburg. Lenin is pointedly *not* an artist; his single-minded dedication to revolution translates stylistically as conversationally "artless" and unfinished prose.

As John Cook has observed (in Bloom 1986, 90), only one similarity binds the three Prologue figures together: all are composing works with the help of paper scraps, a coincidence that permits a joke in which the papers become switched (Joyce mistakenly picks up a slip dropped by Lenin) and which will be repeated on a grander scale when the next mix-up occurs. This second confusion is the Prologue's only reference to Wilde's *Importance of Being Earnest*, whose fable will be imitated by the inner play. Joyce's assistant, Gwen, mistakenly switches folders with Lenin's assistant, Cecily, in an echo of the baby-manuscript switch narrated near the close of Wilde's play. As in Wilde, the switch is not discovered until the final scene where it reinforces Stoppard's politicizing of Wilde's pointedly apolitical play. The characters' discovery of the switch near the play's close becomes another occasion for underscoring their ideological differences, with Joyce calling Lenin's work an "ill-tempered thesis purporting to prove, amongst other things, that Ramsay MacDonald is a bourgeois lickspittle gentleman's gentleman" (97) and Carr (speaking as a philistine) describing Joyce's work as "inordinate in length, and erratic in style, remotely connected with midwifery" (97).

Three of the major figures, ideologies, and texts central to *Travesties'* art-politics debate are cited in the Prologue. Only Oscar Wilde and his play are absent, a clue to the singular function assigned Wilde's "quintessential English jewel." When the light comes up on "Old" Carr, we discover the narrator/parodist and, eventually, the text (*Earnest*) through which we will see the remaining scenes. Carr himself warns us that his narration will be neither reliable nor "objective." The title tells us to expect travesty, the mocking distortion of particular source texts. But the gamut of recycling procedures actually used is more various than this suggests.

Certainly the dominant procedure is parody — Stoppard's distorted repetition of *Earnest* recognized as a fiction by the spectators but not by narrator Carr.[10] The choice of *Earnest* is not gratuitous. Having played the role of Algernon Moncrieff in James Joyce's Swiss production of Wilde's play, Henry Carr inadvertently conflates its lines and plot with his subjective recollection of Zurich during the War.[11] Carr significantly never acknowledges that he is repeating Wilde's play, a discovery left to the spectators, but Stoppard offers a fictional reason (based mischievously on historical fact) why it should be plausible for him to do so.

Stoppard's parody of Wilde both distances the spectators, encouraging them to hear the differences between Stoppard's play and its model, and offers them a familiar line of action in a bewildering array of comic texts and styles. By virtue of its centrality as a structural underpinning and of its persistence as an echo in Stoppard's lines, Wilde's play holds a place of special privilege unlike that of the Joyce, Tzara, or Shakespeare texts. On the one hand, Carr resists *Earnest*, misquoting its lines and subverting its art-for-art's-sake ideology to suit his argument. On the other hand, he insists upon *Earnest*, building his entire recollection upon its fable. We are reminded of the paradox of parody — even in mocking, parody reinforces.

The first Wildean scene of Stoppard's play rewrites the opening *Earnest* dialogue between servant and master and then rewrites its own revision. Stoppard's rewrite substitutes for light references to music a cumulative description of the politics of World War I disguised as Bennett's "consensus of London dailies." Michael Issacharoff cites Stoppard's multiple rewrites of *Earnest*'s second scene, the arrival of Jack Worthing at Algernon's flat, and Cecily's lecture opening *Travesties*' second act, as further examples of what he calls Stoppard's ideological subversion of *Earnest* (1989, 43–44). The subversion amounts to attributing to Wilde's characters a concern for their political beliefs not to be found in Wilde's "delicate bubble of fancy." Wherever Stoppard splices the art-politics conflict into the narrative frame of *Earnest*, he is using parody to create a space for the question of *his* play: what is the role of the artist in politics? While none of *Travesties*' recycling procedures points to an authoritative answer to this question, Stoppard's parody of Wilde's play offers the common ground upon which an answer is attempted.

The next scene reveals more clearly how Stoppard subverts *Earnest*'s philosophy while adhering to its structure. The first time Tzara arrives at Carr's door, he is a travesty, "*a Rumanian nonsense*," followed immediately by a travestied James Joyce, Stoppard's equivalent of Wilde's Lady Bracknell. This scene, minus Joyce, restarts two more times, each time moving closer to the language and performing idiom of Wilde's text, which thus functions as a kind of stylistic (if not thematic) norm. When we repeatedly depart from and return to a text that looks and acts like *Earnest*, we perceive it to be relatively stable.

In lieu of the verbal sparring between Algernon and Jack in Wilde's second scene, Carr and Tzara square off on the art vs. politics question, with Carr claiming that wars are fought to make the world safe for artists and Tzara arguing that wars are fought for oil wells and coaling stations. In the symmetrical presenting of these scenes, neither Carr nor Tzara can be said clearly to win or lose. Their standoff is signaled by their identical use of epithets, the first set hurled at Tzara by Carr: "My God, you little Rumanian wog—you bloody dago—you jumped-up phrase-making smart-alecy arty-intellectual Balkan turd!!!" (40), and the second set aimed at Carr by Tzara: "My God, you bloody English philistine—you ignorant smart-arse bogus bourgeois Anglo-Saxon prick!" (47) Later in the first act, Tzara dismisses Joyce in similar terms: "By God, you supercilious streak of Irish puke! You four-eyed, bog-ignorant, potato-eating ponce! Your art has failed." (62) The hostility between Joyce and Tzara, while echoing that of Algernon and Jack, is based upon their competing ideological views of art rather than upon their jealousy of each other's bunburying schemes.

Stoppard's parody substitutes politics for Wildean themes whenever possible. We hear the substitution most clearly in near quotes of Wilde's play, such as when Stoppard's Tzara (the equivalent of Wilde's Jack) asks Gwendolyn (Wilde's Cecily) what he must do to secure her love: "You don't mean that you couldn't love me if I didn't share your regard for Mr. Joyce as an artist?" Her response is swift and sure: "But you do" (55).

Stoppard's parody of Wilde does not point to a solution to the relative claims of art and politics; instead, it makes those claims unusually clear by virtue of presenting them in the discordant fictional context of what Wilde called "a trivial comedy for serious people." Parodic recycling re-energizes our responses to texts by making us aware of our expectations for their significance. But parody is not the only kind of borrowing Stoppard uses to bring us to a reconsideration of the competing claims of art and politics.

In addition to the Prologue's "direct" citation of Joyce and Lenin (assuming for the moment that the Prologue is not filtered through Carr's memory—a question begged in Stoppard's stage directions), *Travesties* recycles fictional works through narrator Carr that the characters themselves acknowledge to be fictional. This kind of recycling, something close to citation, also serves the art-politics debate, but it involves the spectator in the debate in a slightly different way. Where parody focuses us upon the discrepancy between how a text customarily sounds and behaves and how it is sounding and behaving in front of us, Stoppard's citations focus our attention upon the difference between what a text seems to say and how the speaker is using it. Joyce's "Dooley" recitation appears to distract gratuitously from the primary purpose of his visit to Carr, which is to ask him for money. But it gives Stoppard the opportunity to show us another Joyce—the cadging producer who blithely retracts the principles of "Dooley" in order to raise money for his *Earnest* production. Joyce succeeds in winning Carr's interest in the play by appealing directly to the kind of philistine nationalism reviled in his poem: "Night after night, actors totter about the raked stages of this alpine renaissance, speaking in every tongue but one—the tongue of Shakespeare—of Sheridan—of Wilde" (51). "Dooley" makes an aggressive polemical statement about the foolishness of war, but that is quite beside the point when Joyce needs to raise money. Ideology proves to be contingent upon practical needs.

Tzara's rearrangement of Shakespeare's eighteenth sonnet is a Dada demonstration designed to woo Joyce's assistant Gwendolyn, an admirer of belles lettres. Thus, it, too, appears to be implicated in the battle of ideologies: will Gwen remain faithful to the Great Tradition of Western Masterpieces, or will she be won over by avant-garde experimentation? She first recites the entire sonnet — a celebration of art's immortalizing power — from memory, then defends the verse in a verbal duel with Tzara conducted through Shakespearean pastiche, and finally consents to reconstructing the poem by drawing its words out of Tzara's hat. Thus, the entire scene reenacts in the terms of a Wildean romance the Dada intention of destroying traditional art and replacing it with poetry "written in the hand of chance" (53). Tzara finally coaxes Gwen to create "his" poem (or is it hers if she has pulled the words from his hat?) after citing the line, "But since he died, and poet better prove, his for his style you'll read, mine for my — love" (54). Now borrowing from the Shakespeare he had reviled, Tzara implies that (like Hamlet and Orlando) the depth of his love may damn the style of his poetry but will at least ensure its sincerity. The resulting poem beginning "Darling" is erotic "by chance," no longer Shakespeare's, but not exactly Tzara's or Gwen's either. Not genuinely parodic (actors and spectators both know it as a fiction) nor authentically Dada (the first word fits too well to be the product of chance), it must be a travesty of a chance composition doubling as a subversive valentine.[12] Its dramatic purpose is to frame the presumed differences between Gwendolyn's traditional and Tzara's avant-garde definitions of the "poetical." At the same time, the new poem reverses Shakespeare's polemic, offering physical love (growing and then declining) in the place of immortality. As in Joyce's recitation of "Dooley," the citation and its Dada deconstruction prove pointless. Gwen has already decided to pursue Jack for the very reason she pretended to resist him: the thrill of avant-garde experimentation. Gwen's commitment to tradition is finally no more fixed than Joyce's commitment to neutrality.

Act 1 concludes with a return to Wilde now doubled by a reference to *Ulysses*. Joyce's interrogation of Tzara echoes both Lady Bracknell's quizzing of Jack and the impersonal catechism of the Ithaca episode of *Ulysses*, while giving us a history of Dada. This is the critic Joyce, adulterating the detachment of the Ithaca narrator by descending to Tzara's level of egotistical display. Much of this scene's humor lies in Tzara's and Joyce's competing gestures — when Tzara dons a carnation, Joyce begins to pull silk hankies out of his pocket. Joyce the critic-ideologue gets the last word in act 1, claiming for his novel the permanence Shakespeare claimed for his sonnet: "I with my Dublin Odyssey will double [the original *Odyssey*'s] immortality, yes by God *there*'s a corpse that will dance for some time yet and *leave the world precisely as it finds it*" (62–63). This claim is not, however, dismantled. In fact, Carr's chat with the spectators closing act 1 amplifies Joyce's claim in a backhanded tribute: "And I *flung* at him — 'And what did you do in the Great War?' 'I wrote

Ulysses,' he said. 'What did you do?' Bloody nerve" (65). While Henry Carr is act 1's spokesperson for the art-for-art's sake doctrine, "Joyce" is its legitimating example, in spite of having been parodied.

Stoppard originally intended to open act 2 with a new set, a new scene, and a new character. He wanted to "stop" the *Earnest* frame, splice in a lengthy documentary reporting of Lenin's political development read by the actors "from clipboards or lecterns," and then restart the parody again (Hayman 1979, 9–10). The previews demonstrated to him that this opening narrative needed to be shorter and more narrowly focused on Lenin. Director Peter Wood also pointed out to him the danger of losing the audience altogether in changing the play's rules in midstream. The spectators have accepted the convention by which the whole play (minus the Prologue?) is set in Carr's memory—except for this documentary section. Our provisional belief could be badly dislocated by such a disruption. Cecily's lecture seems to have been a compromise: a character (barely) familiar from the *Earnest* frame delivers a narrative history of the Lenins in front of an unlit set in a direct, pseudo-Brechtian style. Whether or not the narrative is contained within Carr's recollection is ambiguous, so that even this compromise represented a dislocation, albeit a less severe one than Stoppard's original plan called for. The resulting shock to the audience was intended to be funny: "Except," Stoppard told an interviewer, "I was the only person laughing" (quoted in Tynan 1980, 113).

Stoppard refused to give the Lenins parts in the *Earnest* plot, claiming that would have "killed the play because of the trivialization" (Hayman 1979, 10). Instead, he assigned them a distinct style and autonomous roles that dramatically demonstrate the incompatibility of Joycean art-for-art's-sake with Lenin's call for revolutionary art. Thus, Stoppard judged the recycling procedures central to act 1 as inappropriate for representing the Lenins. He solved this problem by assigning to them a unique method for repeating their written work. The Lenins narrate historical information through citations and what Rabinowitz calls "retellings" that present the audience with a new version of a text it knows exists but has never read (1980, 247). (Some of the audience will have read Lenin's *Collected Writings* and his wife's *Memories of Lenin*, but a good share will not have done so, and of those who have, few would seem likely to recall those texts in detail.)

In spite of basing his retellings strictly on his written sources, Stoppard nevertheless manages to surprise the spectators by selecting the more striking and unlikely incidents from the great mass of historical detail. Nadya's first English words on stage tell the story of her husband's response to hearing about the 1904 St. Petersburg revolution (reported in Russian in the Prologue and repeated in both Russian and English immediately following Cecily's lecture). She quotes from his 19 March 1917 letter to Ganetsky in Stockholm:

> I cannot wait any longer. No legal means of transit available. . . . The only possible plan is as follows: you must find two Swedes who resemble Zinoviev and me, but since we cannot speak Swedish they must be deaf mutes. (79)

This is neither a story we expect to hear nor a Lenin we recall having read about. Stoppard uses Nadya to humanize the Lenins, to represent what Corballis calls the "ambivalent" "private" as opposed to the "clockwork public" Lenin (1984, 89) and thereby to complicate the spectators' reading of the couple.

Lenin's act 2 speech on art and artists, the most crucial of the retellings, occupies a central position in the act outside of narrator Carr's control and placed after the narrative sequence describing Lenin's departure for Russia. It is the play's most vivid portrait of Lenin, staged to parody an actual photograph, and one in which the editorializing presence of author Stoppard is most strongly felt, exposing the contradiction between Lenin's call for a free press and his suppression of writing that strays from the communist party line:

> Everyone is free to write and say whatever he likes, without any restrictions. *But* every voluntary association, including the party, is also free to expel members who use the name of the party to advocate anti-party views. (85)

Stoppard augments this quotation with excerpts from letters documenting Lenin's view of the artist's responsibility. Employing Beckettian rhetoric, "Firstly 'A' then minus 'A'," Stoppard follows this authoritarian, philistine Lenin with another version of the (private) man deeply moved by Beethoven's "Appassionata" and troubled by the contradiction between artistic beauty and social injustice.

The effect of retelling (rather than parodying) the Lenins' writings is to place our full attention on the narration itself rather than on the imaginative space between a source text and its copy. But as Corballis has noted, there is a further difference between the Lenins' narratives. Where Nadya's stories invariably surprise and delight us, Lenin's public pronouncements on art have a familiar ring to them. In this comic play of echoes and re-echoes, Ulyanov's position on art and politics has already been voiced in Cecily's act 2 argument with Carr (twice restarted). The striking quality in Lenin's major address on art and literature is thus not its ideas but its self-canceling illogicality. Where such self-defeating mistakes made by Carr or Joyce arouse our laughter, the same mistakes when made in the relatively "straight" or pseudo-documentary style of the Lenin section arouse our antipathy and/or ridicule. Lenin loses credibility as the parodic Carr and Joyce cannot, because he does not see himself as fictional. Stoppard has attempted to defend the fairness of his portrayal of Lenin by arguing that the full complexity of his character was available only during performance:

> In theatrical terms Frank Winsor and Barbara Leigh-Hunt are . . . blood heat, they're so human. When they walk on the stage you don't really think that man has contradicted himself throughout and condemned himself out of his own mouth. You think he really had a burden to carry, and [meanwhile] . . . Ashkenazy is doing his bit in the loudspeaker, playing the Appassionata. The equation is different, and even I am seduced by it. (Quoted in Hayman 1979, 11)

Whether or not Stoppard succeeds in conveying Lenin's burden, he does succeed in establishing him as the ideological opposite of Joyce. For a moment, we have a clear image of art vs. politics, but then the play moves on as the "Appassionata" gives way to more frivolous music. The Wildean reconciliation of lovers occurs to the tune of "Mr. Gallagher and Mr. Shean." And, in a final joke on Carr's travesty of history, "Old" Cecily, wife to "Old" Carr, insists on exposing the distortions of fact that gave his narrative its shape. The final "retelling" dismantles the fiction of the play.

In its self-reflexive complexity, its demonstration of virtuoso technique, and its steady focus upon the question of artists' debt to their society, *Travesties* celebrates the craft of comedy as no single Stoppard play has since its 1974 premiere. But while the outcome may be a stunningly funny and virtuosic representing of literary and theatrical history, it is by no means precious or flawless. Stoppard took risks with the second act because he needed to state his question as fully and clearly as he knew how. The second act falters because the Lenins are insufficiently fictionalized; they are parodied, in the general sense that they are represented as fictional characters in Stoppard's play, but they remain outside of the *Earnest* frame. In asking us to take Lenin more literally than we have taken the play's other characters, Stoppard finally undermines the parodic assumption governing most of the action and exposes Lenin to ridicule rather than the laughter of recognition typical of parody. The portrait of Lenin moves toward satire, while the other portraits remain firmly in the realm of comedy. So that while Stoppard may have hoped to balance a statement of art as ahistorical and apolitical against a statement of art as the handmaid to politics, his treatment of the major spokesmen for these positions skews the balance in favor of a (mock) Joyce and Wilde. *Travesties* marks the end of one kind of writing for playwright Stoppard but it does not answer the overwhelming question it poses. His major plays since *Travesties* address the question in surprisingly new ways.

Chapter 4

Silence and the Turn toward Satire

Stoppard's so-called political plays have led some to suggest that he underwent an awakening marked by a radical shift of subject and treatment culminating in an inevitably more liberal ideological stance. Kenneth Tynan seemed positively heartened by this group of plays as they promised to redeem Stoppard from the political purgatory to which Tynan himself had consigned him. And while it is true that Stoppard's play writing underwent a shift in the mid-1970s, the explicit politics of this group of plays is only one element of that change.

The ideology of this small group of satires, here described by Michael Hays in a review of a book on Stoppard, has already been encountered in a different form in his major parody plays discussed in chapter 3:

> Stoppard's late work, while it does not suggest that the individual can be certain of the correctness of his or her beliefs or actions, demonstrates that, in the face of a structure or system that disempowers by claiming the right to stage truth or meaning, one is always free . . . to orchestrate an alternative . . . that denies the authority of all monolithic interpretations. (Hays 1988, 596)

The heroes of Stoppard's satires are typical of his earlier protagonists in resisting the systems attempting to delimit their choices. They fend off, expose, debunk, deny, and generally sit out of the political culture oppressing them. In *Every Good Boy Deserves Favour* hero Alexander refuses to play an instrument; *Professional Foul*'s Pavel Hollar refuses to place the ethic of the state over that of the individual; and actor Cahoot of *Cahoot's Macbeth* refuses to remain silent. But there are important differences between the parody plays and the satires. Where the artist characters like Albert, George Moore, and Henry Carr are tolerated but ignored by those in power, the heroes of the satires are punished and confined by those in power for resisting officially sanctioned "stagings" of truth or meaning. With a change from West to East, from bourgeois liberal capitalist democracy to (pre-perestroika) Iron Curtain communism, comes a corresponding hardening of character and situation.[1]

The oppressors now represent a stable ideology realized through force rather than a vague pastiche of positivist thought. The heroes no longer reflect on their mental paralysis or uncertainty; instead they insist quietly – sometimes silently – upon their right to dissent, a right about which they are completely certain.

Taking Aim: *Every Good Boy Deserves Favour*

In a 1963 *Encore* review-essay, Stoppard adopts his *Scene* persona to lament the absence of genuinely satiric plays in a London otherwise fascinated with the genre of Swift and Ben Jonson. While reviewing a series of failed stage satires, Stoppard gives his own quite conventional definition of the genre: the exposure of vice, folly, hypocrisy and pretension communicated by humor. The comic element, insists Stoppard, must be the means rather than the end of a true satire ("A Very Satirical Thing," 34). But his own practice proved more complex than his precepts would suggest. Twelve years later, when he began to address his plays to the abuse of human rights in contemporary Czechoslovakia and Russia, he aimed his comedy toward both the "extramural" target of social and political wrongs and the "intramural" target of borrowed literary texts and other artistic works. Although his comedy became more aggressive, it did not surrender its customary playing on and with its artistic precursors.

Stoppard wrote *Every Good Boy Deserves Favour* at the suggestion of London Symphony Orchestra conductor André Previn. As described by Mr. Previn in the notes accompanying the RCA recording of the play, its earliest form was comic but not satiric:

> His first sketches . . . were about a madman millionaire who, having made his bundle on tinning fruit, now owned a symphony orchestra body and soul, to play at his bidding. . . . And then, one day, Tom phoned to tell me that his mind had raced off on another tack.

Stoppard subsequently made the orchestra the delusion of a lunatic triangle player and, after a punning diversion into Euclidean geometry inspired by triangle playing, he reached a dead end. His April 1976 meeting with Russian exile Victor Fainberg proved to be the next and most crucial event in this play's genesis. Fainberg, who had in fact been imprisoned in Soviet mental hospitals and was attempting to publicize the plight of others like himself still behind bars, gave Stoppard a hero and a political target: official Soviet vice, folly, and pretension. The comedy had become a satire supported by parodic moments in the symphony's score—the musical mimicry of the Doctor's gestures and the brief excerpt of Tchaikovsky's *1812 Overture* mocking Ivanov's Napoleonic posturing as he threatens Alexander.

Effective satire implies a clear moral norm against which the demonstrated excesses of its target can be measured. In Stoppard's plays, the norm is usually signified negatively, by the heroes' resistance to official domination of art, language, and education, based on their recognition "that power arises from knowledge of the staging mechanisms themselves" (Hays 1988, 596). This play's hero, Alexander, represents the norm (he even calls himself "normal") and actively resists the Soviet authority's attempts to conceal their staging of social and individual control through their domination of music, education, and language. Stoppard encodes Alexander's dilemma in terms of doubles—double (even triple) characters, double orchestras, instruments, and scores, one of them real, the other imaginary. The "real" orchestra is heard by all, while the private, hallucinatory orchestra—sometimes overheard by the spectators—is regularly heard only by Alexander's mad cellmate, Ivanov. Relying on a grammar he had learned while writing for radio, Stoppard uses the cutting in and out of sound and a gradual gain in volume to signify to the spectators that they are not hearing but overhearing imaginary music.

> *The orchestra tunes up. The tuning up continues normally, but after a minute or two the musicians lapse into miming the tuning up. . . . Ivanov stands up, with his triangle and rod. The orchestra becomes immobile. Silence. Ivanov strikes the triangle, once. The orchestra starts miming a performance. He stands concentrating. . . . Then, very quietly, we begin to hear what Ivanov can hear.* (9–10)

Unlike the spectators, Alexander never overhears Ivanov's private orchestra and steadfastly refuses to acknowledge the public orchestra identified with official Soviet control of its citizens. Both orchestras are compulsory: the public orchestra imposes a score on the players, and Ivanov's private orchestra plays when and where it chooses for him and for him alone. Alexander is literally enclosed by the official orchestra on the one hand and is threatened by the violently anarchic private orchestra on the other. Demonstrating the distinction between the real and unreal orchestras gets laughs, but recognizing their difference is crucial to Stoppard's satiric intent: the orchestras function metaphorically as thought. Alexander thus must refuse both forms of thought—the imposed public form and the entirely private, anarchic form (allied to Albert's, Gladys's and Dorothy Moore's incipient madness). But unlike Stoppard's Western heroes who recognize the need to balance their sense of obligation to a public social realm and a private imaginative realm, Alexander must shut himself off to music altogether in order to resist these threats to his mental freedom.

The suggestion of replication occurs among human characters as well. We learn rather late in the play that Alexander, his hostile cellmate Ivanov, and Alexander's son Sacha (the diminutive form of the Christian name) are identically named, a coincidence apparently planned by Colonel-or-rather-Doctor Rozinsky, the semanticist who has taken personal control of Alexander's case and, according to the Doctor, chose his ward mate carefully. The tripling of characters' names may have been Stoppard's sleight-of-hand solution to the release of Alexander at the play's close (Corballis 1984, 110), but it is also plausible as an additional device by which the authorities have systematically attempted to blur the distinction between the sane and the insane. Housing Alexander with an identically named but genuinely insane double could be read as an attempt further to shake his sanity, literally to drive him crazy and thereby prove the justice of imprisoning him in a psychiatric hospital. But as Alexander nowhere claims knowledge of the coincidence of names, the point remains moot.

Another kind of doubling occurs in the second "scene" of this piece, set in the acting area designated "school," where we learn that Alexander's son, Sacha, plays Ivanov's (and Stoppard's) instrument, the triangle, in the school orchestra. Ivanov's triangle playing is lunatic and involuntary, while Sacha's is compulsory. Both players fail to conform to the official orchestra, but for entirely different reasons. Sacha, like his father, is "unmusical" and unwilling to comply with an orchestrated society that has imprisoned and punished his father.

Alexander's first significant speeches, addressed in frontal style directly to the audience, tell of official attempts to confuse the seeming and the real. Stoppard will include a form of documentary reporting in each of his satires, always at those moments when the heroes are describing the facts of their personal histories as dissenters. These significantly nonparodic reports are distinguished by their apparently factual content and sober delivery in an otherwise largely comic event. In this way, Stoppard distinguishes the heroes of the satires from the other characters and provides them with a unique idiom for telling their stories. These stories are, as it were, "too real" to submit to artistic modeling, although Stoppard does not wish to fool us that he has not selectively reported and paraphrased them. Alexander's story uses the facts of the Victor Fainberg case as described in Clayton Yeo's 1975 essay published in *Index on Censorship,* but adds to those facts an (apparently gratuitous) allusion to alphabetical letters doubling as musical notes, when presenting Alexander's narration of his life:

> My friend, C, demonstrated against the arrest of A and B. I told him he was crazy to do it, and they put him back into the mental hospital. . . . until [my son] was seven the only faintly interesting thing about me was that I had a friend who kept getting arrested. Then one day I did something really crazy. (21)

This crazy thing was to tell the truth about his friend who was put in mental hospitals for speaking against the government.

The tension between art as a form of modeled reality and documentary fact was vividly brought home to Stoppard and the actors in the London production of the play when Vladimir Bukofsky (the real-life referent of "C" above) attended a rehearsal at Covent Garden. "He was," wrote Stoppard in the album notes, "diffident, friendly . . . but his presence was disturbing. . . . There was a sense of worlds colliding. . . . One of the actors seized up in the middle of a speech which touched on the experience of our visitor."

Preserving distinctions between art and life, sanity and insanity is essential both for the actors producing the satire and for the spectators responding to it. The result is a much flatter treatment of the art-life relationship than that offered in the later Western plays like *The Real Thing* or *Hapgood.* This satire insists upon distinguishing the official Soviet intent to label sane political prisoners lunatics and to imprison so-called dissidents in mental hospitals from the absurdities of genuine insanity like Ivanov's. The officials' misuse of language is a cynical attempt to mask the harassment and torture of political dissenters. Unable to speak out, Alexander further attempts to expose the reality of psychiatric torture by silently resuming his hunger strike begun some months before, intent on keeping his actual treatment and that of others vividly before the authorities and the spectators. When he does speak, he grotesquely compares his physical deterioration to another physical — but merely decorative — procedure:

> If you don't eat for a long time you start to smell of acetone, which is the stuff girls use for taking the paint off their fingernails. When the body runs out of pro-

tein and carbohydrates it starts to metabolise its own fat, and acetone is the waste product. To put this another way, a girl removing her nail varnish smells of starvation. (23)

Alexander's Doctor later advises him in direct quotes from Yeo's essay: "Your opinions are your symptoms. Your disease is dissent. . . . I can't help you. And furthermore your breath stinks of aeroplane glue or something—what have you been eating?" (30). Alexander's answer is bitterly comic: "Nothing." Grotesque humor is the humor of dissent.

Stoppard carefully dissociates Alexander and Sacha from the ambiguous farce humor of Ivanov's madness. In a key scene near the play's close we see Ivanov's farce set against the bitter comedy of father and son as Alexander attempts an explanation of why he must risk death by starvation. The madman Ivanov has taken the Doctor's chair while the Doctor joins the violinists in the orchestra. Having been summoned to the hospital to plead with his father to break his hunger strike, Sacha approaches the desk, believing Ivanov to be the real asylum doctor. Terrified by the Doctor's lunacy, Sacha pleads with him, "Don't make me stay. I'll go back in the orchestra!" to which Ivanov retorts, "You can be in mine" (34). Ivanov delivers his musical puns on geometrical axioms with an increasing threat of violence, driving Sacha back into the orchestra from which he sings his refrain, "Papa, don't be rigid! / Everything can be all right!" summarizing his desperate desire to be reunited with his father even at the cost of capitulating to the authorities. Sacha is not so much fully surrendering to the orchestra here (Corballis 1984, 111) as he is falling back on the only position left him, membership in the dominant social system. Children cannot be heroic in the same sense that adults can and to make Sacha a little adult would distort the documented practice by which Soviet officials use dissenters' family members to break down their resistance (Fainberg 1975, 68). When Sacha eventually finds his way to his father's cell, Alexander's responses to his son clarify the moral purpose guiding his actions. It can't be right to tell the authorities that he has been "cured," he explains to Sacha, because such lying helps them to go on being wicked. Alexander must refuse to lie and the authorities must prevent him from dying. We are, says the Doctor, at a logical impasse. But the impasse invokes no real suspense, as it has been anticipated by Alexander in one of his early narrative accounts of his history as a dissenter. He went on hunger strike once before, while a prisoner in the Leningrad Special Psychiatric Hospital on Arsenal'naya Street. After two months on his first hunger strike, they brought Sacha to him, but the boy could not speak.

And then they gave in. And when I was well enough they brought me here. This means they have decided to let me go. . . . But it has to be done right. They don't want to lose ground. They need a formula. It will take a little time but that's all right. . . . Everything is going to be all right. (23)

The formula, as we know, was the pairing of identically named prisoners which permits Colonel Rozinsky to appear to mistake one for the other and thereby release them both without having to admit to an error. As a parodic deus ex machina, the Colonel cuts a farcical figure on stage, appearing in something like a long, flowing cloak to the pompous accompaniment of an organ. Stoppard's commentary on this scene as well as his stage directions to the written text reveal that the Colonel knows exactly what he is doing when he releases both prisoners and that a failure to show that he knows this is a mistake (Interview with Joost Kuurman 1980, 53–54). By implication, it is also mistaken to present the authorities as a zany bunch of lunatics or to equate their corruption with Ivanov's genuine madness. Their rationale and intentions are crystal clear as they attempt consciously and systematically to break down dissenters. To view the Doctor, the Teacher, the Colonel, and Ivanov as interchangeable lunatics is to deny their differences and to cancel the play's satiric intent.

If any inadvertent confusion occurs in this piece, it lies, as Richard Corballis has noted (1984, 108), in the relation between the verbal and musical scores which, on one or two occasions, contradict one another. The dominant signification of the public orchestra ties it to official repression. All of the play's officials, with the exception of the Colonel, play in the orchestra which dominates not only the sound score but also the playing space. The hospital cell, Sacha's schoolroom, and the Doctor's office are all located in small islands surrounded by the orchestra. But the music occasionally embellishes Alexander's performance, in one case representing his nightmare and in the other coloring his personal narrative, which suggests that it is a neutral and omniscient commentary on the action rather than a fixed symbol of social control. Whether this inconsistency resulted from Previn's unwillingness to surrender completely the symphony's evocative power, or whether it reflects the difficulty of collaborating in a maverick form—neither opera nor recitation—it is a minor flaw in an otherwise provocative and unusual satire.

Writing for the purpose of exposing and ridiculing the compulsory staging mechanisms of totalitarian regimes gave Stoppard an extramural target at which to aim his ridicule. Not only the humor but also the structure of his satires reflect this shift in purpose from playfully representing his Western artists' paralysis to demonstrating his Eastern heroes' courage. The conclusion of the play following the Colonel's release of the two prisoners forfeits the reconciliation scene typical of comedy for an ominous suggestion of further trouble to come. Sacha's wish that "everything can be all right" is annotated by a musical score of disturbing menace.

Through Western Eyes: *Professional Foul* as Satire

Ignoring for the moment their significant differences of medium and form, *EGBDF* and *Professional Foul* could be companion pieces, telling the same story, one from the observer's and the other from the participant's point of view. We encounter Pavel Hollar, the Czech dissenter in *Professional Foul*, through the eyes of a visiting British professor of philosophy, Anderson, who knows little of the Czech political situation. As Anderson becomes aware of the official treatment of dissenters, so do we, learning through the television's documentation of hidden facts the authorities' methods for harassing and imprisoning their critics. Showing us what Anderson sees as Anderson sees it, Stoppard slowly introduces to us the differences between Eastern and Western liberties, capped by the sudden revelation of police intrusion into a dissenter's life. Framed by the ironical difference between Western expectation and Eastern reality, the satire in *Professional Foul* is initially cooler and more complex and finally more powerful than the frontal attack launched in Stoppard's piece for actors and orchestra.

According to Stoppard, he had begun preparation for a television play on the subject of Russian political prisoners early in 1976, several months before meeting Victor Fainberg, an exile of Russia's hospital prisons who was campaigning on behalf of the similarly imprisoned Vladimir Bukofsky (Introduction to *Squaring the Circle*, 19, 21). This was followed by a trip to Moscow and Leningrad with the assistant director of Amnesty International early in 1977, where Stoppard met people who had witnessed first hand the movements of the KGB against so-called dissidents. This activity led to a creative burst of energy, one of whose products was his prize-winning television play, *Professional Foul*, aired on BBC-TV of 24 September 1977 after an unusually short composition period of "about three weeks" (quoted in Hunter 1982, 13). Stoppard later explained the occasion of his drama in medium-specific terms:

> Amnesty International had decided to make 1977 Prisoner of Conscience Year
> and I thought a play on TV might help their cause. . . . . On a subject like this

a TV play would have more impact than a play for the stage. After all, on TV you would get a large audience on a single night. In a theater, the impact would be spread over weeks and months. (Shulman 1978)

He had from the first conceived of his play about political prisoners as a TV drama, not simply because television has more viewers than live theater but also because TV is the medium of the broadcast fact as in news programs, news features, and documentaries. Stoppard wanted to exploit the mimetic bias of TV, its historical association with the exposing of hidden facts, in writing his satiric fiction of a British don suddenly confronted with political repression in Czechoslovakia. The inspiration and several key scenes in the play are based on Stoppard's knowledge of real events in the arrest of Czech playwright Vaclav Havel (the play's Pavel Hollar and the real-life president of Czechoslovakia) and on the testimony of a Russian dissident's wife to whom Stoppard spoke during his 1977 tour.[2]

Professional Foul picks up Stoppard's use of a two-track language from the spy thriller *Neutral Ground,* but extends it to include two levels of action corresponding to the comic surface and the menacing underside of the dramatized events. Stoppard leads the viewer into the secret underworld gradually, opening and closing the play with scenes in the airplane carrying British professors Anderson and McKendrick to the Prague philosophy colloquium and home again. The opening of the play's four sections completes the practical business of introducing two of the play's main characters whose dialogue establishes the three events to be interlinked: the approaching colloquium, the World Cup Soccer Match, and the oppression of Czech artists and intellectuals.

We recognize Anderson and McKendrick as Moon and Boot types, respectively, and also as Stoppardian types from earlier plays—Anderson a more confident and successful George Moore and McKendrick a less flashy Archie Jumper. Having caught Anderson reading a girlie magazine, McKendrick warns him that Czech officials, being Marxists, are prudish about pornography. In the conversation that follows, McKendrick leaves Anderson (who is not fully attending to the conversation) behind by first claiming to be a Marxist and then switching his topic to sex and inquiring after extracurricular activities that might develop during their stay.

> *McKendrick*: They won't let you in with that, you know. You'll have to hide it.
> *Anderson*: As a matter of fact it doesn't belong to me.
> *McKendrick*: Western decadence you see. Marxists are a terrible lot of prudes.
>   I can say that because I'm a bit that way myself.

> *Anderson*: You surprise me.
> *McKendrick*: Mind you, when I say I'm a Marxist . . .
> *Anderson*: Oh, I see.
> *McKendrick*: . . . I don't mean I'm an apologist for everything done in the name of Marxism.
> *Anderson*: No, no quite. There's nothing antisocialist about it. . . . The rich have always had it to themselves.
> *McKendrick*: On the contrary. That's why I'd be really very interested in any extracurricular activities which might be going. I have an open mind about it.
>
> (50–51)

While not all of the lines of this exchange make obvious sense (Anderson's two "it's" cannot with perfect sense refer to pornography or sex or Marxism), the conversation as a whole functions as a remarkably clever prologue in which not only the themes of secrecy and dissent but also the action of concealing illegal writing are raised in an apparently apolitical context.

The comic cross talk of this early scene extends to the first meeting between Anderson and his former student, Pavel Hollar, who asks him to smuggle out his thesis on individual rights. This entire scene draws on the spy thriller formula for secrecy and coded communication already seen in *Neutral Ground,* but developed comically here by Anderson's failure to understand that Hollar's predicament is real rather than academic. After objecting to Hollar's precautions, including the use of a child's "magic eraser" pad to avoid being overheard, Anderson consents to hear Hollar's argument, which the Czech summarizes as follows:

> I conclude there is an obligation, a human responsibility to fight against the State correctness. Unfortunately, that is not a safe conclusion. (61)

Anderson misunderstands Hollar's use of the word "safe," thinking it refers to the academic battleground rather than to the warlike conditions of dissidents' daily lives:

> *Anderson*: Quite. The difficulty arises when one asks oneself how the *individual* ethic can have meaning by itself. Where does *that* come from? . . .
> *Hollar*: I mean, it is not safe for me.
>
> (61–62)

But even in this tense scene Stoppard plays with the viewer's expectations, teasing us with the emergence of a suspicious-looking, dark-suited man from the room next to Anderson's at a suspenseful moment. We wait several scenes before learning that the dark stranger is not the secret police but a Western journalist covering the World Cup Soccer Match.

Scene 4 extends the cross-talk gag, as Anderson and McKendrick meet soccer players Crisp and Broadbent in the hotel elevator. Both Anderson's intensely cerebral analysis of the Czech team's probable strategy and McKendrick's breezy philosopher's small talk are returned by the players' blank stares. The failure of language to connect with thought or feeling provides much of the humor in the drama's fifth scene, where McKendrick learns that he had mistaken the soccer players in the elevator for philosophers and that Anderson's real purpose in attending the Colloquium is to see the World Cup. While sitting in the Colloquium auditorium listening to the speakers, their private conversation coincides with Professor Stone's public lecture to underscore the point:

> *Anderson*: Perfectly understandable mistake.
> *Stone*: Nor must we confuse ambiguity, furthermore, with mere synonymity. When we say that a politician ran for office that is . . . merely an instance of a word having different applications. . . .
>
> . . . .
>
> *McKendrick*: So this pressing engagement of yours is a football match.
> *Anderson*: A World Cup qualifier is not just a football match.
> *Stone*: Again, there is no problem here so long as these variations are what I propose to call reliable.
>
> (77)

Suddenly — and mistakenly — called upon to respond to Stone's remarks, Anderson delivers a parody of one of Wittgenstein's early propositions in the *Tractatus Logico-philosophicus*:

> Ah . . . I would only like to offer Professor Stone the observation that language is not the only level of human communication, and perhaps not the most important level. *Whereof we cannot speak, thereof we are by no means silent.* . . . The importance of language is overrated. . . . the important truths are simple and monolithic. The essentials of a given situation speak for themselves, and language is as capable of obscuring the truth as of revealing it. (74–75; my emphasis)

A translation of Wittgenstein's premise reads: "What we cannot speak about we must consign to silence" (151). Anderson's inversion is not anti-

Wittgensteinian, however, as the philosopher himself reversed his position in his later works, arguing that language is not restricted to verbal utterances and that the meaning of words does not reside in their referents but in the uses to which they are put. Stoppard's dramatic translation of the philosopher's idea takes the form of mimed action supplementing, substituting for, and/or contradicting spoken words. The dramatic significance of Anderson's impromptu speech lies less in its propositional content (how are we to take "truth," "simple," and "monolithic"?) than in its rejection of a single system for making meaning. By the scene's end, Anderson has concluded that language is not reliable at all—"The importance of language is overrated. . . . the important truths are simple and monolithic. The essentials of a given situation speak for themselves, and language is as capable of obscuring the truth as of revealing it" (75). Which brings us to scene 6, the dramatic and conceptual dead center of the drama.

In this scene, Anderson stops briefly (so he thinks) to return Hollar's thesis, and discovers that he has blundered into a search of Hollar's apartment. The comic surface of the play's first five scenes momentarily collapses under the weight of the new "reality" of mute terror. Away from the enclave of his Western hotel, Anderson is helpless to intervene or to escape. When ordered inside the Hollar apartment by a Czech-speaking policeman, he reacts by reversing his earlier dismissal of language, insisting upon being shown respect for both his rights and his rank: "Now look here, I am the J. S. Mill Professor of Ethics at the University of Cambridge and I demand that I am allowed to leave or to telephone the British ambassador!" (78). The police respond by shoving him inside the Hollar flat. Both comic and menacing, this is the first of a series of shocks marking the awakening of Anderson—and the viewers. We laugh at seeing Anderson's pretensions fall flat even while we cringe at the brutality of the police. The sudden and unexpected use of force against a person of high rank and class signals the beginning of a new game played by a new set of rules different from those governing the action in the opening scenes.

As our eye on the scene, the camera creates its own commentary on the action. Anderson and the camera move from the exterior front door to the door of the Hollar apartment, to the interior Hollar front door, to the interior flat's hallway, to the inside of Hollar's small front room, and finally to his bedroom where the search is underway. As we penetrate deeper to the core of Hollar's home, the impression of entrapment intensifies. Doors open and mysteriously close again; fearful neighbors peek out from adjoining rooms; Mrs. Hollar repeatedly pulls open the door to the bedroom; the police come and go, shouting in Czech. Much of the spoken dialogue in the scene is Czech, but the viewers nevertheless comprehend the "essentials of the given situation": the search operation is a setup to justify Hollar's arrest and detention. The immediate effect is one of documentary directness, unmediated by aesthetic concern for the shape or appearance of the scene.

However, a second look reveals it to be drily comic, particularly at those moments when the search operation occupies the full frame. While Man 1 *"is going through the books, leafing through each one and looking along the spine,"* Man 2 *"is sorting out the fluff from a carpet sweeper.* Man 4 *is standing on a chair examining the inside of a ventilation grating"* (80, 82). Meanwhile, Anderson continues his comically frustrated attempts to escape to the soccer match, eventually resigning himself to listening to the game on Mrs. Hollar's radio after being forced to relinquish his tickets to a plainclothesman. Thus, the scene concludes with the serio-comic coincidence of Hollar being charged with a trumped-up currency offense while the radio simultaneously announces British player Broadbent's foul against Czech player Deml, preventing him from scoring a certain goal. The seriousness of what is happening to Hollar is brought home by referring it to a form of sport. At a moment of high suspense, Stoppard invites us to compare the ethos of professional soccer with that of the communist-controlled Czech regime: both require that when an individual player's sense of "natural" justice conflicts with the team's need to win, the group ethic will prevail over the individual's sense of fair play.

As in a Hitchcock thriller, Anderson has been unwillingly drawn into a dangerous game to imprison Pavel Hollar from which he will not be freed until he boards the plane to return home. He leaves the Hollar apartment shaken and "out of his depth," with his former student's thesis still in his briefcase and with a new obligation to help him and his family. He returns to his hotel in the following scene, exhausted and relieved, where he overhears two sports reporters dictating copy in the private language (interlaced with telephone dictation codes) that youthful Stoppard had spent several years writing:

> Grayson (*into phone*): Dickinson and Pratt were mostly left standing by Wolker, with a W, and Deml, D for dog, E for Edward, M for mother, L for London . . . who could go round the halls as a telepathy act, stop. Only Crisp looked as if he had a future outside Madame Tussaud's. (91)

Stoppard is not only having fun with journalese here but also satirizing hack prose—"Wilson looked elephantine in everything but memory, stop" (92)—as well as the ethnocentricity of the British references in the dictation. This, together with the philosophers' incomprehensible quibblings, are the sorts of excesses that democratically protected free speech can produce.

Finally, in choosing to help Hollar by smuggling out his thesis in McKendrick's briefcase and by altering his colloquium talk to reflect the gist of Hollar's argument, Anderson reverses a principle—that of respect for one's colleague and host—after experiencing his host's treachery. As long as Anderson, like the agent Philo in *Neutral Ground,* could view his choices from a single vantage point (the propriety of an Oxbridge don), he could be certain of the morally correct way to behave. But when events conspired to give him a more complex vantage on his conduct (that of a British witness for a Czech dissident), he could no longer be absolutely responsible or just, merely relatively so.

The pace of the play's fourth movement quickens as Stoppard cuts between Anderson's revised address on the subject of human rights and a secret police search of Anderson's room. The hidden police menace, now shown directly on screen, suddenly raises the level of threat and suspense undercut by the concluding airplane scene. Once safely aboard the Britain-bound plane, Anderson informs McKendrick that he hid Hollar's paper in his briefcase and uses McKendrick's "catastrophe theory" postulating the necessary reversal of all moral principles to rationalize it. As McKendrick's outrage following the discovery of Anderson's action suggests, it was merely a theory after all, a dashing statement of McKendrick's impatience with the bounds of moral theory that could not withstand its first practical test.

If "satire is militant irony" (Frye 1957, 223) running the gamut between overt invective and the implicit assertion of a satiric norm, then we can identify *EGBDF* with the militant end of the spectrum and place *Professional Foul* somewhere closer to the middle, with its double focus pointing to the sharp differences between communist-bloc East and democratic West. The final example of Stoppardian satire resembles more closely the first: *Dogg's Hamlet, Cahoot's Macbeth,* another maverick hybrid of dramatic fragments and texts, takes us directly into the living room of Czech dissenters where we observe police attempting to upstage a covert performance of Shakespeare's *Macbeth.*

Dogg's Hamlet, Cahoot's Macbeth: Old Dogg Learns New Trick

Like the wall built during each of its two parts, Stoppard's satiric parody grew from a series of distinct "gags" knitted together by a play on Wittgenstein's notion of the language game. The separate components of the play—*Dogg's Our Pet* and *The (15 Minute) Dogg's Troupe Hamlet* (*Cahoot's Macbeth* having been conceived as part of a diptych) — were all produced as occasional pieces for one of Ed Berman's various theatrical enterprises. *Dogg's Our Pet*, an anagram for Berman's "Dogg's Troupe," written to celebrate the opening of the Almost Free Theatre in London's Soho district, provided the platform-building gag with dialogue in English and Dogg, culminating in a mock-scatalogical dedication ceremony very like the one prefacing the later *The (15 Minute) Dogg's Troupe Hamlet*. Stoppard wrote the abbreviated *Hamlet* also at Berman's request, who explained to the playwright that he needed a play to perform while driving around in a double-decker bus. As Stoppard told Nancy Hardin in 1978, *The (15 Minute) Dogg's Troupe Hamlet* did not, in fact, take to the road, but was instead performed outside the National Theatre with the ramparts of the theater serving as Elsinore (164–65). The catalyst for joining *Dogg's Our Pet* and *The (15 Minute) Dogg's Troupe Hamlet* was yet another Berman project — a new British American Repertory Company (BARC) — composed of equity actors from both countries. *Cahoot's Macbeth,* the second half of the double bill, is dedicated to Pavel Kohout, whom he later met in a visit to Czechoslovakia in June of 1977. During this visit, Stoppard also learned about actors Pavel Landovsky and Vlasta Chramostova, all banned from the Czech stage following their involvement with Charter 77, a document calling for the defense of human rights in their country. As Stoppard explains in his preface to the 1980 Faber edition of the play,[3] these actors collaborated in a piece of "Living Room Theatre," a seventy-five-minute *Macbeth* performed privately in people's flats. In *Cahoot's Macbeth,* Stoppard exposes official Czech harassment of dissenting artists and intellectuals while parodying the form of living room theater. The abbreviated *Macbeth* is set inside a private home, is performed by actors banned from the public Czech stage, and is overheard by eavesdropping secret police. As much as any of his works, this piece shows us that even when he writes "seriously," from an attitude of "militant irony," Stoppard attempts to draw the spectator into collaboration with the ideas at play.

In addition to Shakespeare, one of the primary source texts holding together this double bill is Wittgenstein's description of the language game in his *Philosophical Investigations*. In the opening scenes of *Dogg's Hamlet*, Stoppard puts before the spectators a live model of a "primitive language" as the philosopher describes it:

Let us imagine a language . . . meant to serve for communication between a builder A and an assistant B. A is building with building-stones: there are blocks, pillars, slabs and beams. B has to pass the stones, and that in the order in which

A needs them. For this purpose, they use a language consisting of the words "block", "pillar", "slab", "beam". A calls them out; —B brings the stone which he has learnt to bring at such-and-such a call. —Conceive this as a complete primitive language. (3e)

For Wittgenstein, the notion of a language game was roughly analogous to that of a simplified model of the much more complex system of language use that we regularly exercise. Stoppard's parody consists of putting on stage a literal enactment of what is, in Wittgenstein's treatise, a model or metaphor, and further, of using the enactment to illustrate the comic implications of the proposition Wittgenstein advanced when employing his metaphor—that is, the possibility that different groups of people might use the same words to mean fundamentally different things. The comedy arises when members of these different groups attempt to talk to one another using these words. When the English-speaking lorry driver, Easy, enters the stage to announce the arrival of his truck full of lumber, he attempts to solicit the help of the Dogg-speaking schoolboys to unload his freight. Easy uses the word "plank" to name a piece of wood of a particular shape and size. However, the same word in Dogg designates the adjective, "ready," which, in the context of the platform-building game, also signifies "throw me another piece of wood," but not necessarily a plank. Accordingly, when Easy calls out "plank," he always receives a piece of wood from the Dogg-speaking boys, but only sometimes a plank. In spite of a multitude of lexical differences between members of the platform-building tribe, they succeed in completing their task by the end of which Easy and the spectators are learning Dogg, a language that will reappear in *Cahoot's Macbeth*.

After its assembly, the schoolboys mount the platform to perform a fifteen-minute version of *Hamlet*. In its parodically diminutive form, Stoppard's mini-*Hamlet* preserves the outline of the plot and the cliché tags of the major soliloquies while creating the impression of a slapstick speed-through of Shakespeare's play. A two-minute abstract of the thirteen-minute distillation follows after, further compressing the action without repeating the dialogue of the opening version. The overall impression of the mini-*Hamlet* is cliché Shakespeare on two counts—both because its lines have been chosen to point up the missing context that gives them sense in Shakespeare's version, and because the boys speak its lines from duty rather than from love, neither knowing nor caring what it is that they are saying. Stoppard's own deadly experience with classics in the schoolroom may underlie his satiric portrayal of the teaching of Shakespeare, which has been explicated elsewhere in terms of Foucault's analysis of power (Diamond 1986).

It is no accident that the author of *Where Are They Now?*, among other things a condemnation of the violence sanctioned by English public school custom, here shows the violent implications of the domination of convention. One of the Dogg-speaking boys is thrice hit (offstage) by Easy when the lorry driver takes the Dogg lexicon "useless," and "git" in its English sense. And Professor Dogg thrice throws Easy into the wall he is building when the lettered blocks spell out obscenities in Dogg. These scenes are apparently intended to be humorous; but onstage violence (give or take a few shootings) and violence against a child (albeit offstage) is rare enough in Stoppard to mark these incidents with a particular sharpness.

The linguistic domination of Dogg in the first half of the double bill is reversed in the second half, when Dogg becomes a clandestine tribal language for circumventing the censors. The second half of the double bill also inverts the circumstance in which Shakespeare is spoken. Where the *Hamlet* of *Dogg's Hamlet* mocks the compulsory recitation of Shakespeare by captive schoolchildren in the West, the truncated *Macbeth* of *Cahoot's Macbeth* – also parodic, but not in the mocking sense – signifies the clandestine recitation of Shakespeare by censored artists in the East. Here the play has been collapsed not to dispatch it as quickly as possible but to preserve it without detection. Its compression serves to remind us of the danger of performing it at all.

The opening section of the truncated *Macbeth* proceeds as far as the King's murder when the line, "Wake Duncan with thy knocking!" coincides with the Police Inspector knocking at the Hostess's front door. His first appearance marks a comic interlude in the tragedy – a parallel to the Porter scene in Shakespeare's play – during which he indirectly explains the nature and purpose of living room theater as an underground forum for banned actors. The Inspector combines the crude menace of the police from *Professional Foul* with the farcical flare of the Colonel from *EGBDF*. As Stoppard pointed out to a group of university actors performing this piece under his direction, the Inspector's authority is implied in his lines which always top those of the actors: "He always has one better. He scores every time" (quoted in Ruskin and Lutterbie 1983, 552). Domination is again demonstrated through language. Those in power effectively compete with and silence the powerless. When the Inspector refuses to leave, the actors resume their performance of *Macbeth* with the indifference of the *Hamlet*-reciting schoolboys from the earlier play – "*The acting is quick and casual*" (56). We have returned to compulsory

Shakespeare. What would, under normal performing conditions, be a moment of dramatic intensity—the announcing of Duncan's murder—is rendered banal by the Inspector's presence. So that while he forbids the actors to perform one version of *Macbeth* when he is around and a second version when he's not—"Now listen, you stupid bastard. . . . You've only got one *Macbeth*. Because I'm giving this party and there ain't no other" (56)—his being around ensures that they will do exactly what he has forbidden.

The actors leave the stage with the announcement that Macbeth has gone to Scone to be crowned. The second interlude between the actors and the Inspector following this announcement takes up, in a figurative sense, where *Macbeth* has left off, with the Inspector now playing the role of tyrant instead of Porter, issuing veiled threats in the form of false charges he might press against those present, should he wish to. The Inspector's success in outmaneuvering the actors is most obvious in his outrageously funny lines and his strong stage presence. It is as if his comic idiom were part of his attempt to victimize the actors by upstaging them. Repeatedly overridden by the Inspector's parody of gangster talk, the actors begin to express their opinion of the governing regime in lines from Shakespeare's play:

> *Inspector*: . . . Would you care to make a statement?
> *Cahoot*: "Thou hast it now: King, Cawdor, Glamis, all
>   As the weird sister promised . . . "
> *Inspector*: Kindly leave my wife's family out of this. . . .
> *Cahoot*: " . . . and I fear / thou playedst most foully for't . . . "
>
> (61–62)

The Inspector exits soon after, but leaves behind the ceiling microphone. As if on cue, his siren can be heard again on the line, "This tyrant, whose sole name blisters our tongues, / Was once thought honest." Macduff rejoins, "Bleed, bleed poor country!" (72). As their performance becomes increasingly circumscribed by the Inspector's threats, Easy arrives with his lorry full of lumber, now speaking only Dogg, and providing the actors with an alternative language that will evade the state's censors. Having already learned the basics of Dogg during *Dogg's Hamlet*, the spectators now unite with the actors in a delightful game of translating the familiar language of Shakespeare using the lexicon of Dogg.[4]

In spite of the Inspector's return, for a few hopeful moments the lorry full of blocks promises to act as Birnham Wood come to Dunsinane. The now Dogg-speaking actors approach the moment of Macbeth's downfall while Easy proceeds with the building of a platform. Macbeth turns to face Macduff: "Rafters Birnam cakehops hobble Dunsinane, / fry counterpane nit crossly window-framed, / fancifully oblong! . . . [Though Birnam Wood be come to Dunsinane / And thou opposed, being of no woman born, / Yet will I try the last]" (77–78). Sensing that he is losing control of the event, the furious Inspector mounts the now completed platform and, in a parody of Dogg, calls the performance to a halt: "Clamp down on poncy gits like a ton of bricks" (82). He calls in his two Policemen and, while the actors complete the final scene, uses the slabs from part one to build a wall that will close off the proscenium and metaphorically silence the actors. The language (that is, wall-building) game from the first half of the play is thus also repeated with a grim difference. Rather than enabling communication, this wall is intended to prevent it. The play ends pessimistically, as first the platform and then the acting space is occupied by the police. For a moment, Dogg has had its day, but the actors are clearly losing their fight against censorship as the play ends.

The complex interplay between parody and satire in this group of plays defines their difference from Stoppard's major parodies and from his "nuts 'n' bolts" comedies. In *R&GAD, Jumpers,* and *Travesties,* for example, parody functions to resist the domination of major works of the literary and artistic past. *EGBDF* uses parody sparingly, such as at the opening when the symphony musicians omit sound while continuing the mime of tuning their instruments. Our first impulse is to laugh at the customary made obvious through the omission of sound. However, we soon learn the logic of this new convention: Ivanov hears the instruments when we do not. Parody initially draws our attention to Ivanov's difference, which appears at first merely comic but soon grows menacing. In a similar way, Stoppard's use of the musical scale and of the extended metaphor of entrapment within an orchestrated society appears initially comic but gradually grows more serious as Alexander's physical condition deteriorates. The Doctor, a mock-physician, parodies official state wisdom in attempting to cure people who were never sick in the first place. He, too, is humorous, but only as the butt of Stoppard's mockery. The musical score also moves between comic parody (instruments imitating people) and satiric exposure (particular scores being cited ironically to suggest particular characters' follies). *EGBDF* may be the most bitterly Jonsonian of Stoppard's satires, but even it allows the Western observer the luxury of laughter.

In *Professional Foul,* Stoppard waits longer than he does in *EGBDF* before changing gears from humor to aggressive satire, as he wishes to point his finger not only at the repressive East but also at the naive West, keeping before the spectators an awareness of their vantage as citizens of democracies. Only after the scene 3 visit of Pavel Hollar, where the striking differences between the two cultures are made obvious, does the humor approach the pointedness of satire. But even then, ridicule of the Czech government parallels ridicule of Western philosophers and journalists whose uses of language are shown to be either hopelessly analytical, as in Professor's Stone's Colloquium address—" 'You cook well,' says John to Mary. 'You eat well,' says Mary to John" (73)—or trivialized and banal, as in the journalists' dictation. But Stoppard points to a clear difference between Westerners' linguistic follies and the censorship of the East. Following the logic of journalist Milne in *Night and Day,* linguistic excesses are the price we pay for the freedom to choose our language. Anderson makes full use of that freedom in his striking adaptation of Hollar's thesis, delivered in the climactic Colloquium scene. Now fully articulated according to the rules and jargon of ethical philosophy, we hear the difference between Hollar's abbreviated scene 3 description of his thesis and Anderson's full development of it not as a mockery but as a linguistic tribute to the Czech's ideas. Anderson gives Hollar an academic voice while, at the same time, covertly revealing the authorities' silent vices.

Two kinds of philosophical discourse are parodied in *Professional Foul,* speeches like Professor Stone's, which mock the extremely mannered and remote nature of academic philosophy, and Anderson's closing Colloquium address, which, in its difference from what we have come to accept as conventional philosophical discourse, does not mock but draws attention to the unacknowledged dissociation between philosophical arguments and the assumptions about individual liberties that permit those arguments to be expressed. Shakespearean texts also take on a double function in *Dogg's Hamlet, Cahoot's Macbeth. The 15 Minute Hamlet* mocks Professor Dogg's appropriation of Shakespeare as a cultural monument to be venerated by the very young, while the abbreviated *Macbeth* is subverted (after its translation into another parodic language, "Dogg") in order to ridicule a tyrant in the "real" world without suffering his wrath.

In general, Stoppard's use of parody is less striking and self-advertising in the satires. He is not so much interested in creating an imaginative space between texts as he is in drawing attention to how extra-artistic conditions can conspire to shrink that space. Writing satire nudged Stoppard toward experimenting with mime, music, and primitive languages. Perhaps he was responding to what Frye calls the "militancy" of the irony in satire, that is, to the satirist's insistence upon the discrepancy between how a world might be and how it is. He was filled with a strong sense of moral purpose, but expressed his moral in negative terms, as a fending off or parrying of systems of thought that restrict individuals' right to free expression. Endowed with this sense of indignation, and suspicious of declaiming it overtly, Stoppard retreats from the virtuosic tapestries of his major parody plays and moves toward a new sublimated virtuosity — the challenge of displaying the limits of logocentricity itself: whereof one cannot speak, thereof one need not be silent!

Chapter 5

Postmodern Polyphony: *Night and Day, The Real Thing, Hapgood*

Night and Day: A Chekhovian Adventure

Between the appearance of *Travesties* (1975) and *Night and Day* (1978), Stoppard wrote several plays that appear to abandon Henry Carr's art-for-art's-sake stance for a quasi-didactic staging of political oppression in Eastern Europe (see chap. 4). Written for television, stage, and symphony platform, respectively, none of these was conceived as a major stage piece on the scale of *R&GAD, Jumpers,* or *Travesties. Night and Day* was to be the next major Stoppard stage play, a romance about the adventures of British colonials and journalists covering a war in a fictional African country. Stoppard modified the conventions of psychological realism for the dialogue and sets of *Night and Day,* conventions he had largely avoided altogether in his stage plays since *Enter a Free Man.* And he deliberately and carefully modified the illusory "likeness to life" as he had in *Free Man,* by giving central characters Guthrie and Ruth Carson scenes of dream and fantasy in which they act out what they wish or fear to be true.

In moving away from the Joycean style shifts of *Travesties* toward a speech and staging closer to the surfaces of "real life," Stoppard was determined to test new ground as a playwright. "What I'd like to write now," he told Ronald Hayman in 1974 after his success with *Travesties,* "is . . . a literary piece — so that the energy can go into the literary side of what I do. I'd like to write a quiet play" (1979, 12). Two years later, again while talking to Hayman, Stoppard indicated he had not yet written the literary play, but he had begun to imagine it as something J. B. Priestley might write: " . . . a professor or a doctor with a grey-haired wife and a problem child, and the maid comes in with the muffin dish and they talk about the weather a bit" (140). Later still,

137

in November of 1979, he told the *New York Times*'s Robert Berkvist that he had hoped not only to find a new style for his new play but also to write a major part in a "straight" story-telling drama for an actress of Diana Rigg's (the original Ruth) stature. His third wish was to write something that would pay tribute to his former profession of journalism (Interview with Robert Berkvist 1979). All of this was to come together in a play that he was writing for Michael Codron, a West-End (thus commercial) producer, which meant that the large cast and elaborate sets of the earlier stage plays would be prohibitively costly. The final result of this turn in Stoppard's stagecraft was actually two plays held not quite successfully together by a remarkable female character.

One of the two, the play involving British journalists covering a story in a remote third-world country, loosely parodies Evelyn Waugh's Fleet Street satire, *Scoop*. As Tim Brassell has noted, Stoppard borrows pointedly from the situation and plot of Waugh's novel, while glancing less directly at its indictment of Fleet Street careerism (1985, 206). Stoppard's loose parody of Waugh bears many of the marks of a traditional romance of adventure culminating in a quest. The essential elements of the romance are all present, albeit in muted form: young hero Jacob Milne is on a lonely and dangerous search for "truth" in the form of a story about the impending civil war in a remote and exotic location. During his quest, he undergoes a struggle against those who would like to block him from the story (unionist Wagner and, indirectly, President Mageeba). He is killed in pursuit of this truth and subsequently is celebrated by the lesser remaining figures, Wagner who writes his obituary, and Ruth, who represents his idealism during a debate on press freedom.

The second play, which Jim Hunter alluded to as a potential "succession to Chekhov at last" (in Bloom 1986, 119), is a romance of living and loving among bored, wealthy "colonials." Its starring player, Ruth Carson, wife to mine owner Geoffrey, is a formidably beautiful and witty Chekhovian heroine for whom love and idealism have faded with the passing of time. Ruth's attempts to grip on to life through casual sex and alcohol resemble those of the far more desperate and exhausted Laura Malquist in Stoppard's novel. But Stoppard has developed Ruth more fully; she has a functioning marriage and can still feel passion, as she feels it for Jacob Milne. It is only when she learns that Milne has been killed that she is driven to seek consolation in bed (again) with journalist Richard Wagner. Stoppard attempts to tie the play about journalism to the Chekhovian comedy through the character of Ruth, who, in spite of her own cynical view of the press, falls in love with a young, free-lance reporter. The fact that she has also shared a hotel room with Wagner during a weak moment on a recent trip to London has given her a second reason to dislike the press and forms a second link between the two plays.

In both the journalists' adventure story and in Ruth's Chekhovian romance, Stoppard moves the spectators smoothly between scenes of violent action, dreamlike reverie, and heated debate. His new muted style of layered comedy is evident in the opening scene. The action begins with an empty stage and a beautifully lit cyclorama suggesting an African sunset and ends — again at sunset — in a garden extending into an elegant veranda/contemporary living room. As the cyclorama darkens, a helicopter approaches and hovers overhead, training a spotlight across the stage. When the spot disappears, a jeep drives on with its headlights pointed at the audience and the sound of machine-gun fire starts up. Photographer Guthrie jumps out of the jeep, shouting, and is gunned down. A light change reveals Guthrie asleep on a lounge chair in the Carsons' garden at sundown. A telex machine chatters "*in bursts like the machine gun*," while African rock music blares from a cassette player. Gradually the spectators realize in the moments following the opening that what they took for "real" was actually Guthrie's dream, and a prophetic dream at that. We learn from Guthrie near the play's close that his nightmare has become fact, that Jacob Milne has been caught in cross fire and killed while attempting to turn his jeep around in the no-man's-land separating rebel and loyal forces. As we discover our error in mistaking dream for stage "reality," we briefly straddle the two realms of night and day between which Stoppard floats his play.

Ruth's entrance immediately after the dream is both "realistic" and parodic, Stoppard taking care to create the impression of ordinariness by mimicking the cause-and-effect relationships of trivial daily events. When we hear a car door slam and see Ruth enter carrying several packages, we seem to be in the realm of domestic comedy. But when she moves immediately to shut off the African rock music coming from the cassette player with the line "Those drums, those damned drums!" (2), we are momentarily in a parodic film about white colonials trapped in blackest Africa. As we soon discover, Ruth plays many parts: loyal wife and attentive mother, cynical woman-of-the-world, seductress, and tart. In her Chekhovian idleness and melancholy, she parodies her own situation as a bored sundowner trying to pass the time with a kind but absent husband. Some of the poses she takes up include Elizabeth Taylor in "Elephant Walk," Deborah Kerr in "King Solomon's Mines," and Tallulah Bankhead cautioning herself, "Watch yourself, Tallulah." Both performer and spectator, she stands inside and outside of Kambawe's provincial vulgarity, literally flying back and forth between Africa and Europe when the need arises.

Stoppard signals Ruth's divided self by giving her two voices. Once she has awakened the sleeping Guthrie on her patio, and Guthrie tells her that he was directed to meet another reporter, Dick Wagner, at the Carsons' home, Ruth splits in half and begins to speak in a second, private voice, "Ruth," not necessarily more "real" than the public voice, but more "inner," pointing to the private woman hidden by the public mask. As "Ruth" lets us in on her thoughts, we form a special intimacy with her, and this intimacy is a common thread, helping us to move back and forth between the two parts of the play.

Act 2 opens with Chekhovian romance in the form of Ruth's dream seduction of Jacob Milne—the second of the play's two fantasy sequences we mistake for real. Even in this dream scene, Ruth occasionally speaks through "Ruth," who thus becomes the fiction of a fiction speaking to Milne about a fantasy she had about seducing him: "Woke up fluttering with imminent risk. . . . Like walking along the top board knowing you don't have to jump" (76). Stoppard's attempt to accommodate a divided Ruth/"Ruth" without confusing the audience about which of her two selves was speaking at any one time required him to make an unusually large number of textual changes—many of them changes to Ruth's lines—in the eighteen months following the play's London premiere (Gaskell 1980, 165). In at least one place, the act 2 Mageeba scene, an entirely new speech was added in what proved to be Stoppard's most daring and perhaps least successful use of her interior monologue. Wagner is questioning President Mageeba about the possibility of civil war. Mageeba tells him that if the rebel Colonel Shimbu does not show at the Carsons', then Wagner may call their conflict "war" at ten o'clock the next morning. The ominous announcement carries dramatic weight in the male world of the journalism adventure drama, but not in the Chekhovian world of Ruth's romantic fantasy. In the pause following this announcement, "Ruth" suddenly reflects on her habit of dramatizing herself using the image of her grandmother's packet of salt with a label showing a girl holding a packet of salt, and so on. She ends with the lines,

> I talk to myself in the middle of an *imaginary* conversation, which is itself a refuge from some other conversation altogether, frequently imaginary. (93)

In case we are confused, Ruth tells us that "Ruth" talks to herself at one and even two removes from the play's other characters.[1] As Diana Rigg put it, this passage is "the key to Ruth" (quoted in Gaskell 1980, 170), but it comes late in the play and at a moment of dramatic intensity that has, heretofore, excluded Ruth altogether. In *Travesties,* we are prepared to jump tracks from one fictional strand to another, but in the more delicate idiom of *Night and Day,* we are emotionally derailed by such abrupt changes of gear.

Stoppard may have intended Ruth's sudden and apparently irrelevant intrusion to be another sort of ambush, like *Travesties'* second act, where two political ideologies bump against one another. And this raises the question of the dramatic relationship between Ruth's Chekhovian drama and the journalists' adventure romance. For the most part, Ruth functions as a sort of still center in the play, around which the journalists furiously search for a scoop— or at least talk about searching for one. In their talk, we hear the variously disguised voice of author Stoppard reflecting on an institution he both knows and respects. Photographer Guthrie, the quietest and most retiring of the group, is the least overtly egotistical and probably the most experienced. Wagner is the most egotistical, competitive, and crude. Milne (perhaps an echo of A. A. Milne, author of *Winnie the Pooh*, whose Edwardian hero, Christopher, Milne resembles) is the youngest, highest born, best educated, and most naive member of the trio.

These portraits offer us further evidence of Stoppard moving away from the sustained highly presentational parody of the earlier plays toward a more fragmentary, muted parody blended with surface realism. The journalists provide Stoppard with an opportunity for the first extended discussion of newswriting in his work, mediated by subtle references to the hardboiled newsman type from films of the 1940s and 1950s. Just as Ruth occasionally sees herself as a film heroine, so the journalists parody the "tough guy" from films about crime and its news coverage. In describing his work on *Night and Day,* Stoppard told the editors of *Gambit*:

> I was . . . interested by the way journalists tend to ape their fictitious models. It's a certain way of behaving which derives from "tough" films. Of course, in naturalism there is a reciprocal thing between the model and life. . . . (6)

Wagner is the most extreme of these tough types, while Milne is a parody of a public school gentleman who gets the scoops and the beautiful women all without seeming to try very hard. While all three journalists seem, at one time or another, to speak for author Stoppard, Milne is given an autobiographical link missing from the other two. When he and Ruth discuss the free press, Ruth quips, "I'm with you on the free press. It's the newspapers I can't stand" (65–66). Milne concedes the point with what is probably one of the rare extended biographical references in Stoppard's plays:

> I started off . . . looking up to Fleet Street stringers, London men sometimes,
> on big local stories. I thought it was great. Some of the best times in my life have
> been spent sitting in a clapped-out Ford Consul outside a suburban
> house . . . waiting to grab a crooked landlord or a footballer's runaway
> wife. . . . . I felt part of a privileged group, *inside society and yet outside it,* with
> a license to scourge it and duty to defend it, night and day, the street of adven-
> ture, the fourth estate. And the thing is—I was dead right. . . . .Junk journalism
> is the evidence of a society that has got at least one thing right, that there should
> be nobody with the power to dictate where responsible journalism begins.
> (66–67; my emphasis)

There is a strand of "reality" both in the parallel between what Milne says and
what Stoppard believes to be true of journalism (Interview with Nancy Hardin
1981, 159), and in the fact that the entire journalism debate in the play is rooted
in a real-life 1970s debate on the merits of the closed shop—a National Union
of Journalists proposal to suppress or "black" news written by non-members.
While the NUJ's original intent in enforcing 100 percent membership was to
strengthen its negotiating position in wage disputes, opponents of the closed
shop, including Stoppard, argued that it could result in a mechanism for censorship, with a single group of self-selected professionals deciding what could
and could not be printed.[2]

Ruth herself, in all of her fictional poses, is finally the link between the
male journalists' romance of adventure and the Chekhovian comedy of frustration. The two plays collide during the second act visit of President Mageeba
when the merits of a free press are discussed from a series of divergent view-
points. Stoppard integrates Ruth more successfully into the journalism debate
in the later part of this scene where she quotes Milne's position on the "closed
shop," passing it off, with a dig at Wagner, as the opinion of her young son,
Alastair:

> Alastair's theory is that it's the very free-for-all which guarantees the freedom
> of each. "You see, mummy," he said, "you don't have to be a millionaire to con-
> tradict one. It isn't the millionaires who are going to stop you, it's the Wagners
> who don't trust the public to choose the marked card. (97)

Ruth seems here to be parodying Milne, to have begun to think as he thinks,
presenting his libertarian position in his absence as a means of keeping him
alive on stage and in her imagination. Once Guthrie announces Milne's death,
Ruth's bitter view of newspapers emerges, colored by her sorrow as well as
by her personal experience with "yellow" journalism several years before: "I'm

not going to let you think he died for free speech and the guttering candle of democracy. . . . You're all doing it to impress each other and be top dog. . . ." (108). Ruth insists upon testing principles against practice. In the real world of real journalism, Jake was a casualty of an ego war. It is against Ruth's attempt to read Milne's death as absurd and wasteful that Guthrie recites the celebrated equation between information and light:

> I've been around a lot of places. People do awful things to each other. But it's worse in places where everybody is kept in the dark. It really is. Information is light. Information, in itself, about anything, is light. That's all you can say, really. (*He exits.*) (108–9)

Stating in positive terms the ideology of the Stoppard play, Guthrie asserts that writers must always be permitted to express their own "truth" even if it is partial, contingent, and at variance from others' truths. This speech metaphorically echoes Milne's earlier defense of a "free" press: "If you've got a free press everything is correctable, and without it everything is concealable" (65). Stoppard created some confusion in claiming for Milne's statement the status of "truth" during a 1980 interview with *Gambit* editors: "What Milne says is true. . . . With a free press everything is correctable. . . . I wanted him to be known to be speaking the truth" (15). This is truth with a small *t,* not the eternal, ahistorical variety. Further, it is one of several such "truths" given a staging in the play, whose "thesis" insofar as it can be said to have one, is that theses in either journalism or literature are to be treated with suspicion.

Travesties' focus on the artist as a producer of meaning has given way to a focus on newspapers as producers of information. But because newspapers, unlike art works, reflect the world in a relatively direct way, Stoppard chooses a quasi-realistic treatment for this play—interwoven with parodic moments—and submits the characters' arguments to the contingencies that impinge upon the actual production of newspapers. Pressures like the journalists' competition for a story, squabbles between labor and management, and the desire to sell papers by printing sensational and cheap news all become part of the staging of news production.

Finally, *Night and Day* shows Stoppard in transition, attempting to write a quiet play touching on his own experience as a journalist while calling attention to its mediation of "reality" in a variety of new and original ways. Ruth/"Ruth" is the most interesting and provocative of Stoppard's experiments in a play that lies halfway between romance and reality, night and day. His next major stage play would benefit from both the strengths and weaknesses of this one, showing him capable of writing at least two naturalistic parts for women and a role for a man demanding considerable emotional range.

The Real Thing: Jamesian Déjà Vu

With Henry James's story by the same title serving as one of his sources, Stoppard's recent play stages in a survey of play-writing styles the Jamesian paradox by which we prefer the represented subject over its real-life model. The artist-narrator of James's story depends upon the income he makes from illustrations to support his "real" vocation as a serious painter of portraits. Like playwright Henry, who sometimes writes science fiction screenplays for money (and author Stoppard, who does movie projects for the same reason?), James's artist has what Stoppard has called "a cheap side and an expensive side" (Interview with David Gollob and David Roper 1981, 13). When an impoverished but immaculately genteel couple presents itself in his studio to act as models for the ladies and gentlemen in a novel that the artist has contracted to illustrate, he agrees to try them out on the assumption that it might be a help to him to work from models who are the real thing—a real English lady and gentleman. But the painter discovers otherwise, learning from their fruitless collaboration the lesson that "in the deceptive atmosphere of art even the highest respectability may fail of being plastic" (James 1977, 132). Playwright Henry reaches a similar conclusion when attempting to write about love. "Loving and being loved is unliterary. It's happiness expressed in banality and lust" (*The Real Thing*, 39). Both artists abhor cliché and must solve the problem of creating a believable illusion without relying upon tried and tested gimmicks. James's narrator triumphs by using his servants, both of them "natural" mimics, as models of gentility and his genteel couple as his servants. Stoppard's Henry triumphs by oscillating between literary and subliterary dialogue, between the articulate and the inarticulate, creating the illusion of real romance at those moments when he gives up on metaphor and simply declares: "I love love. I love having a lover and being one. . . . . I love you so" (43). Both works attempt to demonstrate that we find pleasing the fictional reproduction of events we have experienced as actual. Both ask the theoretical question posed by Anne Ubersfeld, "Why do these reproductions . . . give pleasure rather than seem like the tedious repetitions of what exists . . . " (1982, 128), by noting that mere reproductions fail to give pleasure at all. In the case of *The Real Thing,* the theatrical copying of human action and speech is interesting for showing how life imitates plays just as plays imitate life. Stoppard's spectators find pleasure both in what Ubersfeld has described as the psychic reassurance of observing this procedure at a safe remove (1982, 128) and in the controlled demonstration of the uncanniness of dramatic illusion. What we see on stage is both real by virtue of being present with the spectator, and it is unreal by virtue of signifying absent people and actions. We believe in the virtual realness of the successfully staged event while simultaneously recognizing its necessary falsity. Given his interest in exploring the fluid frontier where the real and the artificial meet, it is no surprise that Stoppard's characters all have careers in the theater. But we are nevertheless surprised when the opening scene turns out to have been the performance of a play.

Scene 1 opens on a contemporary living room set where an architect husband sits building a house from a deck of playing cards while awaiting the return of his wife from a supposed sales trip to Switzerland. Having found her passport in her recipe drawer, the husband deduces (falsely, as it turns out), that the trip was a cover for an illicit love affair. When his returning wife enters the stage, he gives her little or no chance to defend herself except by exiting, suitcase in hand, like Ibsen's Nora who left her illusory "house of dolls" for something more like the real world. Scene 2 opens as actress Charlotte, the accused wife from scene 1, re-enters the stage in what appears to be her real-life living room. Rumpled from a night's sleep and clearly frustrated with her role in the previous night's performance, she loses no time telling her "real" husband, playwright Henry, what she thinks of his play, *House of Cards*. The joke is on the spectator, who, cued by an illusionist set and dialogue, has read the opening scene as a slice-of-life marriage play.

But the "life" in *House of Cards* begins to fade like an insubstantial pageant before the domestic comedy of scene 2, where we learn that Charlotte's objection to her role in husband Henry's play rests on its failure to be more like real life. As she tells her co-star Max during a visit with his actress wife, Annie, the problem with her character is that she is "a victim of Henry's fantasy—a quiet, faithful bird with an interesting job, and a recipe drawer, and a stiff upper lip . . . trembling for him" (20). That is, she is too unlike the real Charlotte, who, we later discover, has had no fewer than nine affairs during her marriage to Henry. "If he'd given [me] a lover instead of a temporary passport," she tells Max, "we'd be in a play" (20). The spectator pays closer attention to the fiction's boundaries after the surprise scene 2 opening, when the frames distinguishing one fiction from the other separate in the first of a series of successive, overlapping fictions. We now look on through (at least) two frames, watching actors playing actors who also play multiple roles. Stoppard had already used this device—twice—at the opening of each of *Night and Day*'s two acts where we mistake dream or fantasy scenes for the larger fiction from which they have departed.

As early as scenes 3 and 4, the set and characters have begun to echo previous speech and action. Scene 3 places us inside Max's living room "with furniture and doors," the stage directions tell us, "reminiscent of the beginning of Scene One" (36). That is, we are about to witness another accusation scene, but this one in the relatively real-seeming frame play. A shaken Max confronts his wife Annie with "ocular proof" of her affair with Henry: a handkerchief stained with their lovemaking. It seems that Henry has been unfaithful to Charlotte with Annie, the actress wife of actor Max from *House of Cards*. Scene 4, set in a "makeshift" living room after Annie and Henry have moved in together, also doubles back to an earlier moment. It should, the stage directions read, remind us immediately of scene 2—the "real" domestic comedy of Henry and Charlotte's dissolving marriage, itself an echo of the opening *House of Cards*. The visual suggestion of replication momentarily blurs the distinction between inner and outer frame. Perhaps the frame play—*The Real Thing*—is an imitation of the inner play—*House of Cards*—whose fable of infidelity it will recycle at least three times.

But we soon discover that the marriage between Henry and Annie is not like any of the earlier marriages we have seen. It appears to be the real thing, an illusion again created by exposing the procedure by which real-seeming characters are created. Both Annie and Henry speak on—at least—two levels, as "real" people commenting on their roles as artists, and as artists commenting upon their "real" lives. Stoppard has learned to create complex characters and to expose the illusion of character building without resorting to the awkward division of *Night and Day*'s Ruth/"Ruth." Both Annie and Henry pass effortlessly between their "real" and professional selves during this intimate scene. It is as a man sorry to have disappointed his lover that Henry confesses to Annie that he can't "write" love: "I don't know how to write love. I try to write it properly and it just comes out embarrassing. It's either childish or it's rude" (40). And it is as a woman that Annie objects to the professional attention Henry feels obliged to give actress Miranda Jessop when she appears in a television play. Is Henry interested in her as a woman or as an actress? Annie tells Henry, "You'll like her. She wears leopard skin pants. . . . I shared a dressing room with her" (41). Later in the scene, when Annie taunts Henry by repeating a political slogan, he taunts her back: "Do you mean real leopard skin or just printed nylon?" (42). The scene stages love in both a mimetic and a non-mimetic style, with Annie advising Henry how to "write love" by quoting Strindberg's seduction scene from *Miss Julie*. "You'll have to learn to do subtext," she offers. "Mine is supposed to be steaming with lust but there's nothing rude on the page" (39–40). As Leslie Thompson has suggested, *The Real Thing* is evidence that Stoppard has in fact learned to "do" subtext, an accomplishment implicitly celebrated in this scene.

The conclusion of act 1 marks a stoppage or temporary stasis both in the fable and in the spectators' interpretive activity. We are beginning a new story, that of Henry and Annie's lives together. In act 2, the continuing romantic fable of Annie and Henry begins to overlap with, to echo and to resurrect, a series of other romantic fables in the fictional past and present. Act 2 opens with another presentation of another writer's art—a script written by prisoner Brodie to publicize his case. In another playful reference to the real Stoppard's life and work, we learn that Annie has suggested that Brodie write for television because "TV plays get talked about, make some impact. Get his case reopened" (49). In 1977 Stoppard had explained his decision to write *Professional Foul* in support of Charter 77 using nearly identical words: "On a subject like this a TV play would have more impact than a play for the stage. After all, on TV you would get a large audience on a single night" (Shulman 1978). And in Henry's irreverent reading of Brodie's play, we hear every preference of real playwright Stoppard violated, from his abhorrence of cliché and overstatement to his suspicion of "messages":

> "You put me in mind of Mussolini, Mary. People used to say about Mussolini, he may be a Fascist, but at least the trains run on time. Makes you wonder why British Rail isn't totally on time, eh?"
> "What do you mean?"
> "I mean it's a funny thing. The Fascists are in charge but the trains are late often as not."
> "But this isn't a Fascist country."
> "Are you quite sure of that, Mary? Take the army—"
>
> (48)

Brodie's writing, says Henry, is not the real thing. Real writing has an absolute obligation to words, regardless of the writer's intention. From Annie's point of view, Brodie has something "real" to write about, even if he cannot write well. From Henry's point of view, the reality of one's subject has nothing to do with ensuring the authenticity of the writing. Stoppard has written this debate scene with its by-now famous analogy between words and cricket bats, with an Aristophanic zest that appears to lift it outside the dramatic frame as a statement by author Stoppard:

> [Words are] innocent, neutral, precise, standing for this, describing that, meaning the other, so that if you look after them you can build bridges across incomprehension and chaos. But when they get their corners knocked off, they're no good any more, and Brodie knocks corners off without knowing he's doing it. (55)

But Annie pulls the purple prose back into the comedy, deconstructing Henry's principle by quoting from his practice. She reads aloud a page of script he has just completed: "'Seventy-nine. Interior. Commander's capsule. From Zadok's p.o.v. we see the green glow of the laser strike force turning towards us. . . .'" (55). Henry defends his compromise by alluding to the ways in which real life can impinge on art, can falsify or downgrade it: "That's not words, that's pictures. The movies. Anyway, alimony doesn't count" (55). If *The Real Thing* attempts to present "a sacramental view of language" (Delaney 1985, 49), it does so ironically. The Annie-Henry debate on writing ends, as all such debates do in Stoppard's plays, at an impasse. In exasperation, Henry echoes the husband in the opening *House of Cards* by implicitly accusing Annie of caring for Brodie: "*Why Brodie.* Do you fancy him or what?" (54). When he realizes his error, Annie refuses to let him take back his words. "Too late" (54), she tells him, a phrase that his daughter will repeat later as she leaves to follow her lover on his fairground tour.

When we next see Annie, she is tactfully fending off the flirtation of a young actor, Billy, on a Glasgow-bound train in dialogue borrowed from Brodie's play. The Billy-Annie scene echoes the real story of Annie-Brodie's accidental meeting on a train which in turn has become the opening scene of Brodie's play which Annie and Billy now playfully recite on their way in a real train to Glasgow to rehearse Ford's play, *'Tis Pity She's A Whore* (which Annie may be, but we never know for certain). Billy has agreed to play the role of Brodie not for the sake of art, but because, like Brodie, he feels "real" love for Annie. In the following scene, the coincidence of life and fiction continues as Henry's ex-wife Charlotte narrates her loss of virginity at the age of seventeen to the actor who had played Giovanni to her Annabella in Ford's play. Stoppard again delays one scene before showing us Annie's now very real affair with Billy during a rehearsal of the Ford play. Her unwitting imitation of both the role and the life of youthful Charlotte recalls the playwright's description of her in scene 2 as *"very much like the woman whom Charlotte has ceased to be"* (15).

As Henry's scene 10 confrontation with Annie verifies, we have circled back to the marriage crisis in *House of Cards*. Annie returns, suitcase in hand, to a suspicious husband who has turned their bedroom upside down looking for positive proof of her cheating. Like the wife in scene 1, Annie refuses to be questioned; like the husband, Henry persists, but he's not nearly so clever as his fictional precursor. The verbal exchange between Henry and Annie reads more like "ordinary talk" than the "written" dialogue of the opening scene, more like compressed speech under emotional pressure, and consequently more verisimilar than its earlier version, more like the real thing:

> *Henry*: I thought you were on the sleeper.
> *Annie*: What's the matter?
> *Henry*: I was wondering what happened to you.
> *Annie*: Nothing happened to me. Have you had lunch?
> *Henry*: No. Did you catch the early train this morning, then?
> *Annie*: Yes. Scratch lunch, all right? . . . .
> *Henry*: I phoned the hotel.
> *Annie*: When?
> *Henry*: Last night. They said you'd checked out.
>
> (67–68)

Like her scene 1 fictional counterpart, Annie refuses to be contrite, but Stoppard leaves teasingly ambiguous the question of whether she has actually committed the deed that the wife in *House of Cards* merely seemed to have done. According to Charlotte's rules of play writing, we are now "in a play," with a genuine affair started and no end in sight. The tartan scarf Henry pulls out of a bag at the scene's close signifies the complex layering of the illusory and the real built up in the first nine scenes. As a trite symbol of Scotland, a love token, a compensatory gift, and an echo of the prop from the opening scene, Annie's gift for Henry is as false as it is predictable. It is the sort of cliché that one expects in a second-rate romance. Once again, by seeming to have come full circle in the narrative, Stoppard has given us a ground of similarity between scenes 1 and 10 on which to detect differences in theatrical illusion. The result is that we accept the greater verisimilitude of the play's later scenes not because we have been tricked to take the unreal for the real but because we have learned to read the "real" as a hybrid of life and art, truth and fiction.

When we next see Henry, he is in fact playing the role of dignified cuck-

old, breaking into tears only after Annie exits the scene. But rather than trans-
forming the comedy into a model of fourth-wall realism, Henry's sobbing
completes the survey of styles—Ibsenite, Strindbergian, Jacobean, pop, and
Shakespearean—through which the playwright and spectator are investigating
the nature of the theatrical real thing. Even here the play evades a mere copy
of reality by echoing itself: we "see" Henry's tears framed by Max's earlier
breakdown at the news of Annie's betrayal. We have learned to read even the
most verisimilar moments as imitations of imitations.

When the real Brodie at last appears on stage in the closing scene, he
illustrates the perversity of James's principle, what his narrator calls the "law
in virtue of which the real thing could be so much less precious than the unreal"
(James 1977, 134). As long as Brodie was the abstract symbol of a cause, as
long as he was represented by others but never directly on stage, he had the
magic suggestiveness of artifice. But once he appears repeating the clichés of
his play, having "become" the Committee's image of a working-class victim-
hero, he loses the appeal of both the real and the fictional and descends to the
merely actual. Without an awareness of himself as either real or unreal, but
now armed with a real-seeming language, Brodie is being portrayed as the
play's Caliban, ungrateful, lecherous, violent, a metaphor for the sinister implications of false literacy already displayed in comic form by Annie and
Henry's daughter, Debbie. However, Brodie's appearance at the play's close
also disturbs, too abruptly introducing a menacing and rather nasty note in an
otherwise thoroughly urbane comedy. Stoppard has not worked through carefully enough his treatment of Private Brodie, except to suggest that in his lack
of self-consciousness, he is something other than the real thing.

Real play writing, as Stoppard would have us view it, is neither the
seamless illusion of reality nor a surrealist departure from mimesis. It is not
a simple reversing or substituting of the illusory for the real but a suggestion
of their reciprocity. Stoppard had already treated this exchange farcically in
Real Inspector Hound; The Real Thing attempts with greater delicacy to create
the impression of lifelike art and artlike life, doubling back on its own narrative, set, and action to create a sense of carefully controlled déjà vu. When
Henry and Annie head for the bedroom at the conventionally comic close of
the play, we stand both in and above the action, Prospero-like, watching the
real thing round into a sleep.

Staging an Experiment: *Hapgood*

Together with her twin brother, Isabel Florence Hapgood (1850–1928) was
the firstborn of Asa and Lydia Hapgood. While growing up in Massachusetts

and New Jersey, Isabel largely taught herself the Germanic and Romance languages as well as Russian, Polish, and Old Church Slavonic. At the age of thirty-six she began a career as a literary translator, providing the first direct translations from Russian to English of the great modern Russian novels of Tolstoy, Gogol, Gorky, and Turgenev. Described by a Moscow professor as "tall, loud, and forceful" (quoted in Whittaker 1988, 64), she appears to have been every bit as extraordinary as her stage namesake. Together with her "twinship," her long and distinguished career as a foreign correspondent, editorial writer, and reviewer for the New York *Evening Post* and the *Nation*, helps to account for her appeal to author Stoppard. Her function as a cultural link between East and West has been duplicated by her fictional double who not only speaks Russian but also has a child by her Russian "joe," agent Joseph Kerner, thus linking the two cultures biologically as well as linguistically.

But Isabel Florence Hapgood is only one of the more directly traceable references woven throughout Stoppard's text. Hapgood's code name, "Mother," puns on the connotations of motherhood in both Russia and England. She received her name while still a green agent by virtue of acting as "mother" at tea-pouring time in her all-male office. Now the "mother" of her own unit, she both pours the tea and makes the operative decisions. When Kerner calls her his "mamushka," or "mommy," he is using the diminutive as a lover's term of affection. But "Mother" also has deeper roots in the Russian concept of motherland, the mystical attachment to the land conveyed by the term that Hapgood uses (claiming to have cribbed it from Nabokov) to describe why Kerner may have been turned back by his Russian sources—*toska po rodine*—"homesickness squared." We eventually conclude that Kerner may have been turned by both homesickness and blackmail resulting from the Soviets' discovery that he had had a son by his British case officer.

Hapgood's reference to Nabokov, whose parody of the thriller formula, *Despair,* Stoppard had adapted for the screen in 1978, is a clue to the play's Nabokovian sympathies. Three sets of twins appear in the course of the action, the nameless Russian twins, Ridley and his twin brother, and Hapgood and her pseudo-twin, Celia Newton. Deploying a real or imagined twin allows the secret agent to be in two places at the same time, a distinct advantage in the realm of espionage. But that is only their practical utility. At their most Nabokovian, twins insidiously undermine all notions of fixity—fixed time, fixed space, personal identity, and reliable perception. "A double agent," says Joseph Kerner, "is like a trick of the light" (10). Twins defeat surveillance because when you know what one of them is doing you can't be certain where she is, and when you know where she is, you can't be certain what she's doing. Invoking Nabokov's name and some of the games he plays with his readers, Stoppard extends his own exploration of the reciprocal relation between the imaginary and the real introduced in *The Real Thing.*

Like Nabokov himself, who, besides literary ability, claimed to have had an early gift for mathematics and whose contribution to the science of lepidopterology is a matter of record, agent Joseph Kerner takes a scientific approach to the art of spying and an artful approach to science. A theoretical physicist, he adores games, especially the spy game, but also verbal games, puns, tactical stratagems, sports, and mathematics. More resilient and dramatically explicit than Nabokov's haunted, old-world cynics, Kerner speaks to his intelligence colleagues Blair and Hapgood in language Stoppard adapted from *The Feynman Lectures on Physics,* especially those in chapter 37, "Quantum Behavior." His similes are code for the behavior of spies and for the nature of reality:

> You can't make a picture of what Bohr proposed, an electron does not go round like a planet, it is like a moth which was there a moment ago, it gains or loses a quantum of energy and it jumps, and at the moment of the quantum jump it is like two moths, one to be here and one to stop being there; an electron is like twins, each one unique, a unique twin. (49)

Kerner is the artful physicist who can think along (at least) two tracks simultaneously, but neither he nor his "lectures" constitute a discursive core justifying the play's two acts. This is not a "thesis drama" any more than was *Night and Day,* but a playful metaphor comparing human behavior to the behavior of subatomic particles whose infinitesimal and lightning-quick movements can only be hypothesized. Feynman explains that scientists must also resort to metaphor when describing the nature of unknown things: "We know how large objects will act," Feynman writes, "but things on a small scale just do not act that way. So we have to learn about them in a sort of abstract or imaginative fashion and not by connection with our direct experience" (1963, vol. 1, chap. 2, 37). When investigating the subatomic level of matter, the physicist must think like Stoppard's artful spy.

The spy thrillers of John Le Carré and Len Deighton turn on the two-handed attempt to retrieve/conceal authentic information, that is, secrets. Stoppard had adapted its conventions twenty years earlier to television (*Neutral Ground* 1968) and, more recently, to radio (*The Dog It Was That Died* 1982; see chap. 2). Both of these works focused on the agent's bitter struggle to sort out lies from truth, loyalty to himself from loyalty to his agency. *Hapgood*'s Joseph Kerner has solved this dilemma by refusing to accept a Newtonian view of physical or human behavior as defined by exclusive causes and effects. When Paul Blair asks him if he is working as a triple agent, Kerner rejects the question's assumption:

> You think everybody has no secret or one big secret, they are what they seem or they are the opposite. You look at me and think: *Which is he*? Plus or minus? . . . We're all doubles. Even you. (72)

Kerner is not, like agent Purvis from *Dog It Was,* genuinely confused about which side he prefers—Russia or Britain; rather, he sees both as relatively corrupt and unjust. Subatomic physics, Kerner's other occupation, saves him from the despair that drives Purvis to suicide by objectifying in mathematical form the extent to which the perceiver constitutes the perceived, the spy-catcher defines the spy. It gives him a model for the dilemma of the double (triple? quadruple?) agent who morally prefers Western political practice— "To me," says Kerner, "[voting] has the power of an equation in nature, the masses converted to energy" (73)—while recognizing the East as his home. Like *Neutral Ground*'s Philo, Kerner lives neither in one country nor the other but somewhere between the two. When Blair asks him to declare what he believes in, he responds, "My estrangement" (72).

In his estrangement, Kerner has much in common with other Stoppard characters. Twelve years earlier, when blindly in love with agent Hapgood, Kerner had felt like playwright Henry from *The Real Thing,* who confessed to Annie, "I can't cope with more than one moral system at a time. Mine is that what you think is right is right. What you do is right" (79). Now long past the first flush of love, Kerner looks back on his involvement with Hapgood much as Henry might look back on his with Annie: "There is something appalling about love. It uses up all one's moral judgement. Afterwards it is like returning to a system of values, or at least to the attempt" (73). His attempt to return to a system of values requires that he take on once again a more complex vision of morality than that dictated by his infatuation with Hapgood. As his love has cooled, his political alliances have again become divided and ambivalent.

In *Hapgood,* Stoppard is also attempting to renew his powers as a comic playwright. His solution is to attempt a total theatrical metaphor for post-Newtonian morality and epistemology in comic terms. Not only do his three sets of twins use one of the oldest comic devices to point up the multiple selves in us all but also his baroquely convoluted spy plot suggests that people do things for more than one and sometimes for conflicting reasons. Neither absolute morality nor straight causality applies to human behavior. What can explain the playfulness of Kerner's multiple betrayals—"Paul thinks I was a triple, but . . . I was past that, quadruple at least, maybe quintuple"(88)? Even Carl Toms's set and David Hersey's lighting extended the metaphor in the London production.[3] The identical dressing-room doors in the scene 1 and scene 6 municipal swimming pool set "conceal occupancy" but don't meet the ground. We can see part of what occurs but not enough to be sure of what is happening. There are four ways of entering and exiting the set. We never know where an actor will come on or leave. Blair, a figure of questionable loyalty and possible treachery, is twice positioned during crucial scenes in the dark of the upper stage, moving into the light only after the action is over. Scene 2, set in the London zoo, uses the bars of the zoo cages and a strong line of shadow on the stage floor to echo Kerner's explanation of particle-wave physics: "Wave pattern happens when light from two slits mixes together but your particles can't do that. . . . there is only one solution. . . . Each bullet goes through both slits" (11).

As Christopher Innes has suggested, the entire presentation of *Hapgood* is infected by game strategems, not the least of which is the game of interpretation. How we interpret a play arises in part from what we expect it to be: Is *Hapgood* a spy thriller, a poetic metaphor, or a joking Nabokovian spoof? At least since *Rosencrantz and Guildenstern Are Dead,* surprise has been the playwright's vehicle for making us aware of our expectations. One of the surprises in Stoppard's post-Newtonian parody of the spy formula is to show us the junction of scientific observation and aesthetic contemplation. Kerner has given this some thought.

> When I have learned the [spy] language I will write my own book. The traitor will be the one you don't like very much, it will be a scandal. Also I will reveal him at the beginning. I don't understand this mania for surprises. If the author knows, it's rude not to tell. In science this is understood: what is interesting is to know what is happening. . . . This is why a science paper is a beautiful thing: first, here is what we will find; now here is how we find it; here is the first puzzle, here is the answer, now we can move on. (47)

Kerner's cliché novel would fail to give the reader the pleasure of discovery. Art and science attempt to model the world in two fundamentally different ways: science attempts to tell us how the world of things works; art attempts to tell us what the world of things means. At the level of subatomic physics, however, science and art come closer together, because the language of mathematics cannot yet provide a single explanatory model of small objects traveling at high speeds. Scientists must resort to metaphors like "particles" or "waves" to approximate incomputable behavior. Stoppard constructed *Hapgood* to illustrate how a scientific paper and a work of art differ and how they overlap. Act 1 leads to a hypothesis; act 2 carries out the experiment. The denouement leaves to us the interpretation of the results.

In both image and word, the opening prologue illustrates the major problem to be investigated by the play. It does not, like Stoppard's two previous full-length stage plays, fool us into taking the fictional for the provisionally real. That particular type of stage foolery has, for the time being, been used up. Instead, it demonstrates a clandestine operation whose failure leads to a surprising hypothesis. But before it does so, the Prologue must teach us the spy idiom, which Stoppard accomplishes by means of a short radio play in which an invisible agent speaks to an invisible Hapgood while we watch a man (American agent Wates) shaving in the mirror of the men's room at a swimming pool somewhere in East London. The radio play narrates the movements of invisible people until they are about to enter the stage—"Four—three—two—," "You're looking at him" (2). Once the "target" and the "walker" have entered, we find ourselves watching a mime, lightly choreographed to Bach (in the London opening) and for this reason, together with Wates's shaving, reminding some reviewers of *Jumpers*. But this mime illustrates, admittedly in lumbering dimensions and at slow speeds, the apparently random motion of electrons flitting about in atoms while being observed by an experimenter. After a total of six actors have entered the men's room, we have seen (but probably not recognized) each member of two sets of twins, a young inexperienced British agent, and one Russian double agent circumnavigating the dressing room while being observed by one of the experimenters, American agent Wates. At one time or another, they occupy one of four cubicles, move past a shower stall, and exit to the swimming pool area while shifting the positions of three briefcases. When the mime is complete, Hapgood and her team attempt to understand what happened during the experiment. Wates explains that the wrong Russian was followed out (there were two), and Ridley (the "real" riddle, posing as a British agent) blows his cover by revealing his knowledge of the Russian twins, a device he could not have known about unless he had been expecting it. This was "a meet," a clandestine meeting for the exchange of real or bogus intelligence, complete with a booby trap (a duplicated briefcase) intended to divulge whether Kerner was acting as a triple agent. But the trap fails when Hapgood discovers that a bag of film has been taken from the duplicated briefcase. Who retrieved the films and how did he circumvent the alarm implanted in the bag? The surprise turn of events at the meet can only be explained by hypothesizing that two Russians and two Ridleys appeared, each creating an alibi for the other. A spy is like a trick of the light.

What we have seen — two sets of two identical people apparently occupying the same place at the same time — visually models the paradox of quantum behavior, as Kerner explains to Blair the following day during their talk at that most predictable of spy meeting grounds, the London Zoo. The remainder of act 1 establishes "what we will find," a Ridley double, and how we will find it, by tricking Ridley into repeating his performance at the swimming pool. That is, in order to prove the hypothesis of the Ridley double, Hapgood must, like any good scientist, repeat the experiment and achieve identical results.

Act 2 opens as a play-within-the-play, with the spectators fully aware that they are witnessing a fiction, or, as we later discover, a partial fiction. The staged scene in Blair's office is necessary to set up Ridley for the experiment; however, in the spirit of Heisenberg's uncertainty principle, truth and fiction become indistinguishable as the assembled group mixes fact and fantasy in an act for Ridley's benefit. Part of what is revealed in the scene is truth: Hapgood has had a son by agent Kerner and the Soviets have found out. But exactly how the Soviets have blackmailed Kerner is never fully established. His story of having passed crucial information in hidden files to the Soviets at the swimming pool meet is apparently a lie, but Kerner has been providing them with information somehow, as Blair later accuses him of doing. In any event, his lie succeeds in laying the trap for Ridley who, secretly in love with Hapgood, agrees to help her deceive Blair by arranging an exchange of information for the safety of her boy, whom Ridley has been tricked into believing is being held by Russian agents. Hapgood convinces Ridley to locate her supposed twin sister, Celia Newton, to dress her like Hapgood, and to use her as a dummy substitute for negotiating the ransom with the kidnappers while Hapgood remains under Blair's watchful eye. The swap is to take place at the scene 1 swimming pool and has been arranged to force Ridley to produce his double as a means of confusing the observers.

"We're all doubles," Kerner told Blair. And when we next see Hapgood, she is her own double, Celia Newton, Hapgood "without the brains or the taste." And while she initially appears to be the mere opposite of her other self, bohemian, sloppy, foulmouthed, promiscuous, slow-witted, she eventually proves to be the complementary underside of Hapgood which comes closer to the surface in the play's closing scenes. The appearance of Celia Newton is another assault on simple binary opposition. As Celia, Hapgood can speak to Ridley personally, warn him away from the trap she herself has set for him: "If you think [Hapgood's] lying, walk away. If you think bringing back her son

will make you her *type*, walk away. . . . take my advice and open the box"
(82).

As in physics, so in play writing. The dramatic interest does not lie in
drawing absolute distinctions between illusion and reality, knowledge and
concealment, but in revealing where they overlap. We are waiting to see Ridley's double; all that remains is to produce the correct laboratory conditions
under which he will appear. The swap occurs in the dark at the scene 1 swimming pool. When the two Ridleys greet one another with a brief and silent em-
brace, we are reminded, in a delicate Conradian moment, that all of the
characters have a secret sharer, the free man has a fugitive, the physicist has
a spy, the executive has an anarchist, the Briton has a Soviet. Hapgood places
the disk under the cubicle door, Ridley #2 picks it up and is confronted by
Wates. When Ridley #1 re-enters to shoot Hapgood, she shoots him first and
fatally. The meet and the murder change the equation for Hapgood, who soon
after quits the agency. The experiment has both succeeded and failed. The
process of confirming Ridley's double (and double cross) also confirmed
Blair's Newtonian rigidity and Hapgood's post-Newtonian flexibility. Not only
does she balk at equating the KGB with "the opposition" ("We're just keeping
each other in business") but she begins to use the off-color language of her twin
to express her frustration: "Christ, Paul, I must have been buying nothing but
lies . . . since Joe was in his pram!" (87). Kerner's prediction has proven
true:

> Ridley is not very nice: he'll turn out to be all right. Blair will be the traitor: the
> one you liked. This is how the author says, "You see! Life is not like books,
> alas!" (47)

In Stoppard's post-Newtonian spy thriller, life and books can be both like and
unlike, distinct but overlapping. The concluding scene is precisely indeter-
minate. Kerner says he will return to Russia but remains fixed on stage, his
interest in language and game rekindled by his son's rugby match.

In *Hapgood,* Stoppard uses the ancient comic cliché of twins to signify
the junction between art and science, hypothesis and fact, imaginary and actual. Plautus and Shakespeare used twins to exploit the humor of mistaken
identity. But even the most farcical treatment of the double testifies to the uncanniness of duplication, the tentativeness of the boundaries demarking the
self, and the impossibility of the unique individual. The ingenuity of this play
lies in its intricate and concrete reference to the mystery of doubling as a metaphor for the mystery of art and science. *Hapgood* does not attempt to improve

upon *The Real Thing* as a treatment of the art-life exchange, but to give it a new theatrical expression that accounts for the presence of the interpreting spectator. In demonstrating that the problems of subatomic physics replicate the problems of the spy thriller, *Hapgood* reaffirms the power of metaphor itself, of the doubleness implicit in the comparison of unlike things. This power finally belongs to the spectators, following clues, watching demonstrations, sifting evidence, making connections. *Hapgood* attempts to present in the theater an image of the mysteries of human behavior that cannot be solved and to recognize that in the act of observing these images, we are in part determining the meaning we will find in them.

Conclusion

Viktor Sklovskij, self-proclaimed founder of Russian Formalism, defined the movement in this way: "In its essence the Formal method is simple – a return to craftsmanship" (quoted in Steiner 1984, 44–45). As I have used the term in this book, craftsmanship means more than technical ingenuity or virtuosic displays of comic skill (although these, too, are the work of a craftsman). In its broadest and most encompassing sense, Stoppard's craft of comedy is his commitment to sharing with the spectators the coded secrets of play. And his chief means of opening up these secrets is parody – the distorted repetition of source texts and genre markers that define the rules of the comic game. Stoppard's recycling of the literary past shares with the Russian Formalist movement a belief in the power of parody to rejuvenate both the artist's creating energy and the spectator/reader's interpreting energy.

For Stoppard, this renewal does not imply a Darwinian model of literary history; parody, that is, is not a vehicle for improving upon literature but for shifting the vantage from which we apprehend it. Parody explores the frontier between art and non-art, a border that interested Stoppard from his earliest days as a journalist, when he showed signs of rebelling against the reporting of facts by fictionalizing the name under which he presented them. His early reporting covered stage, film, and sport events – all of them forms of theater in the broadest sense of the term, and all of them social games informed by a well-articulated set of conventions or rules. Spectatorship, for Stoppard, meant knowing the rules well enough to appreciate how they could constrain the choices open to the players at any particular point in the game. When he began to write plays, he carried over to them his interest in rules and conventions as the basis for involving spectators in comic action.

In his smaller-scale comedies for radio and television, Stoppard often includes the conventions of the medium in what there is to laugh about – whether

159

it be the "blindness" of the radio medium or the directness of the television's documenting eye. By the same token, virtually all of his stage plays contain inner plays, foregrounding the conventions of stage presentation and its particular rules for signaling the suspension of disbelief. In his use of both medium and genre, Stoppard points up the shared ground of convention upon which spectators and actors collaborate in the dramatic illusion.

Stoppardian parody also includes the spectators in the recycling game, although their degree of involvement will be determined by their awareness of the sources being recycled. With the exception of *R&GAD* and *Travesties,* whose effect depends heavily upon recognition of particular sources, Stoppard's textual and generic parody is discontinuous and fragmentary but persistent. Through parody, Stoppard has continued to patrol the frontier, posing the dilemma of the artist as divided between a public and a private world, between joining and resisting literary tradition, copying and distorting literary models. In Stoppard's treatment, the artist must tolerate the uncertainty and ambiguity following from the realization that art and life intermingle and mutually constitute one another. His artists who retreat from the frontier into the presumed safety of a haven run the risk of sterility or madness.

Finally, Stoppard's craft of comedy clears a space within which the Stoppard artist and spectator can view comic models of human experience under the pressure of doubt and uncertainty about their meaning and value.

Notes

Chapter 1

A version of the first part of this chapter on Stoppard's journalism has appeared in *Modern Drama* 33, no. 3 (1990): 380–93.

1. My journalism colleagues assure me that, even in the 1950s, this indeed would have been an impossible dream, as such roving correspondents generally worked in an extremely competitive environment and on a free-lance basis that could not be expected to provide a living wage. Stoppard's dream tells us something about the intensity of his ambition to become known and of his desire to work outside of any kind of system, including the staff of a newspaper. When hard-boiled reporter Richard Wagner from *Night and Day* describes young idealist Milne as "somebody who wants to impress the world and doesn't know that the world isn't impressed by reporters," he could be speaking as author Stoppard recalling his younger self.

2. I base my hunch that Stoppard used the initials "D. D. F." and later the pseudonym David Foot upon two coincidences: first, the initials appeared after a *WDP* theater review published shortly before Stoppard's resignation (and we know that Stoppard wrote these reviews regularly); second, the byline "David Foot" begins appearing almost immediately upon his arrival at the *BEW* after front-page feature stories, soccer reports, and theater and film reviews—all of them beats assigned to Stoppard.

3. Whether or not this was a common practice among British journalists, it suggests that Stoppard had begun playfully to fictionalize himself in a way that becomes a writer of fiction rather than a reporter of facts. Thus, his identity as a writer rather than a reporter/reviewer may well have been established by this time. The name "David Foot" may have been Stoppard's parody of "William Boot," the bumbling reporter in Evelyn Waugh's novel about journalism, *Scoop,* also parodied in the later stage play *Night and Day.* Two years later, after leaving the *BEW,* Stoppard adopted the William Boot pseudonym outright because, as he has explained it, he then felt (but no longer feels) it to be a conflict to review plays and interview actors and playwrights as the same person (Interview with Editors of *Theatre Quarterly* 1974, 17).

4. For the suggestion that Saunders's play provided some of the images for *R&GAD,* see Neil Sammels (1986, 32–39).

5. Stoppard's journalistic essays written since 1963 include the following:

"But for the Middle Classes." Review of *Enemies of Society,* by Paul Johnson. *Times Literary Supplement* [London], 3 June 1977, 677.

"A Case of Vice Triumphant." Review of *Venice Preserv'd,* by Thomas Otway. *Plays and Players,* March 1967, 16–17, 19.

"The Definite Maybe." *The Author* 78 no. 1 (1967): 18–20.

"Dirty Linen in Prague." *New York Times,* 11 February 1977.

"The Face at the Window." *Sunday Times* [London], 27 February 1977.

"I'm Not Keen on Experiments." *New York Times,* 8 March 1970.

"In Praise of Pedantry." *Punch,* 14 July 1971, 62–63.

"Just Impossible." Review of *The Impossible Years,* by Bob Fisher and Arthur Marks. *Plays and Players,* January 1967, 28–29.

Letters to: the *Times* [London] (7 February 1977, 11 August 1977, 17 October 1977, 3 November 1980; the *Sunday Times* [London] (15 June 1980); the *Daily Telegraph* (17 March 1979).

"Looking-Glass World." *New Statesman,* 28 October 1977, 571–73.

"Nothing in Mind." *London Magazine,* February 1978, 65–68.

"Orghast." Review of *Orghast,* by Ted Hughes. *Times Literary Supplement* [London], 1 October 1971, 1174.

"Playwrights and Professors." *Times Literary Supplement* [London], 13 October 1972, 1219.

"Prague: the Story of the Chartists." *New York Review of Books,* 4 August 1977, 11–15.

"Prague's Wall of Silence." *Times* [London], 18 November 1981, 10.

"Something to Declare." *Sunday Times* [London], 25 February 1968, 47.

Review of *A Supplement to the Oxford English Dictionary, Vol. 1, A–G,* ed. R. W. Burchfield. *Punch,* 13 December 1972, 893–94.

"Tom Stoppard on the KGB's Olympic Trials." *Sunday Times* [London], 6 April 1980, 16.

"A Very Satirical Thing Happened to Me on the Way to the Theatre Tonight." *Encore,* March–April 1963, 33–36.

"Wildlife Observed. The Galapagos: Paradise and Purgatory." *Observer Magazine,* 29 November 1981, 38–51.

"Yes, We Have No Banana." *Guardian,* 10 December 1971, 10.

6. The language of the story appears to be very close to autobiography:

As he later told it (laughing), the closest he ever came to being trapped was when after a luckily timed letter written on a whim he found himself being interviewed for a job by the editor of the *Evening Standard.* . . . The editor . . . was oldish and not at all frightening. . . . What are your special interests? he asked. Well ah reading. The editor seemed to think his question had been misunderstood. Interested in politics at all? Oh yes, indeed, politics, too. Who then, for instance, was the Foreign Secretary? Afterwards . . . he decided it had not been a fair question." (1964, 126)

He explained the actual interview to *Theatre Quarterly* this way: "The job was actually on their 'Londoner's Diary,' and I got on very well with Nick Tomalin . . . but

Charles Wintour did ask me about some politician I couldn't name. . . . So I stayed with the *Western Daily Press*, till I got . . . poached by the *Bristol Evening World* in 1958" (Interview with Editors 1974, 4).

Chapter 2

1. The Third Programme was the BBC's vehicle for esoteric and demanding plays as opposed to the more popular plays aired on the Home Service, later called Radio 4. The radio plays of Samuel Beckett and Harold Pinter also aired on the Third Programme.

2. Stoppard will use disjointed "moon" lyrics again in *Jumpers* (1972) to signal the mental breakdown of moon-loving chanteuse Dorothy Moore. *Jumpers* opens after Dotty's collapse, whereas *Albert's Bridge* closes with Albert's.

3. See Stoppard's autobiographical comments in his *Theatre Quarterly* interview, 3–4.

4. Elissa S. Guralnick, "*Artist Descending a Staircase*: Stoppard Captures the Radio Station – and Duchamp," *PMLA* 105 (1990): 298, suggests additional artists and works Stoppard may have had in mind when shaping his artists and their philosophies.

5. I have declined to consider among Stoppard's television plays his television adaptations of his stage play *A Walk on the Water* (1963), his radio play *The Dissolution of Dominic Boot* (called *The Engagement*) (1970), and Jerome K. Jerome's *Three Men in a Boat* (1975). I am also excluding *The Boundary,* an unpublished television play co-written with Clive Exton in 1975. The latter is described by Tim Brassell (1985, 172–78).

6. The self-reflexivity of the television in *Moon* disappeared in the 1985 revival of the stage play, *Jumpers*, whose oversized TV back projection (specified in the stage directions to the Grove Press edition) was replaced by an actual small TV.

7. Stoppard described his mistrust of the film medium in an interview excerpted in the *New York Times*: "A play is something which happens behind closed doors between consenting adults; and a film is a kind of three-ring circus. . . . The director is the elephant act, and the writer is a sort of clod who comes on afterwards and cleans up the mess" ("I'm Not Keen on Experiments," 1970).

8. The Goldsmith source was noted by Ronald Hayman in his review of *The Dog It Was That Died* in the *Times Literary Supplement* of 24 December 1982: 1419.

9. As with all of the television works, my comments will refer exclusively to the published text of *Squaring the Circle* and will therefore exclude references to features of the edited film such as camera angles, lighting, and cutting.

Chapter 3

1. The technique of direct and indirect quotation Stoppard uses in this play has been interpreted as a failure of imagination and as a cynical resort to riding the coattails of established masterworks (Cohn 1976, 217). But such explanations point to a fundamental misunderstanding of parody, which is never the simple copying of another's words or actions but, in the words of one theorist of parody, a "repetition with difference" rely-

ing upon "the rhetoric of irony" for its critical effect (Hutcheon 1985, 5). I have not used the critical term "intertextual" in this book, as I am taking parody to be a declaration of intertextuality: the term is redundant when applied to parody. And as I am not extending any particular use of the term along the lines of any particular theory (Harold Bloom's "anxiety of influence" or Julia Kristeva's semiotic discussion of intersubjectivity and intertextuality), my using it would seem pointless.

2. Stoppard's fidelity to Shakespeare's script together with the variety and intensity of the humor in the play raises questions about any direct influence upon it of W. S. Gilbert's 1891 farce, *Rosencrantz and Guildenstern,* which freely changes both Shakespeare's language and his plot, concluding with Rosencrantz and Guildenstern sending Hamlet off to England, leaving Denmark (and Ophelia) for themselves. Two comic bits Stoppard might have transformed from Gilbert's play are the "choice of deaths" (dagger or revolver) presented the prince, perhaps echoed by the Tragedians' multiple enactments of death; and Hamlet's use of a real pipe to illustrate the Courtiers' "playing upon" him. In Stoppard's play, the Tragedians' entrances are signaled by flute playing.

3. Richard von Mises, *Probability Statistics and Truth,* 2d rev. English ed. (London: Allen and Unwin Ltd., 1957), 29. Stoppard told Kenneth Tynan early in 1970 that he had been reading the logical positivists with "fascinated revulsion" (Tynan 1980, 90), but it would appear that his reading of this particular positivist began long before 1970 and, while he may have been revolted, his meticulous translation of Mises's definitions suggest more fascination. Even while illustrating a mathematical definition of probability, Stoppard takes care to deform his source, conflating Mises's definition with the popular notion of probability expressed by the idea that monkeys could produce Shakespeare if left alone with a typewriter for a sufficient length of time. "The law of averages, if I have got this right, means that if six monkeys were thrown up in the air for long enough they would land on their tails about as often as they would land on their—" (Tynan 1980, 13).

4. June Schlueter uses this term to acknowledge the parodic status of Rosencrantz and Guildenstern, but reaches conclusions about their significance markedly different from mine. See "Moon and Birdboot, Rosencrantz and Guildenstern," in Bloom 1986, 75–86.

5. Charles Marowitz argues the latter point (1973, 124–25). In commenting upon the capitulation scene, June Schlueter provocatively argues that "it is only when Rosencrantz and Guildenstern step fully into the *Hamlet* play and resume their roles without resistance that they realize their sole raison d'être is those roles" (1987, 83). She continues: "That there is no other life for Rosencrantz and Guildenstern outside of the Shakespeare play, outside of their roles, is affirmed by Stoppard's final tableau. . . . Rosencrantz and Guildenstern are indeed heroes, having fulfilled (though less than nobly) their obligation . . . to perform" (in Bloom 1986, 84). As I have attempted to suggest, the characters as we have come to know them are no longer the property of either Shakespeare or Beckett but of an imaginative stage between them. Consequently, they could not recognize Shakespeare's roles as their sole objective. Even their capitulation scene repeats Shakespeare with difference.

6. The 1984 London revival of *Jumpers* (after which Stoppard issued a new [Faber]

edition of the text) exploited the grisly humor of the shooting by showing McFee dragging himself into Dotty's bedroom, dying as he grabs at her breast.

7. Thomas Whitaker typifies commentary on this play when describing *Travesties* as "more brazenly trivial and more insistently serious" than its Wildean model (1983, 119).

8. I have adapted Felicia Londre's translation (1981, 168).

9. In his study of Joyce's *Ulysses*, Stuart Gilbert quibbles over which term to use, narrowing "parody" to repetition with a mocking intent (1952, 296). I am indebted to Gilbert's study in my discussion of Joyce here.

10. I am here attempting to paraphrase Peter J. Rabinowitz's (for me) somewhat confusing distinction between authorial and narrative audiences described in " 'What's Hecuba to Us?' " 244.

11. Carr is therefore closer to George Moore than to Rosencrantz and Guildenstern in his awareness of creating a fiction, and in his failure to recognize his fiction's basis in another fiction.

12. Kinereth Meyer's intertextual analysis of this scene argues that Stoppard treats Tzara's rewrite of Shakespeare's sonnet not as a canceling but as a doubling (and humanizing) of the written word (1989, 111).

Chapter 4

1. This group of plays was written as an indictment of abuses in Eastern Europe before the extraordinary political changes that have occurred there and in Russia in the late 1980s and 1990. While Stoppard could not in 1990 characterize the polarization between communist bloc East and democratic West as he has characterized it in these plays of the late 1970s and 1980, the intensity of his indictment suggests that he will be slow to reverse his opinion of the communist bureaucracy in Eastern European countries.

2. Stoppard used at least two case histories in constructing the details of the Hollar plot: the arrest of his friend and playwright colleague, Vaclav Havel, and the report of a Soviet dissident's wife. He mentioned in the play all three causes to which Havel attributed his 1978 arrest: his participation in Charter 77, his open letter to Dr. Husak, and his handing over to the press the memoirs of a former Czech minister (see Havel 1978, 25–27). Some of the details of scene 6 were provided by the wife of a Russian dissident. Stoppard also drew on his own responses during the Amnesty International trip in rendering Anderson's fright and discomfort in the face of these events. For further details, see Stoppard's article "The Face at the Window."

3. Each of the published versions of this play (Inter-Action, French's acting version, and Faber's edition) differs markedly from the others. I have consulted the Faber edition as it is the most recent (1980).

4. Easy has brought on stage a Dogg phrase book, but even so, the actors learn Dogg remarkably quickly. As if to explain their speed, Cahoot states, "You don't learn it, you catch it" (74). Stoppard does not attempt to explain rationally how this has happened—perhaps the intensity of their purpose combined with their professional skill has made them quick studies.

Chapter 5

1. Stoppard's restrained use of the internal monologue resembles more closely its use in Virginia Woolf's 1920 novel, *Night and Day*, than its use in Eugene O'Neill's *Strange Interlude*.

2. For a relatively impartial summary of this controversy, see the *Royal Commission on the Press Final Report*, especially chapter 17. Another summary focusing on the possibility of censorship as an outcome of the closed shop appears in *Index on Censorship* 4, no. 2 (1975): 72–75. Stoppard has mentioned that he reads this periodical.

3. See Christopher Innes's additional descriptions of the surreal objects and distortions of perspective signaling the spectators' need to check their perceptions of *Hapgood*'s setting (Innes 1989).

Works Cited

When citing from Stoppard's play texts, I have favored the most recent Grove Press editions, where available. With three exceptions, these editions incorporate the playwright's most recent revisions. The Grove Press edition of *Rosencrantz and Guildenstern Are Dead* exists in multiple versions. In this case, as in all others, I have attempted to quote from the most recent. In line with this attempt, I have cited the Faber 1986 revision of *Jumpers*, not printed by Grove. For a trenchant summary of the multiple versions of Stoppard's plays in print, see the introductory essay of Richard Corballis's bibliography in *Stoppard: The Mystery and the Clockwork*.

The Writings of Tom Stoppard

Plays and Stories

After Magritte. In *The Real Inspector Hound*, 61–105. New York: Grove, 1975.

Albert's Bridge. In *Albert's Bridge and Other Plays*, 7–42. New York: Grove, 1977.

Another Moon Called Earth. In *The Dog It Was That Died and Other Plays*, 89–108. London: Faber and Faber, 1983.

Artist Descending a Staircase. In *Albert's Bridge and Other Plays*, 71–116. New York: Grove, 1977.

Dirty Linen. New York: Grove, 1976.

The Dissolution of Dominic Boot. In *The Dog It Was That Died and Other Plays*, 47–58. London: Faber and Faber, 1983.

The Dog It Was That Died. In *The Dog It Was That Died and Other Plays*, 9–46. London: Faber and Faber, 1983.

Dogg's Hamlet, Cahoot's Macbeth. London: Faber and Faber, 1980.

Dogg's Our Pet. In *Ten of the Best British Short Plays*, edited by Ed Berman, 79–94. London: Inter-Action Imprint, 1979.

Enter a Free Man. New York: Grove, 1972.

Every Good Boy Deserves Favour. Music by André Previn. RCA Recording ABLI-2855, 1978.

Every Good Boy Deserves Favour. In *Every Good Boy Deserves Favour and Professional Foul: Two Plays by Tom Stoppard*. New York: Grove, 1978.

Hapgood. London: Faber and Faber, 1988.

If You're Glad I'll Be Frank. In *Albert's Bridge and Other Plays*, 43–70. New York: Grove, 1977.

Jumpers. London: Faber and Faber, 1986.

"Life, Times: Fragments." In *Introduction 2: Stories by New Writers*, 126–30. London: Faber and Faber, 1964.

Lord Malquist and Mr Moon. New York: Grove, 1966.

'M' is for Moon Among Other Things. In *The Dog It Was That Died and Other Plays*, 59–68. London: Faber and Faber, 1983.

Neutral Ground. In *The Dog It Was That Died and Other Plays*, 109–64. London: Faber and Faber, 1983.

New-Found-Land. In *Dirty Linen*, 53–66. New York: Grove, 1976.

Night and Day. New York: Grove, 1979.

Professional Foul. In *Every Good Boy Deserves Favour and Professional Foul: Two Plays by Tom Stoppard*, 41–124. New York: Grove, 1978.

The Real Inspector Hound. New York: Grove, 1975.

The Real Thing. London: Faber and Faber, 1983.

"Reunion." In *Introduction 2: Stories by New Writers*, 121–25. London: Faber and Faber, 1964.

Rosencrantz and Guildenstern Are Dead. New York: Grove, 1967.

A Separate Peace. In *Albert's Bridge and Other Plays*, 141–74. New York: Grove, 1977.

Squaring the Circle. London: Faber and Faber, 1984.

"The Story." In *Introduction 2: Stories by New Writers*, 53–55. London: Faber and Faber, 1964.

Teeth. In *The Dog It Was That Died and Other Plays*, 69–88. London: Faber and Faber, 1983.

Travesties. New York: Grove, 1975.

Where Are They Now? In *Albert's Bridge and Other Plays*, 117–40. New York: Grove, 1977.

Articles

"The Definite Maybe." *Author* 78, no. 1 (1967): 17–19.

"The Face at the Window." *Sunday Times* [London], 27 February 1977.

"I'm Not Keen on Experiments." *New York Times*, 8 March 1970.

"Something to Declare." *Sunday Times* [London], 25 February 1968.

"A Very Satirical Thing Happened to Me on the Way to the Theatre Tonight." *Encore* 10 (1963): 33–36.

Reviews in the *Bristol Evening World*

"As a Shout Against the Folly of Our Time." 8 March 1960.

"Guinness Seems a Trifle Too Clever." 5 April 1960.

"It's a Joy to Watch This Detective." 21 June 1960.
"Look Out for More Films from the 'Little Fellows'." 19 March 1960.
"Tear-jerker: *Conspiracy of Hearts*." 19 April 1960.
"Teenage Problem." 8 March 1960.
"Tom Stoppard Treads the Beatnik Track." 8 March 1960.
"Was Their Journey Really Necessary?" 16 April 1960.

Reviews and Essays in *Scene* (Titled reviews only)

"After Lawrence, Oscar, Bill . . . " 12 December 1962, 6–9.
"The Asylum Seekers." 26 January 1963, 34–35.
"Author in Agony." 12 October 1962, 4.
"Big Fish Little Fish." 28 September 1962, 22.
"Bits of Bert." 14 September 1962, 21.
"A Case of Double Vision." 16 January 1963, 38.
"Crying Till You Laugh." 26 October 1962, 19.
"Everything But Joan." 8 November 1962, 19.
"Fine Hand at Work." 29 November 1962, 19.
"How Much Rubbish . . . " 23 March 1963, 25–27.
"Knight Errant." 22 November 1962, 19.
"New Wave Olivier." 12 December 1962, 44.
"Off the Shaftesbury Fringe." 1 November 1962, 19.
"O'Toole of Arabia." 19 October 1962, 1, 10–12.
"Peer's Progress." 5 October 1962, 22.
"Revue? Never Again." 21 September 1962, 21.
"Theatre Now." 23 March 1963, 20–23.
"Tom Stoppard on a . . . New Writer." 9 February 1963, 46–47.
"Tom Stoppard on Baal . . . " 23 February 1963, 40–41.
"Tom Stoppard on the Blood Knot . . . " 9 March 1963, 40–41.
"Tom Stoppard on the MRA play . . . " 6 April 1963, 36–37.
"Tom Stoppard on the Strange Fact . . . " 23 March 1963, 42–43.
"Tom Stoppard on Why Directors . . . " 20 April 1963, 34–36.
"Twelve Years without Trousers." 21 September 1962, 5.
"The Ultimate Distillation." 15 November 1962, 19.
"Waiting for Scofield." 15 November 1962, 19.
"Who Killed Peter Saunders?" 27 December 1962, 30–31.
"With Vacant Possession of Course." 27 December 1962, 18–19.

Interviews with Tom Stoppard

Interview with Mark Amory, "The Joke's the Thing." *Sunday Times Magazine* [London], 9 June 1974, 65–74.
Interview with Leslie Bennetts. *New York Times*, 18 June 1988.
Interview with Robert Berkvist, "This Time Stoppard Plays It (Almost) Straight." *New York Times*, 25 November 1979.
Interview with Editors. *New Yorker*, 4 May 1968, 41.

Interview with Editors, "Ambushes for the Audience: Towards a High Comedy of Ideas." *Theatre Quarterly* 4, no. 14 (1974), 3–17.

Interview with David Gollob and David Roper, "Trad Tom Pops In." *Gambit* 10, no. 37 (1981), 5–17.

Interview with Nancy Hardin, "An Interview with Tom Stoppard." *Contemporary Literature* 22 (1981), 153–66.

Interview with Keith Harper, "The Devious Route to Waterloo Road." *Guardian*, 12 April 1967, 7.

Interview with Joost Kuurman, "An Interview with Tom Stoppard." *Dutch Quarterly Review* 10, no. 1 (1980), 41–57.

Interview with Alastair Lack. BBC Radio, 4 July 1976.

Interview with Richard Mayne from the BBC's "Arts Commentary." 10 November 1972. BBC recording provided courtesy of the National Sound Archive, LP34898 b01.

Interview with Barry Norman. *Times Saturday Review* [London]. 11 November 1972, 1.

Interview with Peter Orr of the Arts Council. 21 September 1972. BBC recording provided courtesy of the National Sound Archive, T7730 WR.

Interview with Janet Watts. *Arts Guardian*. 21 March 1973, 12.

Secondary Sources and Other Works Cited

Beckett, Samuel. *Krapp's Last Tape*. New York: Grove, 1960.

——. *Proust*. In *Proust and Three Dialogues with George Duthuit*. London: John Calder, 1965.

——. *Waiting for Godot*. New York: Grove, 1954.

Bennetts, Leslie. "Five Top Playwrights in a Dialogue." *New York Times*, 18 June 1988, 12Y.

Bentley, Eric. *The Life of the Drama*. New York: Atheneum, 1967.

Blau, Herbert. *Blooded Thought*. New York: Performing Arts Journal Publications, 1982.

Bloom, Harold. "Introduction." In *Tom Stoppard*, edited by Harold Bloom, 1–6. New York: Chelsea House, 1986.

Bradshaw, John. "Tom Stoppard, Non-Stop." *New York*, 10 January 1977, 47- 51.

Brandt, George W. "Introduction." In *British Television Drama*, edited by George W. Brandt, 1–35. Cambridge: Cambridge University Press, 1981.

Brassell, Tim. *Tom Stoppard: An Assessment*. New York: St. Martin's, 1985.

Brustein, Robert. "A Theatre for Clever Journalists." *New Republic*, 12 January 1980, 23–24.

——. "Waiting for Hamlet: *Rosencrantz and Guildenstern Are Dead*." In *The Third Theatre*, 149–53. New York: Simon and Schuster, 1969.

Cantor, Muriel G., and Suzanne Pingree. *The Soap Opera*. Beverly Hills: Sage Publications, 1983.

Cohn, Ruby. *Modern Shakespeare Offshoots*. Princeton: Princeton University Press, 1976.

——. "Tom Stoppard: Light Dirges in Marriage." In *Contemporary English Drama*, edited by C. W. E. Bigsby, 109–20. Stratford-Upon-Avon Studies, 19. London: E. Arnold, 1981.

Corballis, Richard. *Stoppard: The Mystery and the Clockwork*. New York: Methuen, 1984.

Davis, Jessica M. *Farce*. The Critical Idiom Series, no. 39. Edited by John D. Jump. London: Methuen, 1979.

Davison, Peter. *Contemporary Drama and the Popular Dramatic Tradition in England*. Totowa, N.J.: Barnes and Noble, 1982.

Dean, Joan. *Tom Stoppard: Comedy as a Moral Matrix*. Columbia, Mo.: University of Missouri Press, 1981.

Delaney, Paul. "Cricket bats and commitment: the real thing in art and life." *Critical Quarterly* 27, no. 1 (1985): 45–60.

Diamond, Elin. "Stoppard's *Dogg's Hamlet, Cahoot's Macbeth*: The Uses of Shakespeare." *Modern Drama* 29, no. 4 (1986): 593–600.

Drakakis, John. "Introduction." In *British Radio Drama*, edited by John Drakakis, 1–36. Cambridge: Cambridge University Press, 1981.

Eagleton, Terry. *Marxism and Literary Criticism*. Berkeley: University of California Press, 1976.

Elam, Keir. "After Magritte, After Carroll, After Wittgenstein." *Modern Drama* 27, no. 4 (1984): 473–85.

Erlich, Victor. *Russian Formalism: History—Doctrine*. 4th ed. New York: Mouton Publishers, 1980.

Fainberg, Victor. "My Five Years in Mental Hospitals." Part 2 of "The Abuse of Psychiatry in the USSR." *Index to Censorship* 4, no. 2 (1975): 67–71.

Feynman, Richard, Robert B. Leighton, and Matthew Sands. *The Feynman Lectures on Physics*. Vols. 1–3. Reading, Mass.: Addison-Wesley, 1963.

Forster, E. M. *Howard's End*. New York: Vintage, 1921.

Foucault, Michel. *This Is Not A Pipe*. Edited and translated by James Harkness. Berkeley: University of California Press, 1982.

Frye, Northrop. *Anatomy of Criticism: Four Essays*. Princeton: Princeton University Press, 1957.

Gablik, Suzi. *Magritte*. Greenwich, Conn.: New York Graphics Society, Ltd., 1970.

Gaskell, Philip. "*Night and Day*: The Development of a Play Text." In *Textual Criticism and Literary Interpretation*, edited by Jerome J. McGann, 162–79. Chicago: Chicago University Press, 1980.

Gielgud, Val. *British Radio Drama 1922–1956*. London: George G. Harrap, 1957.

Gilbert, Stuart. *James Joyce's* Ulysses: *A Study*. New York: Vintage Books, 1952.

Gruber, William. "Artistic Design in *Rosencrantz and Guildenstern Are Dead*." In *Tom Stoppard*, edited by Harold Bloom, 101–18. New York: Chelsea House, 1986.

Guralnik, Elissa S. "*Artist Descending a Staircase*: Stoppard Captures the Radio Station—and Duchamp." *PMLA* 105 (1990): 286–300.

Gussow, Mel. "The Real Tom Stoppard." *New York Times Sunday Magazine*. 1 January 1984, 28.

Havel, Vaclav. "Breaking the Ice Barrier." *Index to Censorship* 7, no. 1 (1978): 25–27.

Hayman, Ronald. Review of *The Dog It Was That Died*. *Times Literary Supplement* [London], 12 December 1982, 1419.

———. *Tom Stoppard*. 3d ed. Contemporary Playwrights Series. London: Heinemann, 1979.

Hays, Michael. Review of Beate Neumeier, *Speil und Politik: Aspekte der Komik bei Tom Stoppard*. *Modern Drama* 31, no. 4 (1988): 594–96.

Hirst, David L. *Comedy of Manners*. The Critical Idiom Series, no. 40. Edited by John D. Jump. London: Methuen, 1979.

Homberger, Eric. *John Le Carre*. New York: Methuen, 1986.

Hunter, Jim. *"Night and Day."* In *Tom Stoppard*, edited by Harold Bloom, 119–26. New York: Chelsea House, 1986.

———. *Tom Stoppard's Plays*. New York: Grove, 1982.

Hutcheon, Linda. *A Theory of Parody*. London: Methuen, 1985.

Innes, Christopher. "Hapgood—A Question of Gamesmanship?" *Modern Drama* 32, no. 2 (1989): 315–17.

Issacharoff, Michael. *Discourse as Performance*. Stanford: Stanford University Press, 1989.

Itzin, Catherine. *Stages in the Revolution: Political Theatre in Britain Since 1968*. London: Eyre Methuen, 1980.

James, Henry. "The Real Thing." In *The Portable Henry James*, edited by Morton D. Zabel, 102–34. New York: Penguin Books, 1977.

Johnson, Paul. "Journalists as Play Actors." *Listener*, March 1981, 362–63.

Joyce, James. *Stephen Hero*. Edited by Theodore Spencer. Rev. ed. New York: New Directions, 1963.

Kelly, Katherine. "Tom Stoppard's *Artist Descending a Staircase*: Outdoing the 'Dada' Duchamp." *Comparative Drama* 20 (1986): 191–200.

Kennedy, Andrew. "Natural, Mannered and Parodic Dialogue." *Yearbook of English Studies* 9 (1979): 28–54.

Lawrence, Karen. *The Odyssey of Style in* Ulysses. Princeton: Princeton University Press, 1981.

Lewalski, Barbara K., and Andrew J. Sabol, eds. *Major Poets of the Earlier Seventeenth Century: Donne, Herbert, Vaughan, Crashaw, Jonson, Herrick, Marvell*. New York: Odyssey Press, 1973.

Londre, Felicia. *Tom Stoppard*. New York: Frederick Ungar, 1981.

Marowitz, Charles. *Confessions of a Counterfeit Critic: A London Theatre Notebook, 1958–1971*. London: Eyre Methuen, 1973.

Meisel, Martin. *Shaw and the Nineteenth-Century Theater*. First Limelight Edition. New York: Princeton University Press, 1984.

Meyer, Kinereth. " 'It Is Written': Tom Stoppard and the Drama of the Intertext." *Comparative Drama* 23 (Summer 1989): 105–22.

Mises, Richard von. *Probability Statistics and Truth*. 2d rev. English ed. London: Allen and Unwin Ltd., 1957.

Mrozek, Slawomir. *Tango*. Translated by Nicholas Bethell. Adapted by Tom Stoppard. London: Cape Goliard Press, 1968.

Rabinowitz, Peter J. " 'What's Hecuba to Us?' The Audience's Experience of Literary Borrowing." In *The Reader in the Text*, edited by Susan R. Suleiman and Inge Crosman, 241–63. Princeton: Princeton University Press, 1980.

Roberts, Philip. "Tom Stoppard: Serious Artist or Siren?" *Critical Quarterly* 20 (1978): 84–92.

Royal Commission on the Press Final Report. London: Her Majesty's Stationery Office, 1977.

Rusinko, Susan. *Tom Stoppard*. Boston: Twayne, 1986.

Ruskin, Phyllis, and John H. Lutterbie. "Balancing the Equation." *Modern Drama* 26, no. 4 (1983): 543–54.

Sammells, Neil. *Tom Stoppard: The Artist as Critic*. New York: St. Martins, 1988.

Saunders, James. *Next Time I'll Sing to You*. London: Heinemann, 1965.

Schlueter, June. "Moon and Birdboot, Rosencrantz and Guildenstern." In *Tom Stoppard*, edited by Harold Bloom, 75–86. New York: Chelsea House, 1986.

Self, David. *Television Drama: An Introduction*. Basingstoke: Macmillan, 1984.

Shakespeare, William. *The Tragedy of Hamlet, Prince of Denmark*. In *The Riverside Shakespeare*, 1135–97. Textual Editor, G. Blakemore Evans. Boston: Houghton Mifflin Company, 1974.

Shulman, Milton. "The Politicizing of Tom Stoppard." *Times* [London], 23 April 1978.

Steiner, Peter. *Russian Formalism: A Metapoetics*. Ithaca: Cornell University Press, 1984.

Styan, John L. *Realism and Naturalism*. Vol. 1 of *Modern Drama in Theory and Practice*. New York: Cambridge University Press, 1981.

Thompson, Leslie. "The Subtext of *The Real Thing*: It's 'all right'." *Modern Drama* 30, no. 4 (1987): 535–48.

Tynan, Kenneth. "Withdrawing with Style from the Chaos." In *Show People: Profiles in Entertainment*, 44–123. New York: Simon and Schuster, 1980. Originally published as a profile of Tom Stoppard, *New Yorker* 19 December 1971, 41–111.

Ubersfeld, Anne. "The Pleasure of the Spectator." Translated by Pierre Bouillaguet and Charles Jose. *Modern Drama* 25, no. 1 (1982): 127–39.

Whitaker, Thomas. *Tom Stoppard*. New York: Grove, 1983.

Whittaker, Robert. "The Tolstoy Archival and Manuscript Project." *Tolstoy Studies Journal* 1 (1988): 61–65.

Wilde, Oscar. *The Importance of Being Earnest: An Authoritative Text Edition of a Great Play*. New York: Avon Books, 1965.

Wilson, Edmund. *The Wound and the Bow*. New York: Oxford University Press, 1947: 272–95.

Wittgenstein, Ludwig. *Philosophical Investigations*. Translated by G. E. M. Anscombe. London: Basil Blackwell, 1953.

———. *Tractatus Logico-philosophicus*. Translated by D. F. Pears and B. F. McGuinness. New York: Humanities Press, 1961.

Yeo, Clayton. "The evidence." Part 1 of "The Abuse of Psychiatry in the USSR." *Index on Censorship* 4, no. 2 (1975): 61–66.

Index